PROTESTANT

MW01031601

PROTESTANTISM IN GUATEMALA

Living in the New Jerusalem

VIRGINIA

GARRARD-BURNETT

UNIVERSITY OF TEXAS PRESS, AUSTIN

Requests for permission to reproduce material from this work should be
sent to Permissions, University of Texas Press, P.O. Box 7819, Austin,
TX 78713-7819.

⊗ The paper used in this publication meets the minimum requirements
of American National Standard for Information Sciences—Permanence
of Paper for Printed Library Materials, ANSI Z39.48-1984.

LIBRARY OF CONGRESS
CATALOGING-IN-PUBLICATION DATA
Garrard-Burnett, Virginia, 1957–
    Protestantism in Guatemala : living in the New Jerusalem / by
Virginia Garrard-Burnett.
        p. cm.
    Includes bibliographical references and index.
    ISBN 978-0-292-72817-2

    1. Protestant churches — Guatemala — History — 20th century.
    2. Guatemala — Church history — 20th century.   I. Title.
    BX4834.G9G37   1998
    280'.4'097281—dc21   97-49864

To my children: WILLIE, GRANT, AND HELEN

Contents

Introduction

O N MY first trip to Guatemala, in 1980, I went, predictably enough, to Panajachel, a tourist town perched precariously on the aquamarine shores of Lake Atitlán. At the time, hard-working Indians, ladino merchants, and foreign "*jipis*" (hippies) lived together there in relative harmony. On my first evening, I was surprised to hear the heavy night air pierced by the discordant sound of hymns being broadcast over a scratchy sound system from a tiny evangelical church.[1] On investigation, I was surprised to find a congregation of women in *traje* (indigenous dress), weeping, clapping, and murmuring in what I assumed at the time to be an indigenous language while a man in an ill-fitting suit preached and sang to them. I was astonished, for this scene flew in the face of my image of the "real Guatemala," a land of the baroque Catholicism of Antigua's churches and Holy Week festivities and the exotically pagan Catholicism of the candles, saints, and *pom* in the altiplano.

I returned to Guatemala in 1983, during the presidency of Efraín Ríos Montt. Among the many changes I encountered—the absent friends, the guarded, hollow eyes of people in the countryside, the civil patrol armed with wooden guns and new hats, and the omnipresent military sentries, even in the mellow streets of Panajachel—was the presence, everywhere it seemed, of Protestant churches. I surmised that this had something to do with the president's own much-touted status as a Protestant, and probably even more to do with the influence of the United States, where the Moral Majority now wielded considerable influence.

Sometime later, a friend and I were driving down a road in El Quiché in a pouring rain. We passed a group of indigenous people walking in our direction. They were carrying guitars and were soaking wet, but their faces were radiant and open. We remarked that they had all the hallmarks of *evangélicos*—and, sure enough, we soon passed an encampment of evangelicals, protected from the elements by plastic sheeting and fellowship. It was at that moment that I realized that the issues of Protestant conversion ran much deeper than political positioning, economic aspirations, or even survival strategies, although these things might also be involved. I asked myself why here, and why now? As a historian, I knew that missionaries had worked in the country for more than a hundred years, but the wave of conversions dated back only a decade or so. What had changed?

The initial premise of my research for this book was that Guatemala's late-twentieth-century affinity for Protestantism was the result of the efforts of North American missionaries, who had, to use a term that frequently appears in some of the hostile literature, been "invading" the country since the late nineteenth century. At that time, I hypothesized, missionaries had come to Guatemala, perhaps with the support or at least the tacit approval of the U.S. government to convert and "civilize" along specifically North American lines as part of a larger expansion of our nation's political and economic hegemony in northern Latin America. I also assumed collusion in this effort with the Liberal government in Guatemala, which presumably accepted the missions in accord with the rubric of "order and progress."

In the twentieth century, the issues, I presumed, were similar but the stakes, now fueled by global politics and modern technology, were even higher. This hypothesis was fed by an image that appeared fairly often in the popular writing on Central America in the early 1980s: that of well-funded American missionaries of the Christian Right working hand in glove with ferociously anti-Communist military governments and using money, handouts, and sophisticated marketing techniques to lure the populace into political, cultural, and spiritual submission.

Yet within this basic set of operative premises lay a conundrum that was evident from the start: the problematic question of agency. At best, it suggested that Guatemalans were opportunists who could cannily manipulate religious institutions to their own political or economic advantage; at worst, it implied that they were "empty vessels" into which foreign beliefs and ideologies could readily be poured. Either scenario seemed to belie the historical resilience of popular religion in Guatemala, where the sacred—whether in its Catholic, pre-Hispanic, or even Protestant guise—continues to inform the conduct of much of everyday life.

The methodology I used to examine these premises was fairly straightforward but extensive. I scrutinized missionary papers from the various denominations, including correspondence between missionaries and their mission boards in the United States, the monthly and sometimes weekly journals that were published in Spanish or English (and, though rarely, sometimes in a Mayan language) for many years by virtually every denomination for the edification of local converts and other missionaries or for the missions' supporters back in the United States. These kinds of documents were augmented by domestic reports, surveys, censuses, and other instruments located in the local archives of churches in Guatemala. These in turn were amplified with numerous interviews with and oral histories from local church activists, pastors, government officials, and lay partisans. An additional lode of information lay in the Archivo General de Centro América in Guatemala City, where the archives of the Ministry of Foreign Relations and the Ministry of the Interior (Gobernación) yielded nearly a century's worth of carefully maintained records of the entry and exit of missionaries and less precise but nonetheless useful reports on their activities in the country.

These varied pieces came together to form a historical mosaic that looked much different from what I had expected. First and foremost, the missionary movement does not seem to fall within any sort of grand hegemonic conspiracy, although certain individual players may have considered themselves actors in that particular drama. It is true that North American missionaries to Guatemala at the turn of the last century did indeed envision themselves as part of something larger than themselves, and that vision was as much embedded in the solidly secular norms of U.S. culture as it was in Protestant spirituality. It is also true that this particular cultural package (particularly in its emphasis on "development," as evidenced by medical clinics, schools, and translation projects) endeared missionaries to the Liberal government, which initially had invited the missions in primarily to irritate its old political nemesis, the Roman Catholic Church.

But despite these obvious congruencies, the record shows clearly that the early missionaries in Guatemala considered themselves not to be political emissaries but agents of Jesus Christ in modern guise. Perhaps because of the strong tradition of the separation of church and state in the

United States or because of their aversion to the authoritarian character of Guatemalan politics, the missionaries accepted but remained suspicious of official support in Guatemala and did not expect it or receive it at all from the government of the United States. Furthermore, while cultural values were strongly encoded in the missionaries' message, they considered "civilized conduct" to be a serendipitous and indeed necessary side effect of conversion, but by no means its central purpose.

Yet American missionaries well into the twentieth century remained either unable or unwilling to extricate culture from spirituality, the result being that they and their work, despite official support, remained highly marginalized and even reviled within Guatemalan society as a whole. In the missionary context, conversion required not merely the rejection of Catholicism, but also the renunciation of a cultural identity that in effect sentenced new converts to a life permanently severed from the coherent and internally logical corpus of custom, kin, and economy that had once defined their world. It is not surprising that the early missions' few converts—often former drunkards, jailbirds, victims of "witchcraft," adulterers, and other malefactors—tended to be those who had good reason to insulate themselves from society at large within the protective cocoon of the missions.

By the middle years of the twentieth century, however, an important shift had occurred. The missions' converts, now reformed and respectable, began to assume some responsibility in the churches, thus transforming them gradually from patriarchal foreign bodies into more autochthonous entities. As it happened, this critical period coincided with dramatic changes in the nation's politics and society—the political opening during the "ten years of spring" from 1944 to 1954, and, of only slightly less importance, the reformation of Guatemalan Catholicism through the introduction of the Catholic Action movement. In the course of all of these changes, Protestantism began to assume a Guatemalan face. It was only then that the evangelical movement started to move from the margins of society into the mainstream, initially in a small trickle but by the late 1960s and the 1970s, in a torrent that poured over into the 1980s.

The expansion of Protestantism across the social landscape corresponds chronologically with the militarization of the state, the increase in public violence, and the "globalization" of Guatemalan national politics that occurred in the postrevolutionary period and accelerated in the 1970s and the early 1980s. Clearly, these elements figure into Protestantism's growing attraction during this period. But as the following chapters will show, by and large, while conversion is a drama played out against a political backdrop, it is not in itself an expressly political act.

I would argue instead that the fortunes of Protestantism in Guatemala are inextricably tied to issues of community. For missionaries and converts alike, conversion has always meant a break with the past and the repudiation of the ties of kinship, custom, and belief that originally formed the parameters of their worlds. Until recently, this break seemed disadvantageous to most. But by the same token, there is also clear advantage to be gained: the convert wins admittance to a new community of believers that is almost entirely self-contained, with its own custom, ritual, language, and even a new set of kin, the *hermanos* (brothers). I suspect that this new type of identity held little appeal as long as what we rather imprecisely call the "traditional community" remained more or less intact. But when the center began to give, through the erosive processes of "development," migration, and war, many beliefs, practices, and institutions that shaped identity gave way with it. It is, at least in part, the attempt to re-create some sense of order, identity, and belonging that has caused so many to turn to Protestantism in recent years.

In many respects, this idea is hardly new. Two of the preeminent scholars of the sociology of religion, Emile Durkheim and Max Weber, viewed Protestantism from a similar functionalist perspective; Weber, particularly, interpreted it as a rationalizing system that helped broker the way into modern, capitalist society.[2] The literature on the topic specific to Latin America has taken much the same view. The Swiss sociologist Christian Lalive d'Epinay's 1969 seminal study of urban Protestantism in South America, significantly titled *Haven of the Masses,* suggests that immigrants to the city seek rigid Protestant religious organizations to "replicate the authoritarianism of the hacienda" (p. 118). Similarly, Emilio Willems's noteworthy *Followers of the New Faith* (1967) draws similar conclusions for rural Protestants in Chile and Brazil. According to Willems, converts tended to be people on the edge of economic transition who converted in part because of the relationship between "Protestant" notions of the importance of the individual and the capitalist "modern" world, but also because that faith helped them cope with the "anomie" (moral meaninglessness) that modernity engendered. More recently, British sociologist David Martin has made a similar case for the popular variety of Protestantism known as Pentecostalism, which, in his words, "is its very own fiesta." "The evangelical believer," he writes, "is one who has symbolically repudiated what previously held him in place, vertically and horizontally."[3] David Stoll sums up the argument in a different way. "At a time when a paternalistic social order is breaking down," he argues, "placing a new premium on individualist initiative, it is not hard to see why a Protestant system will be favored."[4]

In general, I, too, subscribe to this basic framework, which Daniel Levine has called the "crisis/adaptation model," although I am reluctant to completely disregard issues of belief and faith in conversion.[5] To do so strikes me as perversely obstructionist as, say, trying to study gender without taking sex into account. Though it goes against the tide of the conventions of social science, it seems reasonable to assume that at least some people make religious decisions based on reasons that have to do with personal spirituality. To say this does not condemn this book as a "confessional" study, but, rather, serves notice that it follows the admonition of Rudolf Otto, who argues that in order to study religion one does not have to be religious, but one does need to believe that some people are. In this regard, Levine's model might be expanded to crisis/adaptation/solace; that is, evangelicals can transcend social dislocation by establishing new forms of community that offer identity and relief, even though this new community may be (and often is) detrimental to the cohesion of other social units, such as the extended family, the town, or even, arguably, the state.[6]

It is because of this that so much of this book focuses on rural Guatemala and the relationship between indigenous communities and the state. Those familiar with Guatemalan Protestantism will know that much of the movement is ladino, urban, and, in recent years, middle and upper class, but there is little of that in the pages that follow. Nor does this book pretend to offer detailed, authoritative histories of the individual denominations, a daunting task that would in any event be of little interest to those outside the particular churches. What it does seek to do is to explore how Protestant actors, institutions, and ideas have merged into the larger flow of Guatemala's more recent history. The reason is that the particular history of Protestant work in Guatemala touches on many of the salient themes of Guatemala's national history, writ small. In this respect, local Protestant history provides us with a yardstick with which to measure Guatemala's enduring and often unsuccessful effort to re-create itself in the image of what nations to the north considered "modern" and "developed" in the late nineteenth and twentieth centuries. This involves many strictly secular themes: the development of an international economy, the various remedies for "el problema indio" (the Indian problem), and, above all, the attempts to establish a unifying national identity. All of these efforts, in turn, pivot around the central goal of government in Guatemala since the late nineteenth century: the creation of a nation-state that is powerful and commanding enough to assert its will in whatever form necessary to defend or improve the *patria* (homeland). These struggles, I believe, are most eloquently played out in the indigenous communities, those spatial and metaphysical localities that scholars once considered ineffably "traditional." It is in these communities where I have particularly tried to chronicle the Protestant story.

When I first began to look at this topic, there was precious little written on Protestantism in Latin America, much less in Guatemala specifically. So in my first writings I tried to cover many bases—from extricating the tangled histories of the various denominations to measuring Protestantism's anthropological, sociological, and political ramifications to, finally, attempting to answer the basic question of just why it is that people convert. In the last few years, the topic of Protestantism in Latin America has attracted many good minds across a breadth of disciplines, and I commend their work to you. Although I have very much enjoyed taking part in this discourse, I will confine myself in the pages that follow to discussing Guatemala's history. As a historian, I know how to use the tools of history best, and I leave it to the anthropologists, the sociologists, and the political scientists to better explain the how and why of the here and now.

Many people have helped me through the long process of putting this book together, and any list that appears in these pages will undoubtedly haunt me forever with important names I've neglected to mention. Nevertheless, explicit thanks must go to the following people: Ralph Lee Woodward, Jr., who was willing to overlook his aversion to religious topics to oversee this project at its inception; Richard N. Adams, who shares the same aversion but whose ideas continue to stimulate and guide my thinking; and David Stoll, whose passion and prodding incited me to action.

My special thanks and admiration go to those "workers in the field" who have been unfailingly generous with their time and insights, especially those many converts and pastors in Guatemala who, though sometimes dubious of my motives, were nonetheless willing to share their stories and take me in as one of their own, even when doing so might put them at risk. I am indebted to those modern-day church leaders like Vitalino Simalox and Dennis Smith, whose efforts, commitment, and energy continue to help so many; to Samuel Berberian, whose patient and animated explanations granted me an insider's view of Pentecostalism; and to David Scotchmer, whose life and work struck such a unique balance between scholarship and praxis.

Special gratitude is due to Naomi Lindstrom, Jim Handy, and Edward Cleary, who offered especially useful critiques of this manuscript. I will be forever grateful to my anonymous University of Texas Press readers, who assessed this book with such acuity and graciousness. I am also indebted to my graduate students at the University of Texas, whose observations and research have added so much to my revisions of this work, with a particular thanks to Joel Tishkin and David Workman, whose careful reading and technical assistance have been absolutely invaluable. Many thanks also go to my friend and colleague Anne Dibble, who has "covered" for me so long and so well at the Institute of Latin American Studies when I've escaped from the office early to go home and write. Finally, I am grateful to the Institute of Latin American Studies of the University of Texas at Austin, for its support in the form of time and money, through the Mellon Foundation, to complete this work.

No acknowledgment would be complete without a word of affection to my family—for my parents, who have supported me from the very start, and my husband, John, who has been patiently waiting for me to finish this manuscript for such a long time. The success of this book is owed to them and to many others for their support and recommendations, with the recognition that the responsibility for the final version rests entirely with me.

CHAPTER I

"ORDER, PROGRESS,

AND PROTESTANTS"

The Beginning of Mission

We implore the benevolent protection of the Virgin of Guadalupe against
the perfidious impostor and poisonous evangelism . . . of the evangelical
sect. Good for 100 indulgences.

—Roman Catholic tract dated 1911

HISTORICALLY, Protestantism has been a damnable heresy in
Central America. In colonial Spanish America, the Roman Catholic Church was so integral a part of government and society that religious heterodoxy was tantamount to unspeakable social and political de-
viance. The Protestant faith was tainted by association with the English,
the enemies of Spain, and the traders and buccaneers who marauded up
and down the coast of Central America carrying messages of heresy and
treason.[1]

Even so, a few Protestants and some Protestant tracts did filter into
Guatemala during the colonial period, and the trials of Protestant
heretics became a preoccupation of the Holy Office of the Inquisition.
Prosecution of Protestants in Guatemala began in 1560, with the "reconciliation" of a teacher named Francisco, and reached a climax between
1556 and 1598, during the reign of Philip II, during which time the Inquisition in Guatemala tried and executed twenty-one convicted Protestants in autos-da-fe.[2] Of these twenty-one, a majority were foreign
born, most of them Englishmen. At least two of the convicted Protestants were allegedly pirates, suggesting that they were neither devout
churchmen nor tried for their religious crimes alone.[3] Yet the fact that
Spanish officials apparently considered Protestantism to be a greater

crime than piracy speaks volumes about the vital linkage in Spanish America between political and religious orthodoxy.[4]

It was not until Guatemala gained its independence, first from Spain in 1821 and then from Mexico in 1823, that there came any major rupture in this relationship; this was the first act of a lasting drama between the Catholic Church and the emerging state in which Protestantism would for many years play only a minor role. For Guatemala, legal independence came virtually without bloodshed or loss of life. Yet the pronouncement of legal independence sparked the transition and change that would flare into full-blown conflagration as the century progressed. These changes at first came slowly and fitfully, as part of the merging political ideologies of the day, which reflected the inchoate nationalism and interests of the provinces that had formerly made up the colonial Kingdom of Guatemala. In 1823, these tiny states—now Guatemala, El Salvador, Nicaragua, Honduras, and Costa Rica—broke away from Mexican denominations to form a loosely confederated republic known as the United Provinces of Central America, with Guatemala City and, later, San Salvador, as the seat of government.

The United Provinces was a brief and unsuccessful experiment in Bolivarian republicanism, marked by partisan warfare between two key political parties, the Liberals and the Conservatives. By 1840, the United Provinces had splintered into five nations, which, with Belize, make up present-day Central America. The reasons for the disintegration of the United Provinces are many and varied, but one major issue that splintered the provinces was the state's relationship to the Roman Catholic Church. In some respects, the question of the role of the Church was the bellwether of Central American politics in the nineteenth century, looming at least as large at times as the controversies over Central American union or foreign investment.

On one side of the battle lines were the proponents of the Conservative Party, members of the elite who wished to frame the government and society of independent Central America along traditional Hispanic lines. A central focus of Conservative concern was support for the traditional function of the Roman Catholic Church as society's preeminent institution. For Conservatives, the Church was the repository of all that was best of Spain's legacy, from the definition of moral context to the legitimization of authority to the mediation of social relations between men and women, kings and peasants, Europeans and Indians, and God and man.

On the other side of the political divide were the Liberals, who, though they were from the same elite class as their rivals, defined themselves as ideological modernists.[5] Wrapping themselves in a self-hatred of all things Spanish, the Liberals borrowed heavily from the economic and political ideals of the Enlightenment. They came into the independence period with ambitious plans to "rationalize" Central America by obliterating the remnants of colonialism and by completely reconstructing Central American government and society, using the capitalized, industrial—and Protestant—nations of Western Europe and the United States as templates for development. Like the Conservatives, the Liberals also saw the Catholic Church as the embodiment of the Spanish past—an intellectual mausoleum that safeguarded the monopoly, paternalism, and inertia that were, in Liberal eyes, the bitter legacy of colonialism.

From 1831 to 1838, Guatemala was governed by Mariano Gálvez, a powerful Liberal governor, whose well-chronicled policies provide a microcosm of the issues, particularly regarding matters of church and state, that separated the Liberals from the Conservatives. Gálvez, using as a model the Protestant nations of the North Atlantic whose modernity he so admired, sought to establish the basis for republican government and a base for capitalist development. To this end, he encouraged foreign investment and tried to regularize relations with Britain, whose hegemony was inching southward along the Atlantic coast from the Belizean district of Guatemala, which the English already audaciously referred to as British Honduras. The Liberals attempted to introduce new judicial codes and medical practices, which, to their political detriment, failed to halt the lethal spread of cholera during a dreadful epidemic in 1837. And, in an effort to combine the religious notions of the philosophes with political pragmatism, Gálvez implemented a series of anticlerical legislation designed to reduce that most colonial of institutions, the Roman Catholic Church, to its barest and most minimal functions.[6]

Among his most sweeping anticlerical measures were the economic reforms, enacted in 1832, that abolished the tithe, placed strict limitations on the size and future acquisition of Church landholdings, and expropriated the national diocesan treasury for the national treasury. That same year, Gálvez secularized the cemeteries, made civil marriage compulsory, and put legislation into effect to gradually decrease the numbers of "religious" in Guatemala while turning the orders' assets over to the state. Finally, in what was intended to be a lethal blow to

Catholic authority, in May 1832, Gálvez, endorsed an amendment to the federal constitution that called for "freedom of conscience and religious freedom" for all religious sects in Guatemala, a striking departure from the original article of the 1824 Constitution of the United Provinces, which stated that "the religion of the United Provinces is Catholic, Apostolic, and Roman, with the exclusion of all others."[7]

For Gálvez and his Liberal counterparts elsewhere, the anticlerical legislation was part and parcel of a larger program of political reform and social modernization, and as such the religious ramifications of such legislation for the general population were of minimal consequence. Guatemala, the richest state of the Central American union and by far the most heavily populated (in 1820, its population, at 595,000, was nearly double that of the combined populations of the rest of Central America), for most of the era served as the capital of the Liberal-controlled United Provinces of Central America.[8]

Yet this efflorescence masked the fact that Guatemala, like the other states of the union, had failed to construct its social, economic, and ethnic independence in the postcolonial period. Indeed, the Liberal-Conservative fissure that so defined the political ideology of most of the nineteenth century was a construction of elite interests that had little bearing on the life of nonelite Guatemalans, at least as long as public policies emanating from the capital did not demand their labor and tribute or impinge on the practices of community custom. Thus, the Liberal task of crafting a "modern" state from colonial materials, without retrofitting, was perhaps doomed from the start, and surely accounts for the political ascendancy of the Conservative Party, which began in Guatemala with the political emergence of Rafael Carrera in the late 1830s.

Nowhere is the discrepancy between the Liberal reform and popular will more evident than in the turmoil surrounding the horrendous cholera epidemic of 1837. This episode sheds light on the great gulf between elite aspirations, informed by foreign models, and domestic reaction, framed by local perceptions and tradition.[9] This pandemic entered Guatemala through British Honduras early in the year and swept through villages and the countryside before afflicting the larger towns of Antigua and Guatemala City. By the end of 1837, the epidemic had killed twelve thousand souls, claiming over nine hundred victims in the capital and the rest in the countryside. Because the epidemic hit first and most devastatingly in nonladino areas, Liberal awareness of the fearful and poorly understood disease became embedded with ethnic and political implications. As noted in the official publication *Boletín de Noti-*

cias de Cólera Morbus, "Two thirds at least [of the victims] have been Indians, and more than three fourths vice-ridden.[10] Believing the disease might be spread by drunkenness and a bad diet of "chile, pepper, cinnamon, coffee, and wild game," the government proscribed these foods, though they were staples of the Indian diet.[11] Liberal leaders also prohibited the sale of liquor in towns where Indians were a majority of the population, ostensibly as a public health measure.

As the epidemic moved to the cities, the government enlisted the most modern public health methods, such as placing a sanitary cordon around infected areas, assuring that cities were clean and brightly lit, quarantining the homes of the sick, marking the homes of the dying with red and black flags, and disposing quickly and expeditiously of the dead through burial or cremation.[12]

While the epidemic played itself out on this level among the elites, for the poor, among whom the disease ran its deadly course most virulently, the disease suggested a different metaphor with powerful religious undertones. While there is little to suggest that Indians and poor ladinos interpreted cholera as the manifestation of God's wrath imposed on an apostate people (an interpretation long put forth by Liberal historians as evidence of priestly connivance and indigenous gullibility and superstition), the evidence is clear that many did understand the epidemic to be the result of the Liberals' willful godlessness, a charge that laid culpability directly at the feet of the new administrators. The nineteenth-century Liberal historian Lorenzo Montúfar reported that village priests, who retained enormous local authority despite the decline in the institutional Church's power, spread rumors that the Liberals had poisoned the water supply, perhaps to make room for European immigrants. This charge so resonated in local understanding that the poor attacked and killed government health agents and smashed boxes of medicines.[13] Moreover, mass opposition to the government's preemptive disposal of corpses in unhallowed ground was so great that Gálvez abrogated his own earlier legislation by allowing new cemeteries to be built and consecrated by Catholic clergy.[14]

Although obviously not the only factor in the equation, the link between Indians, revolt, and cholera took on a logic of its own. In 1837, Rafael Carrera, an illiterate and able soldier, recruited an army of Indians and poor ladinos (non-Indians) from Los Altos to topple the Liberals; significantly, Carrera's first act of rebellion was to abandon his post with the military who were enforcing the sanitary cordons in Mita and to take up the cause of resisting the quarantine of the area.[15] Fearful that his movement would unleash a widespread peasant rebellion—a bête noire that had been a dark subtext to political ideologies since colonial times—elite Conservatives quickly co-opted Carrera and made him president for life, a term fulfilled by his death in 1865.

Carrera's long rule was conservative in both philosophy and content in that it created an unapologetic ideological construct for Guatemala's continuation of the colonial order. This was represented most clearly by his paternalistic policies toward the Indians, which included physical segregation in their traditional lands in the western Highlands and a re-vival of some of the "protective" statuses provided for in the old colonial Laws of the Indies.[16] Carrera encouraged traditional latifundial agricul-tural forms, which began to produce a new and transformative com-modity, coffee. He also rejuvenated key colonial power brokers, above all, the institutional Roman Catholic Church.[17]

During this long Conservative interregnum, the Church did in fact regain a modicum of its old power.[18] Through legislation and personal fiat, Carrera reintroduced Holy Orders into the country and reinstated the archbishop, who had been exiled under Gálvez. In an ostensible ef-fort to revive the Church's old political and economic status, Carrera also restored clerical privileges and properties to such an extent that, as Douglass Sullivan-González has shown, more than one third of Guate-mala's land again lay in the hands of the Church and the upper-class when the Liberals regained power thirty-two years later.[19]

Earlier Liberal assaults on the Church's secular activities, however, had made inroads against Church power that Carrera was unwilling to reverse. As Hazel Ingersoll has suggested, Carrera's rhetorical support for the Church was tempered by a wary pragmatism.[20] Nowhere was this more apparent than in the matter of Church lands, which had been sold off under the Liberals and had been subsequently put into lucrative coffee production or had been sold to Carrera's political allies. Carrera's commitment to ecclesial reinstatement did not include expropriations of these types of real property, nor did it extend to the kind of funda-mental political "power sharing" with the Church that had characterized the colonial period. To the contrary, Carrera explicitly forbade clergy from holding any type of public office, and he also declined to allow the Church to reinstate mandatory tithes, a key source of Church wealth.[21] Thus, despite the Carrera administration's public support of the Catho-lic Church, the Church's political and particularly its economic power continued to erode slowly as the century progressed, making it vul-nerable to further Liberal encroachments after 1870.

Yet the slow seepage of secular power did not necessarily reflect a loss of spiritual authority. Throughout the nineteenth century, the Roman Catholic Church's spiritual hegemony remained largely unaffected by the shifting political discourse. In Guatemala in the mid-nineteenth century, virtually everyone across political, class, regional, and ethnic lines considered themselves to be Catholic, with the exception of some Liberals, who called themselves atheists for politically fashionable reasons. This Catholic identification had virtually nothing to do with orthodox theology or even with religious sentiment, for Guatemalan Catholicism then as now spanned a wide spectrum of belief, ranging from the ultraorthodoxy of European-trained clergy to the highly syncretic mixture of Mayan and Catholic beliefs adhered to in varying degrees by much of the indigenous population. Yet despite its variegation of form, Catholicism was so integral a part of the nation's fiber that Henry Dunn, a British Anglican bishop to the country in 1827, remarked, "I could dispose of any number of these products [Bibles and tracts]: but I am not sanguine as to the good which might be expected to result. It is not for us to decide where God will give or where He will withhold his blessing, but viewed as a means, I conceive millions might be circulated without the conversion of a single soul from the legal and idolatrous system of Popery."[22]

Dunn was one of a handful of foreigners associated with Protestant denominations or Bible societies who insinuated themselves into Guatemala in the postindependence decades. Gálvez had allowed legalized non-Catholic religions practiced as part of a larger package of anti-clerical legislation in 1824, but the six Protestant itinerant ministers and Bible vendors (known as *colporteurs*, from the French word for peddlers of devotional literature) who came to Guatemala during this period would probably have slipped into the country even without official sanction, since their efforts were part and parcel of a separate social and political ideology, that of British imperial expansionism.[23] All of the early *colporteurs* were British subjects, most employed by the British and Foreign Bible Society, which was also active in Africa and Asia in the dispersal of religious and morally uplifting materials.

Though none had any official ties with the British government and three were "dissenters" (that is, they did not belong to the Church of England), the *colporteurs* were part of the growing British influence in Central America during the first decades after independence. The most visible British presence was along the Caribbean rim, stretching south from British Honduras, along Guatemala's Lake Izabal region to the northern coast of Honduras and Nicaragua's Atlantic coast, to the coast of northeastern Costa Rica. In this regard, the *colporteurs* may certainly be seen (and perhaps would have been satisfied to see themselves) within the context of the larger scheme of British expansion in the early and middle nineteenth century, which sought to incorporate the Atlantic coast of Central America into the British sphere of influence for economic and, ultimately, political ends.[24]

While most of the *colporteurs* were content to visit Guatemala, preach, distributes tracts and Bibles, and hurry back to British soil, one, a naturalized Englishman and former sailor named Frederick Crowe, was not. The Belgium-born Crowe came to Guatemala from British Honduras via Abbottsville, a British colony on Izabal. In 1843, he moved to Guatemala City, where he sold tracts and opened a school offering courses in "Bible, reading, religious conversion, and English." The school was attended, briefly and propitiously, by young men from prominent families who would later be influential in crafting a new national political agenda.[25] Crowe eventually ran afoul of Carrera, who had outlawed non-Catholic religious expression in 1842, and who suspected Crowe of subversion. Frederick Crowe left the country under duress in 1845, but his two-year stay, highlighted by the establishment of the school, became an important footnote to the creation of the Liberal reform in the last decades of the nineteenth century.[26]

The death of Rafael Carrera in 1865 marked the beginning of the end of the Conservative era. Technically, that era came to a close with the military victory in 1871 that ushered in the Liberal rule that endured well into the twentieth century. That six years elapsed between the death of Carrera and Conservatism's defeat is telling. The decline of Conservatism occurred gradually, as a consequence of the change in the national zeitgeist wrought by the expansion of coffee as an export commodity. Coffee, which was introduced into Guatemala on a large scale in the 1850s, had expanded so rapidly that one decade later, this single commodity made up 50 percent of all Guatemalan exports.[27] As David McCreery has shown, the expansion of coffee production stressed conservative ideological structures beyond their limits. The protective cocoon of economic control, xenophobia, and neocolonial patterns of land ownership and labor and ethnic relations that had enveloped Guatemala during the Carrera era now threatened to suffocate the new prosperity.[28]

In 1871, Justo Rufino Barrios, a general, and Manuel García Granados, a Liberal politician, seized power. García Granados was a liberal aristocrat from the old school, whereas Barrios was initially known more as a military strategist than a political partisan. In 1872, García Granados stepped down so that Barrios alone might assume the office of the presidency.

Although Barrios was more autocrat than ideologue, he surrounded himself with advisers who included some of the great minds of the era, including Lorenzo Montúfar, the noted statesman and historian. It was this inner circle that redefined Guatemalan liberalism in the latter part of the century, giving it a more coherent focus and imperative.

As chief executive, Barrios defined his central task to be no less than the creation of a nation that commanded the primary loyalty of all those who lived within its confines. The new liberal vision was to create a modern, unified nation from a disparate mix of ethnicities, languages, classes, customs, and conflicting bonds of loyalty and association. As Benedict Anderson has pointed out, the notion of nationalism in the nineteenth century was relatively new, and it was a most unfamiliar concept in Central America. The abstraction of a citizen's loyalty to a corporate nation, or state, as opposed to a more tangible fealty to a ruler or to an anthropic god, had first emerged from the Enlightenment in the late seventeenth century. But in most of Latin America it was not until the second half of the nineteenth century that nationalism, or the primary allegiance to the organic state, began to replace these ancient loyalties.[29]

In 1870, no Central American state, with the arguable exception of Costa Rica, had succeeded in "building nationhood." Of the five countries on the isthmus, Guatemala was perhaps the most factionalized, and deeply divided along political, economic, and ethnic fault lines. The liberal-conservative struggle between the self-defined "European" and ladino elites that had so dominated the political landscape for most of the century had masked the larger issues confronting the establishment of nationhood: the disarticulation and even the disinterest of the majority of the population.

In 1870, Guatemala had a population of slightly over one million; approximately 70 percent were Indians, and all but a fraction of the remaining 30 percent were poor people of mixed Indian and European blood (ladinos).[30] Despite the Indians' majority status, centuries of servitude, oppression, and geographic isolation hardly provided fertile ground for the germination of nationalist sentiments. Since colonial times, the Indian experience of inclusion within the larger abstraction of the state had generally occurred only when they found themselves pushed into the bottom of the wage labor force or impressed into one or another private army. The deep divisions that prevented Guatemala from claiming its nationhood were perhaps best represented by the repeated efforts of the highly populous (and predominantly Indian) region of the western highlands of Los Altos to secede from the state, thus dividing Guatemala into two separate countries: an indigenous Los Altos, and a more Western, ladino "Guatemala." While Los Altos's several attempts at secession all ended in failure, the last and what was briefly one of the most successful rebellions took place in 1848, fewer than thirty years before Barrios took power.

Yet the indigenous aversion to incorporation into the nation-state, in the minds of liberal thinkers, served only to illustrate its necessity. The imperative for building nationhood was as much pragmatic as ideological, for Indians and poor ladinos were to serve an integral part in the plan for what Liberals simply called "progress": the expansion of capitalism through the export of key commodities, particularly coffee.

As McCreery has shown, the expansion of capitalism was both the central focus and the enduring legacy of the Barrios regime. Early in his administration, Barrios replaced the old colonial-era commercial *consulado* (council) with a modern Ministry of Development (Fomento), which was devoted exclusively to the task of promoting national economic expansion. The work of the Ministry of Development, fueled by the influx of foreign (mainly German) capital, meant that by the time of Barrios's death in 1885 Guatemala produced more than fifty-one million tons of coffee annually, a fivefold increase from 1871.[31]

The cost of the full-blown development of an export economy was to fall largely on the native population, whose traditional patterns of land use and labor were no longer tenable in the new export economy. The immediate need for Indian (and, to a lesser extent, poor ladino) labor to plant and harvest, combined with the eventual need to convert Indian communal lands into coffee *fincas* (farms) required an element of coercion. This the Liberals readily accomplished through such measures as the reestablishment of forced labor levies (*mandamiento*), but the philosophical rationale for coercion and the revival of old colonial methods of servitude was not so easily come by.[32]

To lessen this dissonance somewhat, Barrios outfitted liberalism in the new social theories of positivism, the intellectual progeny of the French social architect Auguste Comte then in vogue in many parts of Latin America. Comte's clarion call for "order and progress" resonated with Barrios's own ambitions and agenda, and the congruencies between old-style liberalism and modern positivism were many.

One obvious point of similarity between old-style liberalism and positivism was a shared aversion to the Catholic Church. The Church was a clear barrier to Liberal reform, primarily because its pervasive hegemony served as an obstacle to the ideology of nationalism. Moreover, the Church's secular power, resuscitated by Carrera, was still formidable in the last decades of the nineteenth century. At the time Barrios seized power, the Church also ran virtually all the schools in the country, monitored educational curriculum (which included the enforcement of a legal prohibition on teaching anti-Catholic doctrine), and censored written material that made its way into the country.[33]

This alone would not have been especially significant (since most Guatemalans in 1873 lived beyond the pale of schools and the written word) had the Church not been intricately linked to local villages through local priests and through religious brotherhoods, or *cofradías*.[34] As we shall see, the nature of the *cofradía* itself underwent considerable transformation during the Liberal period as Church control weakened and the Indians reconstructed the brotherhoods as religious loci of community identity, political coherence, and economic parity. In its initial form, the *cofradía*, with its loose ties to the formal Church and *cura* (clergy), posed a potential obstacle to state construction. Transformed into a more autochthonous Indian-based institution, however, it was an outright threat. As Tim Steigenga has noted, "*cofradías* created an autonomous Indian social structure that was aligned with the Catholic Church and isolated from national society"—a dangerous pairing of religion and ethnicity that was anathema to Barrios's vision of the integrated, autonomous state.[35]

It is important to note that, despite the underpinning of positivist thought in Barrios's brand of liberalism, neither the caudillo nor many of his close advisers called themselves formal adherents to positivist doctrine: in the true spirit of Comte, they freely selected and discarded political ideologies according to pragmatic application. It was within this context of progress, development, and Catholic universality that Barrios seized on the idea of introducing Protestantism into Guatemala. To that end, on 15 March 1873, Barrios issued a Freedom of Worship decree (*libertad de cultos*), which eliminated Catholicism as the state religion (a redundancy, since Rafael Carrera had either intentionally or negligently allowed Gálvez's law of religious toleration to remain on the books during his administration), thus allowing for the open practice of Protestant worship.[36]

Theoretically, Protestantism seemed, from at least two perspectives, to be the ideal vehicle to further the Liberal agenda. On the most prosaic level, Barrios believed that no desirable "civilizing" foreigners from such modern, capital-rich nations as Germany or the United States would immigrate without the assurance that they could practice their own religion; this concern was made explicit in an 1876 treaty with Germany that specifically stipulated that German Lutherans be permitted to worship freely and construct church buildings without restriction.[37] That Barrios imagined that this type of legislation would provoke a mighty influx of Protestant immigrants was clear in the wording of the decree, which reads in part: "The right to freedom of religion in Guatemala would remove one of the principal obstacles that has heretofore impeded foreign immigration to our country, for many do not wish to settle where they are not allowed to exercise their religion."[38]

Second, Barrios also reasoned that competition might eat away at what was still very much a Catholic religious monopoly. In this respect, the decree as such was only one component of a larger body of anti-clerical legislation that reproduced earlier Liberal provisions such as the expropriation of monastic properties, the suspension of ecclesiastical *fueros* (which here referred only to ecclesiastical courts' jurisdiction over clergy), the secularization of cemeteries and marriage ceremonies, and the strict limitation of the number of Catholic clergy who could be present in the country. These laws were designed, of course, to strip the Catholic Church of all but its strictly spiritual function and, as in the case of marriage, even to intrude into this arena. Seen as a whole, the anti-clerical legislation severely truncated the influence of the one "national" institution that competed with the state for the loyalty of the populace.[39]

The introduction of foreign religions, particularly the brand practiced in the nations that were the historical enemies of the Hispanic, Catholic world—most notably England, the home of the Black Legend, and the United States, which had recently gobbled up more than half of Mexico in its own Protestant Manifest Destiny—carried a strong racial message. Although not articulated by Guatemala's Liberals as clearly as it would be a few years later by Porfirio Díaz's *científicos* in Mexico, liberal thought in Guatemala enthusiastically embraced the pseudo-scientific philosophy of social Darwinism. Although it employed a convoluted "scientific" lexicon, social Darwinism was the simple notion that society evolved like any biological matter, and that some people or societies were more highly evolved (civilized) than others. In Guatemala, as well as in other Latin countries with large ethnic populations, "progress," "evolution," and "civilization" became synonymous with northern European and North American, and not coincidentally Protestant, values and beliefs. Thus, the transformative potential inherent in Protestantism existed on not one but two levels: Protestantism could break the bonds of community and atavistic faith that hindered the development of the nation-state, and in doing so it might introduce and nurture the very characteristics that could mold even the most backward members of the state into productive citizens.

There is little evidence to indicate that the Guatemalan Liberals of this period were attracted to Protestantism for the Calvinist and Puritan elements that the German sociologist Max Weber would later link so closely to the rise of capitalism; indeed, Barrios and his advisers, predating Weber by slightly more than a generation, may very well never have made any intellectual connection between the two.[40] Yet it is clear that the Liberals envisioned Protestantism to be very much a "civilizing agent," most specifically in the area of education.

Just as in Mexico under Juárez and Díaz, education lay near the forefront of Guatemala's liberal reform, at least in theory. And, as in Mexico, where President Benito Juárez once issued an invitation to American missionaries to come teach Indians to "read, rather than light candles," Protestant missionaries seemed ideally suited to play a central role in Guatemala.[41] In Guatemala, as in all of Latin America, education had historically fallen under the prerogative of the Roman Catholic Church. During the reform, Liberal usurpation of education had, as planned, greatly reduced the Church's secular power and had opened a new venue for furthering the Liberal agenda. The motives behind the introduction of public education were mixed, shadowing the debate of *científicos* Francisco Bulnes and Justo Sierra in Mexico on the same topic. For Guatemala's more progressive Liberal intellectuals, education was seen as a leaven to hasten the social evolution of the general population. For the more racist of the Liberal policy makers, public education provided an opportunity to indoctrinate and tame the "irredeemable" masses with Liberal propaganda, if little else.[42]

Even in the most cynical assessment, the introduction of public education was an opportunity not to be missed. But given the Church's long domination of the field, Guatemala, like many newly secularized Latin American countries, was sorely lacking in teachers, modern curricula, and pedagogical methodology, which foreign Protestants were unusually well equipped to provide. During the latter decades of the nineteenth century, Protestant educators in England and the United States were active in promoting the innovative British Lancasterian pedagogical system. The fact that several members of the Liberal inner circle, including Lorenzo Montúfar and Barrios's close friend Buenaventura Murga, had both attended Frederick Crowe's school and were convinced of the merits of Protestant educational projects undoubtedly entered into the equation.[43]

Despite this pressing imperative, ten years passed after the Freedom of Worship decree became law before any denomination in the United States sent a single missionary to Guatemala, and this transpired only after Barrios, on a trip to New York to negotiate a border dispute with Mexico, approached a foreign mission board personally. In 1882, the caudillo persuaded the Presbyterian Board of Foreign Missions to reroute John Clark Hill, a pastor designated to work in China, to return with him to Guatemala. Hill was reluctant; in the hierarchy of mission work, China, with its hundreds of millions of "heathens" was considered a more worthy destination than was Guatemala, which boasted only a million or so people who were already Christian, albeit of the wrong variety. Moreover, Hill was singularly unsuited for the tasks that Barrios had in mind for him. In Thomas Bogenschield's description, "the conservative Presbyterian theology and Victorian social attitudes offered by Hill . . . were far removed from the modernists' ideologies that were popularized and promoted by the developmentalist state."[44] But even at that, the board's hesitation stemmed mainly from the bottom line; Hill was to receive a twelve-hundred-dollar salary in 1883, more than twice what it cost to sustain missionaries in the Far East, and even this princely sum was hardly enough to allow Hill to keep up with the lifestyle of the national elite in the new prosperity of Liberal Guatemala.[45] With benefit of hindsight, Hill's reticence and Guatemala's low priority offer a glimpse of the kinds of problems that would plague the medium-range future for Protestantism in Guatemala.

Nonetheless, Hill permitted himself to be sent to Guatemala. In early 1883, using a building lent by Barrios himself, just off Guatemala City's Parque Central, Hill established a small congregation and a school called La Patria. These initiatives proved less than successful, however; Hill, who declined to learn even the rudiments of Spanish, became embroiled in political intrigues and invested heavily in bonds to finance the Northern Railroad, that "precise symbol of modern capitalism" that was to link the capital with the northern coast.[46] The railway project failed after two capital-intensive attempts, leaving Hill deeply in debt. Yet Hill claimed that his involvement in the railway scandal indicated not a moral lapse, but the mission board's failure to support him in a way that would allow him to keep up appearances among Guatemala City's elites, the specific target of his mission efforts.

The school, however, despite Hill's inattention, was a modest success. Barrios sent his own children to study at La Patria, as did most of his cabinet officers; there the nation's future leaders learned English, pedagogy, Christian living, social growth, and personal finance.[47] Since many of Barrios's colleagues were professed atheists, one must assume that the attraction of the school was its political cachet and its offerings in the English language, for which there was an increasing demand as Guatemala entered the world market.

Despite the pedigree of the students in attendance, local hostility toward Hill, the mission, and the school was high, so much so that Barrios at one point offered the pastor use of his personal bodyguards.[48] Bad feelings toward the endeavor apparently did not abate over time; by 1885, hostility was sufficiently visible that an American visitor to the capital remarked, "Both the church and the school received the hearty support of Barrios; not so much because he favored this form of religion as because he recognized it [as] a civilizing and progressive power, the power he admired above all others. . . . Since he favored it, no one dared offer any opposition, for his word is law, but the people call [the school] in derision a *protestantería*."[49]

With the death of his sponsor, Justo Rufino Barrios, in 1885, Hill's fortunes plummeted. He continued to dally in railroad schemes and moneymaking scandals, claiming that the Board of Missions' failure to adequately support the mission and its refusal to allow the mission to accept subsidies from the Guatemalan government necessitated such activity. In November 1886, the Presbyterian Board of Missions abruptly dismissed Hill, and he returned to the United States.[50]

Barrios's death and the recall of John Clark Hill the following year might well have spelled the end of Protestant work in Guatemala, but in fact they set the stage for what might be called the pioneer era in mission work in the country. Barrios's death did little to change the prevailing political ethos in Guatemala. His brand of liberalism continued to define the political landscape throughout the presidencies of his immediate successor and of Manuel Estrada Cabrera who, during his more than two decades in office, carried the aging precepts of liberalism into the twentieth century. Barrios's immediate successor, José María Reyna Barrios, adopted his uncle's developmentalist agenda wholesale, including the work to be done by Protestant missionaries.

A second factor was also at play. The Presbyterian Board of Missions by the late 1880s had begun to reevaluate the low priority it had given to Latin American mission work, primarily because of the denomination's unexpected successes in Porfirian Mexico, at least in terms of official support from the government, if not from the population in general.[51] Even so, the surprisingly high cost of living in Guatemala at that time and its general lack of foreign cachet (which was important for attracting contributions for mission support) suggest that it is unlikely that the Presbyterians would have replaced Hill immediately had not a twenty-seven-year-old preacher named Edward M. Haymaker volunteered for the post.

Haymaker, a Missourian who had studied at Yale Divinity School, came to Guatemala fresh from a three-year stint in Zacatecas, in Central Mexico. Fluent in Spanish and at home with Latin culture, he was one of a new breed of young missionaries who practiced an evangelical Calvinism tempered by the Social Gospel, a radical and controversial movement that was being taught in only a few influential North American seminaries at that time.[52] Unlike many of the missionaries who would follow him, Haymaker was attracted to missionary work by the Social Gospel, with its dual message of social concern in this world and salvation in the next.

The Social Gospel was itself a response to the turmoil of industrial society in the late nineteenth century. It called on Christians to address issues of societal reform and was a dramatic departure from traditional Protestantism's preoccupation with the salvation of individual souls or, for that matter, Catholicism's emphasis on sin and penance. In some respects, the Social Gospel's emphasis on the here-and-now imperative foreshadowed the "praxis" called for by Liberation Theology in the mid-twentieth century, but this is not to suggest that it prevented Haymaker, perhaps unwittingly, from taking his place in the government's grand plan of national development.

To the contrary, Haymaker's Social Gospel orientation placed him squarely among those whom the Liberals believed to be most in want of civilization: poor Indian and ladino urban workers whom Haymaker affectionately (and patronizingly) referred to as "the Great Unwashed." In part, Haymaker's enthusiasm for working with the poor stemmed from practical considerations, since wealthy elites and liberal intellectuals found Freemasonry and agnosticism to be more attractive alternatives to Catholicism than was Protestantism.[53] Haymaker did maintain friendships with the influential Montúfar family, who lived across the street from him, and with German Lutherans and American and British expatriates, for whom he surreptitiously conducted services from the Anglican *Book of Common Prayer* until the Presbyterian Board of Missions found him out and put a stop to the practice in 1902.[54] But, as Haymaker himself was quick to point out, it was generally not the elites but "the lowest class who have nothing on earth to lose" who were the ones most likely to associate with the mission.[55]

In the United States, the Social Gospel was most concerned with the earthly needs of the urban immigrants, so it is not surprising that in the early years of his ministry, Haymaker's greatest interest lay in the largely ladino urban working class. For Haymaker, the dismal realities of Guatemala's vast gulf between rich and poor, Indian and non-Indian, fit readily into the framework of his own theological-social understanding. Although he was ultimately concerned with the saving of souls, he attributed "sin" and "vice" as much to oppression and environment as to moral failing. Catholicism, he believed, had stunted the process of social evolution, engendering a social environment of oppression, drunkenness, and greed.

Confident in the belief that Protestantism could counteract these corrosive forces and provide a wholesome venue for moral instruction, Haymaker initiated a variety of social organizations and educational programs targeting the urban poor. In 1881, he established the Workingman's Temperance and Improvement Society (Bolas de Plata), designed to provide "innocent and useful diversions" for working-class men and boys, and in 1889, he opened a recreation center with a small library and gymnasium for the working poor in the capital.[56] Prosaic though these projects were, they were innovative for the day, perhaps too much so; both failed after a few months.

Haymaker's more successful projects were also more ambitious. Between 1893 and 1906, he founded a satellite campus of La Patria school and established a vocational school in El Progreso. In 1888, he imported a printing press to publish tracts and a newsletter, *El Mensajero* (The Messenger), and to provide an additional source of revenue for the mission (a practice that came to a halt when one disciple was caught printing beer labels on the church machine).[57]

In 1890, the Presbyterian mission board sent down a male pastor to assist Haymaker in his work; he was soon followed by two married couples and later still by two female teachers and a doctor—Guatemala's first female physician. All three women were single, the first of a disproportionately large number of well-trained, well-educated single women who worked, often alone, in the mission field during those early decades.

Despite this expansion, the Presbyterian effort made little impact in terms of conversion or social assistance among the urban poor, as Haymaker was well aware. By the end of 1887, he reported to his board that 125 people had attended the mission's Christmas service, but admitted that average attendance on Sundays in the flagship church in the capital was usually closer to 20.[58]

Given this discouraging situation, Haymaker began to cast his sights toward the countryside, where the real objects of liberal religious designs resided—the Indian population. In September 1898, Haymaker offered his board the following suggestion: "It is not for me to forecast the views of the Board, as the question of [Indian work] has never been stated, but I am free to say that I would favor the development of work on behalf of these Aborigines for the Mission."[59] Interpreting a lack of response as a positive sign—which it most certainly was not, for the issue of Indian-language ministry later proved to be a bitter point of controversy between board and missionaries in the field—Haymaker opened a small Presbyterian mission in Quetzaltenango in the last months of 1898 and set himself to the formidable task of learning Ki'ché, the language of that region.[60] Two years later, in 1901, the Presbyterians established their second permanent Indian congregation, a Spanish-language mission in San Marcos, near Mexico's southern border.[61]

While Haymaker plodded along in Guatemala, his contemporaries in the emerging field of sociology were plotting out the scientific study of religion. In 1912, Emile Durkheim published *Les formes élémentaires de la vie religieuse,* which posed a series of seminal hypotheses that formed the basis for the discipline of the sociology of religion. His central premise, that religion's role becomes increasingly circumscribed as society becomes more complex, was underscored by a complicated causal linkage between urbanization, industrialization, religious conversion (usually to Protestantism), and, ultimately, the secularization of society.

For our purposes here, the fact that Haymaker's experience fell utterly outside the Durkheimian paradigm may open a small window on the structural dynamic of urban Guatemala in the late nineteenth century. In 1880, Guatemala City was a nonindustrialized metropolis that served, to a limited extent, a large, intensively cultivated rural hinterland. Although Guatemala was undergoing dramatic change as liberal economic reforms transformed postcolonial agricultural systems into commercial, capitalist enterprises, it would be some time before these changes would affect the urban workers as profoundly as they immediately did rural Indians and other small-scale *agricultores* (farmers). In 1880, the demographics of the capital were relatively stable; its population, while not static, still did not have the constant and heavy infusion of rural immigrants that characterized the city a century later. This suggests, perhaps, that the sector of the urban poor was more constant and more stable—perhaps even relatively less "poor" (in a psychological sense, if not in an economic one) than its counterpart in the next century. In this context, neither Haymaker's projects nor his message offered much that could not be found in traditional venues, such as the extended family, the community, or the Catholic Church, and at a significantly lower social price.

Haymaker's efforts also shed light on the status of the Roman Catholic Church in Guatemala in the late nineteenth century. For most of that century, the stumbling fortunes of the Catholic Church were a metaphor for the issues that faced Guatemala as it entered nationhood. For Liberals, a strong Church—institutionally vital, wealthy, and emotionally evocative, the locus of loyalty and authority—was not merely a powerful contender for the hearts and minds of the populace, but a Goliath to be slain before the issues of nationhood could effectively be addressed. The Liberals sometimes waged this war as an assault, sometimes as a war of attrition, but even given the respite of the Carrera era, the Catholic Church steadily hemorrhaged money, power, labor, and authority throughout the nineteenth century.

Yet, even in these straitened circumstances, the Church still retained its spiritual hegemony. A "Catholic" identity was still strong in the late nineteenth century, even among those who never attended mass or who practiced folk religion so far removed from orthodox Catholicism that some called it "witchcraft" (*brujería*). In late-nineteenth-century Guatemala, Catholic identity had shifting and sometimes contradictory levels of meaning and valence, but it was nonetheless an identity that held utility and value across virtually all class or ethnic lines, though just what that value and utility were might vary considerably. In this respect, "Catholicism" as identity (as opposed to belief) was still so universal that, although one might drift away from the orthodox practice of the faith through the heterodoxy of local practice, backsliding, Freemasonry, or even the professed agnosticism of many liberal intellectuals, it was neither acceptable nor desirable to throw one's lot in with the competitive variety of Christianity—even when it was directly associated with the promise of "modernity," the hope of reform, or the allure of foreign lifestyles.

CHAPTER 2

"BETTER THAN GUNSHIPS"

The Institutional Expansion of Missions

Our institutions will do more than gunboats.

—Dr. Mary Gregg, Presbyterian Mission, 1909

BY THE last decade of the nineteenth century, important shifts in the Zeitgeist of North American missionary work brought, if not a flood, then at least a trickle of new missionaries into Latin America and to Guatemala in particular. The reason for this shift lay in the United States' growing influence in the world arena in the days following the Civil War. The rapid expansion of the U.S. Navy and Merchant Marine, the acquisition of coaling stations in the Pacific, and American involvement in the Spanish American War all generated among North American Christians a lively discourse on the larger implications of empire. To some extent, the "Christian response" broke down along what were soon to be (but were not yet) described as modernist-fundamentalist lines.

To some future modernists, the expanding political hegemony of the United States called for isolationism and peaceability in world affairs—two time-honored principles in theory, if not in practice, in both conventional Protestantism and the American political tradition. But to others, some of whom were modernists but most of whom would be better described as evangelicals, the expansion of political hegemony carried with it an obligation and opportunity that might be termed a spiritual manifest destiny. Starting in the mid-nineteenth century, evangelical theologians and scholars of the new science of sociology began to visualize Protestant missions as the handmaidens of empire. Like the secular liberals of Latin America, mission theorists beginning in the 1870s often employed Darwinian terminology and conceptualized Protestant Christianity as a means of "arrest[ing] the downward trend of degenerate races."[1]

This militant and aggressive missionary thrust took shape first in England in the mid-nineteenth century, where evangelical refugees from the Anglican Oxford Movement, Methodists, and other Protestant dissenters sought to spread the light of Christian civilization to the darkest corners of the Pax Britannica. In North America, the movement took a decidedly scientific bent. Among the most influential framers of the movement was Harvard theologian John Fiske, whose classic *Outlines of a Cosmic Philosophy* (1874) was among the first works to attempt to reconcile Darwin's theory of evolution with conventional Christian teleology. Fiske was profoundly influenced not only by the work of Darwin, but also by that of Herbert Spencer, whose ten-volume *Synthetic Philosophy* applied Darwin's biological theory to human morality and society, therein producing both the popular philosophy of social Darwinism and the foundation of modern social science.

In the late 1870s, Fiske produced a series of essays that added a religious element to the cold theories of social and biological evolution. For him, social evolution was not an inexorable process, but one that could be manipulated and controlled, in much the same way that a child grows to adulthood: physical maturity occurs through an unalterable biological process, but social development is molded and formed by "a good upbringing." To Fiske, two forces—Protestant religion and democracy—could provide a similar mitigating effect in the social evolution of primitive societies. This he articulated in a series of works beginning with *The Unseen World and Other Essays* (1876). Here, Fiske sounded a call for social evolution under North American tutelage, a new global order characterized by political expansionism, Anglo-Saxon greatness, and Protestantism in the post–Civil War era.

The fusion of Darwinism and Protestant belief might seem incongruous, given the post-Enlightenment animus between science and religion. It did not seem so, however, to a handful of prominent North American theologians to whom the theory of evolution, with its focus on selection and its implicit suggestion of a larger evolutionary plan, was congruent with a broad understanding of traditional Calvinist teachings, particularly the doctrine of predestination. For example, John Fiske's contemporary, the noted Congregationalist preacher and controversial social activist Henry Ward Beecher, called himself a "cordial Christian evolutionist" and, in 1885, published a book entitled *Evolution and Religion,* which did much to make the notions of evolution—both biological and social—palpable to the religious public in the United States.[2]

When distilled to the popular level, the emphasis of Christian evolutionists shifted from the abstract to the concrete, and from this was born the movement for spiritual manifest destiny. The notion was arresting in its simplicity: American missionaries, blessed by sagacity, prosperity, and charitable temperaments, had a divine obligation to hasten the evolutionary development of unreached people by teaching them proper Christian doctrine and civilized behavior.[3] One of the most articulate North American spokesmen of spiritual manifest destiny was Josiah Strong, a celebrated social commentator of the post–U.S. Civil War era. In a widely disseminated book published in 1885, he sounded a missionary call to arms that so resonated that by 1900 almost every major North American denomination had established or revived an overseas mission society. Wrote Strong: "[The Anglo Saxon] is divinely commissioned to be, in a peculiar sense, his brother's keeper . . . It is chiefly to the English and American people that we must look for the evangelization of the world that all men may be lifted in the light of honest Christian civilization . . . God is training the Anglo-Saxon race for its mission."[4]

Nowhere was the movement of spiritual manifest destiny more apparent than in Cuba, where twenty-four Protestant denominations established missions during the ten-year American military occupation of the island following the Spanish American War.[5] Cuba, of course, was a crucial test case in both spiritual and political manifest destiny. The island having been liberated by Protestant Anglo Saxons from the yoke of Spanish, Catholic oppression, it is no wonder that one of the commanders of the U.S. occupation troops felt moved to write, "We must lift them up by a generous and noble Christian series of efforts. It is our God-given mission, and the whole Christian world is watching to see if the great American republic is equal to the strain."[6]

Guatemala, on the other hand, a place that most mission boards still considered a backwater, received only one sixth as many new missions as Cuba did during the same period. Still, even there, the fervor generated by this divine mandate was infectious; even Haymaker, who normally considered his sympathies to be with the underdog, waxed enthusiastic. In 1917, he wrote these words in a typewritten guide called "A Study in Latin American Futures," which he produced single-handedly to distribute to potential American investors in Guatemala: "The missionary corollary of the Monroe Doctrine is that Central America is our responsibility. Others will not evangelize it, America must. The spirit of the Monroe Doctrine rules out more than European armies; it chills European mission efforts and keeps it away."[7]

The missionary movement also breathed new life into some of the older Bible societies that had been born out of the upheaval of the Great Awakening in the United States during the last years of the eighteenth century, an awakening that had languished during most of the nineteenth. Such was the case with the American Bible Society, which established Guatemala as its base of operations for all of Central America in 1892. The next year, the British and Foreign Bible Society, having not pursued work in the country since the eviction of Frederick Crowe during the Carrera era, sent an agent to Guatemala. So diligent were the agents of the two societies that in 1901 Haymaker remarked to his mission board that "the country is deluged with Bibles."[8]

But there was another dimension to the late-nineteenth-century missionary thrust that was less triumphalist; indeed, in tone and focus this second impetus was downright apocalyptic. While the last decades of the century were a time of expansion and growth in the United States, they were also a time of rapid change and domestic turmoil. This was an era when old verities about religion and faith became the subject of sometimes irreverent scrutiny and public dissection, when time-honored "American" (read Protestant, North Atlantic) values and tradition seemed ready to submerge beneath waves of Jewish and Catholic immigrants from Eastern Europe, when America's frontier disappeared and its cities bloated, and when, in 1893, the nation's worst economic depression to date seemed to make a mockery of the "land of opportunity."

It was this crucible that produced the eschatological vision of the Central American Mission (CAM), one of several missionary agencies and new denominations that emerged in the United States in response to this era of crisis. The Central American Mission was founded in 1888 by a group guided by a Dallas businessman by the name of Cyrus I. Scofield. Scofield and the other founders of the CAM were premillennialists who believed that the social tumult in the United States was the period of Great Tribulation, which was to precede the dawn of the thousand-year reign of Christ described in the Book of Revelation. Messianic millenarianism, of course, has found expression in virtually every religious tradition in the world, but its distinctive expression in this context came from the theological construct known as dispensationalism.

Emerging first in England and the United States in the latter part of the nineteenth century, dispensationalism was the belief that history was divided into linear epochs, or "dispensations," in which God progressively revealed His divine nature and plan to humanity. The Final Dispensation would culminate in the end of the world and the beginning of the thousand-year reign of Christ.[9]

Although dispensationalism's emphasis on teleological evolution would seem to suggest a liberal theological slant, it was nonetheless a profoundly conservative ideology, in both a theological and a social sense. It views human action as largely peripheral to God's unfolding blueprint, except where that action contributed directly to the coming of the Kingdom. Clearly, this lay in stark contrast to the social activism of the Social Gospel and placed dispensationalism solidly within the camp of conservative Protestant ideology.

The CAM's missionary thrust, however, fell wholly within the paradigm of dispensationalist activism. Scofield believed that the time for the world was nigh and that the entire world must hear the Word of God before the Kingdom could come. In Scofield's vision, Central America was particularly ripe for this latter-day conversion and the existing Protestant denominations were remiss in their neglect of the region. To remedy this failure, Scofield and his backers founded the CAM in an effort to save Central America and to hasten the coming of the Millennial Kingdom.[10]

The CAM sent its first missionary to Guatemala in 1896, one H. C. Dillon, who succumbed within a matter of months to "tropical fevers." Three years later, the CAM's first permanent missionaries, the Rev. and Mrs. Albert E. Bishop, arrived in Guatemala City. Within three years, at least nine more missionaries joined the CAM in Guatemala.[11]

Because the CAM was not technically a denomination, the organization was not concerned with the niceties of church buildings and pastors' salaries and was thus able, at least in the beginning, to pour all of its human and economic resources into straightforward evangelization. Within a few years, CAM missionaries had sprinkled tiny missions all over the country, although the organization focused most of its efforts on the capital and the densely populated indigenous zones of the western highlands.[12]

By benefit of its fairly generous and well-placed resources, the CAM enjoyed some modest successes. Its largest church, established in 1889, was in the capital and located at a busy intersection where five streets came together, thus inspiring the name Iglesia Evangélica Cinco Calles.

After a promotional revival during which its pastor, Albert Bishop, conducted boisterous but well-attended services for 150 consecutive nights, the Cinco Calles Church was off to a solid start. By October 1889, Bishop could report, "God is blessing—large attendance every night at our meeting."[13]

Much of the CAM's growth was at the expense of the Presbyterians, however, who had neither the money nor the staff to compete effectively with the interlopers. Shortly after the opening of the Cinco Calles Church, Haymaker complained to his mission board that "the only thing I can do is to be as ubiquitous as possible and try to hold out against . . . Central American missionaries who persistently steal my sheep. I think that it must be admitted," he added, "that the odds against me are heavy."[14]

It was not long before the competition between the missions in the capital took an ugly turn. Theoretically, the differences between the Presbyterians and the Central American Mission were purely theological in nature and, on the surface, relatively superficial. The CAM was premillenarialist; the Presbyterians, as a group, were not, although some individual missionaries did subscribe to that doctrine. The CAM baptized by immersion, the Presbyterians by "sprinkling." CAM missionaries accused the Presbyterians of "sectarianism" and berated them for working on salary rather than "on faith."[15]

But what most fueled the flames was the fact that Haymaker and Bishop had what would be called a century later a "personality conflict." The relationship between the two had gotten off to a rocky start when Bishop had first come to Guatemala City. Although Haymaker met with Bishop soon after his arrival, the latter wrote to the CAM office in Dallas that the city was "a virgin field where no work has been done." The letter infuriated Haymaker, and relations between the two men deteriorated further as Presbyterian converts began to drift away to attend CAM services.[16]

By the first years of the new century, the ill feeling between the two missionaries had degenerated into an outright feud. In mission reports for 1901, Haymaker referred to Bishop as one "whose spirituality . . . consist[s] of crankiness and fanaticism" and claimed Bishop and his organization discredited the entire Protestant effort in Guatemala. "They go blundering away in the most public and obtrusive style," Haymaker wrote, "making the course they represent rediculous [sic] in the extreme and imagining that they are doing these foolish things when in reality it is the cause of Christ they are bringing into ridicule by coupling all this stuff with evangelical Christianity."[17]

The animosity was mutual, as evidenced by letters to his board in which Bishop accused Haymaker of being "sectarian, unconverted, worldly, and faithless." He also pronounced the Presbyterian Church to be as corrupt as the Roman Catholic Church—a remark that must have cut Haymaker, who was a true catholophobe, to the quick. At one point, the war of words between the two reached such a low ebb that Bishop called the Presbyterian mission an "institution of the Devil."[18]

The feud between Haymaker and Bishop reached its nadir in 1902, when an earthquake destroyed the Presbyterian mission in Quetzaltenango. With the Quetzaltenango station gone and the congregation in Guatemala City greatly depleted by the CAM, the Presbyterian Board of Foreign Missions began to make quiet inquiries into the possibility of turning the Presbyterian work over to the Central American Mission. The Presbyterian board ultimately concluded that such a move was inadvisable, but the episode did little to smooth the relationship between Haymaker and Bishop.[19]

The conflict between Edward Haymaker and Albert Bishop, personal and pettish though it often was, served as a metaphor for the much larger struggle that engulfed the Protestant world at the turn of the century between the modernists and the conservatives, who were at that point just beginning to refer to themselves as "fundamentalists." The modernist stream of Protestant thought—typified by preachers such as Henry Ward Beecher—attempted to carve out a consensus between modern science and traditional religious belief. Through such means as the "higher criticism" of biblical texts and the allegorical interpretation of biblical teachings, and by expanding the social role of churches, modernists sought an accommodation between the physical world of modern science and the metaphysical sphere occupied by religion. The impact of modernist thought spread rapidly in the last decades of the nineteenth century and touched virtually every major Protestant denomination. By the 1890s, however, conservative critics of modernism in mainline denominations began to call for a return to "traditional" and "fundamental" Christian doctrine. The touchstone issue for conservatives was textual criticism of the Bible, which they believed to be an unalterable sacred text, inerrant and literally true. The transformation of conservative orthodoxy into outright fundamentalism was a protracted process that drew from most mainline Protestant denominations, although some, such as the Baptists, were more caught by the groundswell than others.

The modernist-fundamentalist rift did not formally splinter until just after World War I, when, in 1919, conservatives established the World Christian Fundamentals Association. But the battle lines in Protestant Christianity were drawn at least a decade earlier, even in Guatemala.[20] The CAM's denouncement of the Presbyterians' "worldliness" and its involvement in social projects marked it as what Thomas Bogenschield has called "protofundamentalist" and cast the CAM as distinct from the modernist-infused Presbyterians as typified by Haymaker.[21]

Yet even in this context, it is important to note that these generalizations were not universal, for many Presbyterians, including some missionaries who came to Guatemala, were attracted to conservative theologies and even to the fiery eschatological doctrines of premillenarianism. Even so, as long as Haymaker continued to dominate the Presbyterian work, the mission retained its relatively liberal focus, couched in the Social Gospel.[22]

While the Presbyterians and the CAM played out on their small stage the drama that continues to divide modern Protestant Christianity, other denominations were beginning to slip quietly into Guatemala. In 1901, two missionary husband-and-wife teams from a small group called the Pentecostal Mission (which later became part of the Nazarene Church) attempted to found a small mission in Livingston, on Guatemala's disease-ridden Atlantic coast.[23] In the first year, all four missionaries died in a yellow fever epidemic. The Pentecostal mission sent two more missionary couples as replacements in 1903 and 1904. Two of these missionaries also caught yellow fever, but both survived. In 1904, the pastors, John Butler and Richard Anderson, prudently moved their work to the more salubrious coffee lands of Alta Verapaz, where they established a Pentecostal-Nazarene church in Cobán in 1904.[24]

At about the same time, another missionary group, the Quakers, or Society of Friends, initiated work in southern Guatemala. In the early spring of 1902, Thomas J. Kelly and Clark J. Buckley, two young men who had impetuously rushed into mission work after hearing an inspirational speaker in California, arrived in the country unable to speak the language and utterly bewildered by the social, political, and geographic landscape. After spending a few months in the capital to learn Spanish, Kelly and Buckley faithfully headed south to what they believed to be a spot chosen by God: the town of Chiquimula, a violent mestizo town on the dry, desolate plateau near the Honduran border. The two Quakers used Chiquimula as a base from which to distribute Bibles at fairs in the larger towns of the area—in Jocotán, Quetzaltepeque, and the revered Catholic pilgrimage destination of Esquipulas—throughout 1902. They established no permanent mission until 1906, when Ruth Esther Smith arrived in Chiquimula to become the matriarch of the Friends' work in Guatemala for the next forty-one years.[25]

Both the Nazarenes and the Quakers were conservative denominations, but combined with the Presbyterians and the CAM, they represented a fairly wide spectrum of Protestant doctrinal diversity. The records left by the various missions suggest a subtext of division and conflict between various groups, but there is no evidence of the type of interdenominational conflagration that flared between the Presbyterians and the CAM. Despite the fundamental differences and competition that divided the denominations, however, by the beginning years of the century, mission records show the formation of a surprising array of pan-denominational cooperative agreements, missionary conferences, and comity accords, which appear to have been forged as much from necessity as from Christian concord. The missionaries' social and geographic isolation from one another may have contributed to this show of unity: in adversity, strength in numbers.[26]

The most important of these cooperative arrangements was one that divided Guatemala into denominational spheres of influence in 1902.[27] Although such a division might seem contradictory, given the competitive aims of the missions, the agreement was modeled on similar divisions of territory by missionaries in Asia and Africa. The impetus for such comity was the practical recognition that no single denomination had sufficient personnel or funding to evangelize all of Guatemala alone. This, coupled with the shared belief that intradenominational differences paled before the specter of Catholicism and—later—that of the more *outré* sects such as Jehovah's Witnesses (then known as Russellites, after their founder, Charles Russell) and Seventh-Day Adventists— precipitated the partition of 1902, later codified into a formal Comity Agreement in 1936.[28]

Because the Comity Agreement was based largely on where each mission had existing work, the division of territory by departments was somewhat random, but did follow some general patterns of ethnic and spatial settlement. These, serendipitously, correspond roughly to Lovell and Lutz's schema of "core and periphery" of social and ethnic relation-

Guatemala

The Comity Agreement

Petén

Huehuetenango

Alta Verapaz

Izabal

El Quiché

San Marcos

Baja Verapaz

Zacapa

Totoni-capán

El Progreso

Quetzalte-nango

Chimal-tenango

Soloá

Guatemala

Chiquimula

Jalapa

Sacate-péquez

Retalhuleu

Suchite-péquez

Jutiapa

Escuintla

Santa Rosa

Presbyterian

Nazerene

Primitive Methodist

CAM

Friends

0   65 mi

65 km

ships in colonial Guatemala; this schema provides a useful model for understanding mission expansion and influence even at the cusp of the twentieth century.[29]

The Presbyterians received what was arguably the most desirable territory, in what Lovell and Lutz call the lowland core and the eastern edge of the highland periphery.[30] This included the heart of the predominantly Kaqchikēl and Ki'ché departments of the altiplano, including the city of Quetzaltenango, which they correctly perceive to be the "Indian capital" of Guatemala, as well as an important commercial center. From Quetzaltenango, Presbyterian country ran east, to include the important departments that lined the Quetzaltenango–Guatemala City corridor.

The Presbyterians also laid claim to the southwestern departments of Retalhuleu and Suchitepéquez, in which lay the *"boca costa,"* the rich piedmont lands that were, by 1902, the heartland of lucrative coffee cultivation. They also included the predominantly ladino departments of El Progreso and Guatemala, long sites of Presbyterian missionary labors. The centrality and productivity of these zones gave them an integral role in Liberal plans for economic development and regional integration. By 1910, Presbyterian land was traversed by a modern system of railroads (including the Pan-American), which ran from the capital to Retalhuleu, and by a new network of roads that connected both the piedmont and Quetzaltenango to Guatemala City.[31]

Thus, Presbyterian work found itself squarely in the middle of the vortex of Liberal development and its concomitant results: the integration of metropolis into periphery, the conversion of subsistence lands into commercial production, the expansion of transportation and communication, the beginning of labor migration, and the redefinition of ethnic relations. Understandably, this would profoundly affect the direction of Presbyterian work in the future.

Most of the territory that the CAM received through the Comity Agreement was geographically more remote, less suited to coffee production, and thus less immediately affected by Liberal policies. Lying mostly on the western side of Lovell and Lutz's "highland periphery," CAM territory stretched in a northwesterly arc from Guatemala City, taking in the Kaqchikēl and Ki'ché lands near Lake Atitlán and reaching up into the Mam and ladino districts of San Marcos and Huehuetenango, along the Mexican border. The CAM also received three departments along the Pacific coast, however, including Escuintla, the industrial city that would emerge as the financial hub of the southern coast as the export economy expanded in the first decades of the century.

The two smaller denominations, the Friends and the Nazarenes, received more circumscribed claims, although even these far outstripped the resources of these tiny missions. Quaker territory lay in the lowland periphery, along the Honduran border and the Atlantic coast, reaching from the established mission in Chiquimula up into Zacapa and Izabal, where one year earlier, United Fruit Company had made its first purchase of Caribbean "hot lands" to convert into banana plantations. The completion of the Northern Railroad in 1912, linking the newly completed entrepôt of Puerto Barrios with Guatemala City, ran a vital artery through Quaker territory.[32] But the Friends' isolation in Chiquimula and the preponderance of women in their organization, who were prohibited by modesty and convention from venturing too far from the mission enclave, prevented them from expanding much beyond Chiquimula and its environs.

The Nazarenes, the smallest of the primary mission agencies, claimed the coffee-rich but peripheral highland departments of Alta and Baja Verapaz and the sparsely inhabited frontier of the Petén. The Verapaces, which were linked by neither road nor rail to the rest of the country, were primarily inhabited by the aloof Qeq'chi Indians and a sizable but insular German population engaged in coffee production. The Germans, who were typically Lutheran or indifferent, made poor prospects for conversion, while the Qeq'chi language was a formidable obstacle to the Nazarenes, who initially expressed a theoretical aversion to non-Spanish ministry. Thus, in the remote Alta and Baja Verapaz, the Nazarenes found themselves unusually isolated from both potential converts and other missionaries.

Despite striking differences in doctrine, geography, and logistics, the basic *modus operandi* of mission work was essentially the same for each denomination. The most common method involved preaching trips, which might last several days or even weeks. During these trips, missionaries would stop in towns and witness door-to-door, handing out tracts and Gospels. Later, often assisted by some "native helper"—a lay preacher who translated the missionary's words into the local language and did follow-up work after a missionary's visit—they would hold a small revival in some public location. For these services, native helpers were paid an abysmally small stipend, an issue that became something of a preoccupation for some of the more thoughtful missionaries. The public revivals, though open to all takers, were generally kept low-key to prevent confrontations with hostile villagers. Haymaker noted that his early preaching meetings seldom even included music, because music would call too much public attention to the gathering. "In those days," he recalled some years later, "we still wanted to avoid publicity."[33]

The missionaries took with them on these preaching trips a number of tracts, Bibles, and New Testaments, which they usually sold to their listeners at a nominal price. Haymaker recorded in 1918 that he normally sold copies of the New Testament for one *real,* then worth about five-eighths of a cent. "We prefer selling them," he explained, "because they (the people) value it much higher if they pay for it."[34] Their more elaborate methods presaged, perhaps, the high-tech ministries of the televangelists of the next century. Haymaker sometimes employed "magic lantern" (a type of slide projector that used a gaslight for illumination) shows on his preaching trips, in which he regularly showed slides of Paris and the Egyptian pyramids as well as of the Holy Land. Other missionaries drew audiences by using stereopticons in their evangelizing efforts.[35]

The preaching trips were notoriously grueling. Rural inns regularly denied board to missionaries, and, if they failed to find lodging with new converts or sympathetic locals, they ended up sleeping outdoors in hammocks brought along for such an eventuality.[36] Local vendors often refused to sell them food, or offered them tainted or inedible fare. Usually, missionaries traveled on foot, but occasionally they rode, as did the women from the Quaker mission in Chiquimula, who astonished residents of remote villages by arriving to preach, often alone or in pairs and astride mules.[37]

Although staff and resources for all the organizations were quite limited, all five missions purposefully set out to establish not only churches, but secular projects designed to bring civilization to the nation and prestige to the missions as well. By 1920, these projects included schools, mobile medical clinics, a hospital, literacy programs, publishing houses, and, eventually, Bible translation projects.

The Presbyterian mission, the only nonfundamentalist denomination, was the most ideologically committed to the development of secular institutions, and it subsequently produced the most extensive outreach program. In addition to the industrial school and two secondary schools in the capital that Haymaker had built up during the last years of the nineteenth century, the Presbyterians also opened schools in Quetzaltenango and Mazatenango. They founded a hospital in Guatemala City in 1910, the Hospital Americano, which, after some initial problems, became the nation's first modern medical facility. By 1920, the mission had established permanent medical clinics from mission outstations scattered throughout the highlands. The Presbyterians also operated two printing presses, one in the capital and the other in Quetzaltenango, from which they published at least two religious journals, religious and secular books, and a variety of tracts and pamphlets in Spanish.[38]

The Central American Mission, a comparatively well staffed and well funded organization, competed with the Presbyterians in secular proj- ects. In this, the CAM was typical of the protofundamentalist missions operating in Guatemala at the time in that it rhetorically eschewed the development of social institutions, but developed them anyway out of practical concerns. The CAM was theoretically interested only in the sav- ing of souls, not in the improvement of this world—a sensible ap- proach, given their belief in the imminence of the Second Coming— but the agency nonetheless opened a large elementary and secondary school in Guatemala City in 1914.

Unlike the Presbyterians, who endorsed secular education as an end unto itself, the CAM valued education primarily as a vehicle for theologi- cal instruction. In 1926, it opened its own Bible institute, the Instituto Bíblico Centroamericano, which soon became a training center for the- ology students from all over Central America and, occasionally, Mexico. The CAM also opened a boarding school for missionary children in Hue- huetenango, as well as several small *colegios* (primary schools) in other parts of the country.[39] In 1909, the CAM permitted itself to engage in the affairs of this world by placing a permanent clinic in San Antonio Aguas- calientes and establishing a training program for itinerant nurses.[40]

The smaller denominations contented themselves with making edu- cation the major focus of their mission, since education, after all, was es- sential to their primary task. The Quakers, whose view of education lay closer to that of the Presbyterians than to that of the CAM, despite their theologically conservative orientation, opened an elementary school in Chiquimula in 1908. In 1912, they founded a coeducational institution called the Berea Bible Training School.[41] The Nazarene mission, too, joined in the evangelical educational effort when it established a small school for girls in Cobán in 1912. During the 1920s, the Nazarenes added two more schools to their roster, a *colegio* for boys and a Bible institute in Cobán.[42]

Since one of the key differences between Protestant liberal and fun- damental ideology was the conservative rejection of social activism, the conservative denominations' commitment to mission schools may ap- pear contradictory; however, this contradiction dissipates when the schools are placed within the conservative understanding of their pur- pose. For the protofundamentalists, mission schools were direct tools of evangelism, something altogether outside a secular agenda to improve a worldly "*buen común.*" For even the most liberal Protestants, mission schools were first and foremost a means of religious instruction, since the ability to read the Word of God is a basic tenet of Protestant faith. But the mission schools were also mandated to instill in students the norms of "civilized conduct," patterned against a strictly North American template. For liberal Protestants, mission schools were a medium of social engineering, meant to craft a better world in the here and now. Fundamentalists, on the other hand, justified the educational ventures as a means of creating uplifting, wholesome lifestyles, which were the sine qua non of the conversion process. But in the final analysis, the structural differences in the missions' educational programs were few.

In this context, it is not surprising that the mission schools offered courses based on a strictly North American curriculum, centered around liberal arts or, less often, vocational training. English-language instruction appeared in every curriculum, and in some schools the higher grades were taught almost entirely in English. Mission schools typically prescribed a dress code for their students (as do government schools in Guatemala to the present day), substituting the *traje* of the Indians for uniforms similar to those worn by North American schoolchildren. They imported Appleton textbooks, journals, and popular (but morally edifying) novels from the United States, such as *Black Beauty* or, significantly, the tales of Horatio Alger and translated them when necessary. They also opened recreation centers and introduced both baseball and basketball to Guatemala. (Edward Haymaker once commented, in a telling jest, "The native teams [take] pride in being capable of winning the 'civilized' sports.")[43] In short, missionaries sought to inculcate their charges, whenever possible, with the cultural values of the United States. For most, the gospel and secular values were virtually interchangeable; "self-improvement" was an integral part of the missionary ideology, and it carried a distinctly American flavor.

While the liberal and even the conservative-fundamentalist denominations subscribed to this ideology, there was a small but ultimately influential body of missions that lay completely beyond the pale of the larger construct of mainline Protestant missionary work. Missionaries for these groups, which the mainline missionaries considered "sects" because of their heterodoxy, began to filter into Guatemala during the first decade of the new century.[44] These included the Seventh-Day Adventists, Russellites (Jehovah's Witnesses), Mennonites, the Plymouth Brethren (which, like the Mennonites, was a nonproselytizing German pietist group), and a smattering of independent preachers.[45]

The Seventh-Day Adventists, who first came to Guatemala in 1916, launched an aggressive program of evangelization and succeeded in winning some converts, may of whom were defectors from the other Protestant churches. Beginning about 1917, the mainline denominations launched a widespread campaign in their periodicals against what they called the "false theories" of the Adventists, and eventually were able to check the Adventists' encroachments in their own congregations.[46] Russellism, introduced in Guatemala in 1918 by a missionary who traveled under the Oz-like name of Dr. Tavel, also spread rapidly, especially in the southeastern coastal and piedmont areas, where it attracted a fair number of converts from Presbyterian congregations. The Presbyterians were eventually able to curb the tide of Russellite incursions by a strategy of "emphasizing great fundamental truths" and by focusing missionary resources intensively on the area.[47]

Although the mainline denominations were able to stem the tide of defections into the "sects," a telling pattern emerges that may be illustrative in understanding the expansion of Protestantism in the latter part of the twentieth century; that is, that those congregations most affected by the Adventists and Jehovah's Witnesses were almost always led by "native helpers" or by Guatemalans educated in mission schools. A standard reading of this phenomenon at that time was that Guatemalan preachers lacked the training or the conviction to hold their congregations under the sway of orthodoxy. A different interpretation, however, might suggest that Protestant conversion carried a different meaning for Guatemalan converts, who might not have conceptualized mainline Protestant belief to be a terminal, hegemonic ideology, but only one of several variable options that could be selected and discarded according to circumstance.[48]

While the impact of Russellism and Adventism was largely ephemeral in Guatemala, the entry of a separate group of Pentecostal missionaries was not. Modern Pentecostalism started in the United States around 1880, and was a product of the same crucible of religious turmoil that forged the fundamentalist-modernist controversy. Like fundamentalism, Pentecostalism, too, was a rejection of modernism, and it was characterized by the literal belief in the "signs and wonders" described in the New Testament. By 1900, two well-known evangelists, Charles S. Pierce and Aimee Semple McPherson, had emerged from the fray to popularize the precepts of Pentecostalism among the American public. Abandoning the worldly confines of the modernist-fundamentalist debate, Pentecostalism sought higher sacred ground by focusing on salvation through baptism in the Holy Spirit, manifested by ecstatic behavior such as "speaking in tongues," as described in the New Testament Book of Acts.

During the first decades of the twentieth century in the United States, a number of new groups espousing the Pentecostal doctrine sprang up. Between 1880 and 1926, some twenty-five "holiness" and Pentecostal churches formed in the United States, most of them splinters from the Methodist Church. Among these new denominations were the Church of God and the Assemblies of God, which sent missionaries to Guatemala in 1934 and 1935, respectively.[49]

The missionaries of the Church of God and the Assemblies of God were not, strictly speaking, the first nontraditional Protestant groups to come to Guatemala, nor were they even the first Pentecostals. The first Pentecostal missionaries to enter the country were Charles Furman and Thomas Pullin, two independent missionaries who came to Guatemala in 1916. Furman and Pullin were only two of a handful of itinerant, independent missionaries of varying theological persuasions who were drawn to Guatemala during these early years; most drifted out of the country as quietly as they had arrived, but a few, particularly Furman, stirred up enough attention to attract the ire of the missionary establishment.[50]

In 1917 and 1919, Furman tried to open a Pentecostal mission in Zacapa and the Petén, but the established missionaries, "with kind Christian courtesy," prevented him from doing so on the grounds that his presence violated the terms of the Comity Agreement.[51] In 1921, Furman contracted out to be a missionary for the non-Pentecostal Primitive Methodist Church, a small branch of the Methodist Church that had come into Guatemala in 1914, and that had been deemed doctrinally sound by the established denominations. For more than a decade, Furman subscribed to the doctrine and teachings of the moderate Primitive Methodist Church, and he established more than a dozen small congregations among indigenous populations in El Quiché and Totonicapán.[52]

In 1932, however, Furman began to introduce Pentecostal practices, specifically glossolalia (speaking in tongues) into the Primitive Methodist missions, and in 1934, he resigned from the Primitive Methodist Church at its request. His fourteen congregations in El Quiché and Totonicapán voted to leave the Church with him. Significantly, these congregations were made up almost entirely of indigenous members, which was unusual in itself, given that most Protestant congregations at the time were predominantly ladino. It is also significant that the small ladino Primitive Methodist congregations did not join Furman's Pentecostal movement, suggesting perhaps that either the format of Pentecostal worship or the autonomy of the churches had some unique appeal to the indigenous members.

Later that year, Furman reincorporated his congregations under the small, loosely affiliated North American Pentecostal denomination called the Church of God, originally based in Cleveland, Tennessee.[53] Unlike the other missionary denominations in the country, which gave Indians at best peripheral and patronizing roles in Church leadership (such as the CAM's "barefoot helpers"), the Church of God from the beginning permitted and even encouraged an indigenous pastorate, which no doubt accounted for its immediate popularity in the heavily populated zones of the altiplano. By 1935, church records show that of the Church of God's seventeen congregations, six (35 percent) had pastors with indigenous surnames, and it is safe to assume that at least some of the pastors of the remaining ten churches were Spanish-surnamed Maya. In striking contrast to all other denominations, Furman and his wife served only a single congregation in Totonicapán, leaving the lion's share of mission work to native converts.

It was around 1935 that another Pentecostal missionary (John Franklin of the Assemblies of God) came into Guatemala and began to proselytize in the Department of Jutiapa. Although Jutiapa fell solidly within the territory designated to the CAM, Franklin established a thriving mission in Atescantempa in 1937.[54]

Both the Assemblies of God and the Church of God missions were immediately successful in attracting converts, although neither denomination had nearly the human or financial resources of the established churches. What made matters worse from the perspective of the other missionaries was that the new converts to Pentecostalism came not from the Roman Catholic Church but from other Protestant denominations. This was true not only for the Primitive Methodist Church, where entire congregations had voted to transfer to the Church of God with Furman, but of every single denomination that found itself in competition with the Pentecostals.

In one voice, the mainline churches denounced the Pentecostals for "dipping from the net." In Chiquimula, the Quakers complained that the members of the mission were "very animated, especially . . . because the Tongues people . . . are tenaciously working against our believers."[55] In the capital, Albert Bishop reported that "some twenty of the Convulsionists or Tongues people . . . have invaded our Eastern territory.

TABLE 1
Church of God Congregations and Pastors, March 1935

Missionaries:
Carlos (Charles) Furman, Totonicapán
Carolina E. Furman, Totonicapán

Foreign missionaries: 2
Congregations: 17
Congregations served by pastors with indigenous surnames: 6 (denoted by *)

Church of God Congregations and Pastors
in El Quiché and Quetzaltenango

Totonicapán (1),	José María Enríquez
Totonicapán (2)	Antonio Enríquez
Paqui	Mariano Robles
Chuisuc	Nasario Monzón
Santa María Chiquimula	*Baltazar Chacaj Tzunux
Chuicaca	*Baltazar Chacaj Tzunux
San Cristóbal	Cruz Figueroa
San Francisco El Alto	*Francisco Matul
Paxixil	Francisco Ramos
Momostenango	*Obispo Lacán
Palemop	José Laureano Par
Patachaj	*José Leandro Tajiboy
Chivarrett	Cristóbal López
San Andrés Xecul	Calletano Aguilar
Quetzaltenango	Raymundo Pacheco
Olintepeque	Eugenio Ramón
Sija	*Juan Agustín Ajucum

SOURCE: AGCA, Ministerio de Relaciones Exteriores, "Religiosos y Asuntos Religiosos," Signatura B104-17, legajo 8320.

A few of the babes in Christ have been disturbed."[56] A visitor to a Nazarene mission reported that "[the] field has been badly torn up due to the work of the Tongues and Holiness people." In San Cristóbal in El Quiché, a CAM missionary complained that his congregation was "badly split up on account of the Tongues people." He reported, "Many who have attended the Tongues' meetings . . . tell us of very strange and disorderly doings on the part of those whose teachings seem akin to Spiritualism."[57]

It was no coincidence, then, that in 1935 the mainline denominations chose to consolidate their work by forming the Evangelical Synod. The formalization of the Comity Agreement in 1936 even more clearly demonstrates the lengths to which the original denominations were willing to go to present a united front against the encroachments of the new groups, which they believed to be heretical. The Pentecostal pastors were enraged, but had little recourse against the Evangelical Synod's censure. Relations between the two groups never improved, and the events of the mid-1930s were the basis for a deep and bitter schism between mainline and Pentecostal churches that still divides Guatemalan Protestantism.

Despite the united effort exemplified by the creation of the Evangelical Synod and the opposition to the Pentecostals, growth within the traditional denominations tapered off during the 1930s and completely plateaued by 1940. In part, this stagnation resulted from the departure of the pioneer missionaries; by the mid-1930s, Haymaker, Bishop, and Smith were all in their twilight years, and all three died in the 1940s.

Exacerbating the situation was the fact that the Protestants seemed to have simply reached the limits of their potential growth. The pioneer missionaries had envisioned that, once having planted the seeds, Protestant work would blossom freely. Operating from this premise, the early missionaries had conducted their most successful proselytization among the very poor and the socially dislocated, in anticipation of expanding their work into the middle and upper classes from this established base. As Haymaker wrote in 1914, "The 'publicans and harlots,' the lowest classes who have nothing by identification with anything on earth to lose are the first to enter . . . the 'Great Unwashed,' the unbleached muslin class, mostly furnished our first adherents."[58]

Yet the facts suggest that this strategy of evangelization was highly flawed and poorly suited to a country like Guatemala, where proper social prerogatives flowed in only one direction: from the top down. A list of communicants of the Central Presbyterian Church in Guatemala City in 1924 reveals that only one of the 275 members would count as a member of the "elite"—and this was a Swiss *finquero* (*finca* owner) who was in all likelihood a Protestant before he came to Guatemala.[59] The list does reflect that petty businessmen and tradesmen, such as tailors and stonemasons, made up some 18 percent of the congregation. By far, though, the predominant occupations for members of the congregation were in the service industries and in the working class. Over 43 percent of the members of the church worked as maids or farmworkers. The remaining 38 percent were simply classified as *"obreros,"* common laborers. The congregation of the Central Presbyterian Church, moreover, was probably more cosmopolitan than any other Protestant congregation in the capital, and certainly more so than any evangelical church in the countryside.

The Presbyterian congregation profile, then, offers clear evidence that Protestantism had not, by the mid-1920s, trickled out from the humble sector into the rest of society. A foreign visitor to the missions in Guatemala in 1926 tried to explain why it was that missionaries seemed to make so few inroads with the Guatemalan upper class:

> The sense of separateness from the foreigner which the Central American retains gives him much of his power and influence with the lower classes of this people, in whom separateness from the foreigner is ingrained. In even a non-material relationship such as religion, the Central American's feeling is distinctly clannish, and it is amusing to discover that in Guatemala all who are not Roman Catholic, be they Jews or Protestant converts, English, French or Negroes, are classified as "outsiders," calmly denominated as "judíos" or Jews![60]

The American diplomat-historian Dana Munro was less bemused and probably more insightful. Observing missionary effort in Guatemala, he concluded that "Protestantism is so utterly unsuited to the temperament of the people that they have made few converts."[61]

It was not only internal factors, however, that were responsible for the plateau of Protestantism's growth. The precarious nature of mission finances also hampered growth during the century's first decades. Every denomination in Guatemala suffered from a chronic lack of funds. The missionaries regularly wrote their mission boards about the surprisingly high cost of living in Guatemala, where inflation and a weakened currency often made rents and food costs in the capital higher than in the United States.[62] Nonetheless, in most denominations, the home mission boards consistently underfunded their Guatemala mission in order to allocate their resources to Asia and Africa, where initial expenditures were greater but the local costs of living were substantially less, and where the exotic venues were more attractive to mission donors.

The Presbyterian Board of Foreign Missions was especially guilty of inveterate neglect of its Guatemalan work. As early as 1905, William McBath, a Presbyterian missionary in Quetzaltenango, summed up other missionaries' feelings when he wistfully wrote to the board: "Perhaps I do get the blues when I realize what it really means to be a missionary on the Neglected Continent." In another letter he charged, "We do not begrudge the work done for the more interesting countries, but we must say that the souls of these people are worth as much as those of the Koreans or the Siamese . . . and it is apparent from the Treasurer's annual report that more money is being spent in the other fields than in Guatemala."[63]

While the Presbyterian mission board in New York condescended to assure its Guatemala station that "poverty strengthens us, [and] affluence weakens us," the meager funding was barely sufficient to support the infrastructure of mission-run schools, presses, and medical centers, in addition to the salaries of the missionaries and their assistants, the so-called native workers.[64] The native workers, though poorly paid and badly patronized by the mission boards, were perhaps the missions' most useful tools for spreading scarce resources over large areas. These workers did most of the follow-up work after missionaries had passed through an area on preaching tours, and they served as pastors of small, isolated congregations, which missionaries could visit only infrequently. Most important, native workers were usually Indians, which enabled them to act as interpreters and, under the most propitious circumstances, cultural emissaries between the missionaries and their converts. In 1921, Albert Bishop described the vital role that the native workers played in the CAM ministry, although, with an eye to his mission board, he chose to emphasize the bottom line. "In our missionary work," he wrote, "the barefoot Indian with his tribal garb and the barefooted half-breed are as essential as the missionary. . . . The work cannot be done by one class. It costs as much to support one good mounted man as it does to support three or four barefooted ones."[65]

Despite their enormous importance, however, native workers normally received salaries that were less than half those earned by the American missionaries, and often the churches were strapped to pay even these paltry amounts. One missionary wrote his board that, if his mission did not receive any further appropriations, he would have to tell his native helper, a man of fifty with a wife and six children, "to go and look for his support elsewhere or starve. And to tell the plain truth," he added, "they are starving now."[66] But when the Great Depression forced mission boards back in the United States to cut back on the meager funds they sent to Guatemala, the missionaries were obliged to cut back on their programs, including the number of native workers they could afford to employ. When they did so, the work as a whole suffered.

Another pervasive problem, which worsened in the 1930s, was the recruitment of missionary personnel. The Protestant missions, with the possible exception of the Central American Mission, which channeled all of its labor into Central America, were perpetually understaffed. In part, the problem stemmed from recruitment in the United States, as young volunteers were attracted to preferred destinations like the Orient and Africa, where they longed to earn their wings among cannibals and heathens, not Spanish-speaking Catholics.

A second problem was that even when a missionary agreed to go to Guatemala, his or her commitment had to be substantial. Most boards considered appointments to a country to be for life, with a yearlong furlough to the United States every five years or so. But in Guatemala, that land of earthquakes and tropical disease, "life" did not necessarily imply a long term of service. Disease of all kinds forced missionaries out of the field, and many returned to the United States permanently to recuperate "from the altitude," to which they attributed a variety of ills. The less fortunate did not return at all; particularly in the years before mosquito eradication and antibiotics, missionaries often succumbed quickly to tropical ailments or from poor medical care, such as the missionary who died from perinatal fever just as she finished teaching local women a course in modern midwifery.

Evidence of the inherent hazards of mission work is clear from a letter written in 1904 from the Nazarene mission board to two missionaries recovering from yellow fever in Livingston. The letter stated that, since the frugal members of the board "presume you will already be dead" by the time the letter arrived in Guatemala, they would send along no salaries for that month.[67] The missionaries recovered anyway.

For those who lived and stayed in the republic, life was often difficult, especially for those who worked outside the capital. Because missionaries were generally unwelcome in the communities in which they lived, their work was often lonely, and a missionary in a remote outstation might go for months at a time without hearing from another outsider or speaking a word of English. In 1905, a young Presbyterian mentioned visiting with a female CAM missionary in San Marcos who had not seen another foreigner in over a year, although this particular problem was remedied when the two married each other sometime later.[68]

One persistent dilemma vexed the mission boards: most of their missionary recruits were single women, who were drawn to mission work as one of the only socially acceptable adventurous careers for virtuous women. Most missions vastly preferred the services of single men or married couples, on the theory that unescorted women needed expensive protection and amenities that men did not require. Single women, moreover, could not lead congregational worship and so were useful to the mission stations only for teaching, nursing, instructing local women in the "domestic arts," or in other secular appointments. Nonetheless, single women dominated the mission staff in several denominations, most notably the Friends and the CAM, where the ratio of women to men was normally about two to one. The problem was acute for all the missions, save the Quakers, whose beliefs permitted women to take part in all facets of church life.[69]

In 1921, Bishop addressed the problem of the imbalance of female missionaries in the CAM in a letter to his home mission board:

> As long as [the women] are confined to work among women and children and in the way of home teaching, we hear no complaint; and we feel sure this kind of service would be the real preference of every one of our lady missionaries, married or single. But let one begin to preach the gospel or teach the Bible to a promiscuous audience, or do any service generally done by men, even tho' there is no one else to do it, and some denounce it and withdraw fellowship and turn against our whole work, as if it was in the hands of the wicked one.[70]

Despite the hardships of the post, however, those missionaries who came to Guatemala before 1940 usually served lengthy tours of duty in the country, even the "lady missionaries." Between 1882 and 1940, the average Presbyterian missionary worked for fourteen and a half years in Guatemala. The average Quaker who arrived in Guatemala prior to 1940 usually stayed for around twelve years, while the average Nazarene who came to Guatemala before 1940 usually stayed in the country for about eleven years. The CAM sent many more missionaries than the other denominations, but they did not tend to stay at a single post for an extended period of time, although a few remained in Guatemala for prolonged terms of duty.[71]

In every denomination, moreover, there were a handful of missionaries who gave their entire adult lives to the Guatemalan work. These missionaries came to Guatemala as young men or women and stayed at their post until they died, in a few cases, more than fifty years later. In the Presbyterian mission, twelve of the fifty missionaries who came to

TABLE 2
Average Term of Missionary Service
by Denomination, 1882–1930

	TOTAL NO. OF MISSIONARIES	AVERAGE TERM	NO. WITH MORE THAN 30 YRS	AVG. STAY FOR THOSE WITH MORE THAN 30 YRS
CAM	85	12.8	15	42
Presbyterians	50	14.5	12	40
Quakers	37	12	6	38.8
Nazarenes	29	11	5	30

Guatemala between 1882 and 1930 served in the country for thirty years or more. Among the twelve, the average term of service was an astonishing forty years. The Nazarene missionaries had a record that was only slightly less impressive. Of the twenty-nine missionaries who came to Guatemala between 1901 and 1930, seven served for terms of longer than twenty years; of these, the average length of service was thirty years.

The Quakers, however, had the greatest number of missionaries per capita who remained at their Guatemala post for life. Because the Quakers allowed women to serve as pastors, there were many fewer missionary couples in the Quaker mission than in any other denomination. Instead, single women usually headed their Chiquimula station, and many stayed at that isolated post for decades. Between 1906 and 1930, some thirty-seven missionaries came to the Friends Mission in Chiquimula. Of these, six stayed at the mission for more than 30 years, at an average term of duty of an impressive 38.8 years. Of these, only two were men; the rest were single women and widows.[72]

Despite the singular focus of these missionaries, Protestant work failed to thrive during this period, at least as indicated by the number of converts. The earliest credible count of religious affiliation is one taken relatively late, in 1940, but even by this late date the number of Guatemalans who identified themselves as Protestants was so small as to be almost unmeasurable, at less than one percent of the overall population.

As this chapter has shown, the failure of the missions to expand was due at least in part to institutional problems within the missions themselves, although, as the chapter 3 will show, critical cultural considerations played an important role as well. The poisonous feud between

Haymaker and Bishop was but one manifestation of the many ills that plagued early mission work, that is, sectarianism, a scattershot approach to expansion, and an overstretching of scarce resources, all of which were exacerbated by the poor support that the missions received from their governing boards back in the United States.

Yet at the same time, missionaries during this period did not measure their successes in terms of numbers of converts—a prudent approach, under the circumstances—but in terms of foundations laid. Most would probably have concurred with Dana Munro's observation that Guatemalans were temperamentally unsuited to be Protestants, but it was precisely that very temperament that they sought to change, either through word and example or by "uplifting" the social discourse in schools and print. Using biblical terminology, they conceptualized themselves as "sowers in a field" that would be "white for the harvest" at some time in the future, perhaps long after their own tenure on this earth.

This long view of the efficacy of the work was entirely in keeping with the two motives for mission that simultaneously and sometimes contradictorily informed the missionary movement in Guatemala in the early twentieth century. On a metalevel, the missionary effort in the early years of the century—encoded in a sophisticated missiology that linked religion with nationality, language, and power—was very much part of the expansion of North American hegemony in the region. Through the exercise of what has been called here spiritual manifest destiny, Protestant religion, evidenced most clearly in church-run schools, helped reformat the "minds and spirits" of Latin Americans to more closely match those of North Americans. But the mission impetus to Guatemala was also fueled by a crisis of faith fostered by the perceived disintegration of "American" or "Christian" values at home, as manifest in the emergence of protofundamentalist groups like the CAM or disaffected groups like the Pentecostals. For these groups, mission work was as much a means of shoring up traditional Christianity as it was of saving foreign souls.

CHAPTER 3

ETHNICITY AND MISSION WORK

I knew that if I would eat one of the flying ants, caught just before the wings were sprouted, I would be more like one of them. So I did, with considerable relish. Their confidence was won. I had found the point of contact.

—Cameron Townsend, Central American Mission, 1921

A T T H E cusp of the nineteenth and twentieth centuries, Protestant work remained closely entwined with the Liberal developmentalist agenda. Although still undergirded by positivism and social Darwinism, liberalism at the turn of the century was also increasingly influenced by the new pseudoscience of *indigenismo,* an autocthonous Latin American body of theory that blamed the contradictions of national development on the presence of a large Indian population. Although the Guatemalan discourse of *indigenismo* never reached the level of articulation or shrillness of its counterpart in Mexico, the two movements paralleled each other in time and concept.[1] Early *indigenista* thought, first put forth in Guatemala by Liberal statesman Antonio Batres Jaureguí in his 1894 tract, *Los indios: su historia y su civilización,* celebrated the golden Maya past, but presumed contemporary Indian inferiority, characterized by indolence, drunkenness, and poverty. Various *indigenista* writers made different claims for the cause of this inferiority, which ranged from biological to historical and phrenological explanations, but all agreed that contemporary Indian degradation stunted the natural growth of the developing nation.[2]

The solutions posed by *indigenistas* fell well within the larger Liberal scheme of development: to civilize the Indian and integrate him into national life. Specifically, this translated into the improvement of Indians' material condition along expressly Western lines—education, *castella-nización* (Spanish acquisition), and improved public health for Indians.[3]

Yet within the discourse of *indigenismo* lay a minefield of internal contradictions that were never fully developed or satisfactorily resolved. First, were Indians, as people of "clogged blood," in the redoubtable words of Guatemala's most famous novelist, Miguel Ángel Asturias, indeed capable of development, and, if so, would their elevation from degradation ultimately truly serve the good of the nation as a whole?

In most respects, Protestant missionaries found themselves in accord with the Liberal government regarding what Asturias would call in his influential 1923 thesis "el problema indio." The primary focus of *indigenista* policy centered on the alienation of the indigenous majority from the relative cultural isolation that they had enjoyed before Barrios's time and on the integration of *indigenistas* into the larger national society. The purpose of *indigenista* policy was twofold and contradictory. First, it was to assimilate a highly identifiable ethnic minority into the developing state, which was "developing" both in the capitalist sense and in terms of nationalism. In this context, assimilation had two meanings. The most complete type of assimilation was vis-à-vis the emerging nation-state, which required the renunciation of identity based on ethnicity and locality. The more ambivalent type of assimilation was toward the capitalist economic system, which required that Indians relinquish enough autonomy to be fully integrated into the wage economy, but not to the extent that they could no longer be readily identified as a cheap and easily exploitable labor source.[4]

The second rationale for Liberal intrusions into Indian community autonomy was to free up Indian-farmed communal lands so that they might be given over to lucrative commercial agriculture, primarily coffee cultivation. The process of absorbing Indian lands into coffee production had begun in the mid-nineteenth century, but even by Barrios's era, the competition between Indian communities and coffee *fincas* had become acute. During the 1870s, a significant increase in litigation and outright violence within indigenous communities to establish proper legal title to land long held in common offers testimony to these pressures.[5]

In neighboring El Salvador, where similar conflicts threatened the expansion of commercial coffee production, Liberal planners cut the dispute short by simply outlawing communal landownership by Indian communities in 1880.[6] But in Guatemala, where communally cultivated lands produced the food consumed by the majority of the population, even the Liberal leadership recognized that the equation was more complex, and their solution therefore more ambiguous. Liberal policies in Guatemala implicitly attempted to rechannel traditional patterns of community fealty into the larger hegemony of the emerging state, but in such a way as to retain the physical dimensions of the Indian communities, which remained essential sources of food and labor for the growing commercial economy. As a result, Liberal legislation in Guatemala did not seek the outright legal elimination of spatially defined communal lands, but it did try to atrophy the role of the community as a metaphysical locus of identity and loyalty. As an abundance of laws, regulations, and newspaper editorials written in the waning years of the nineteenth century attest, this was to be accomplished through the partial assimilation and, more important, the proletarianization of the indigenous population.[7]

The dual goal of assimilation and proletarianization was codified in Guatemala's Labor Code of 1894, which became law during the brief and largely undistinguished administration of José María Reyna Barrios. The Labor Code outlawed the *mandamiento,* a variation of the old colonial system of forced rotational labor for Indians that Barrios had reinstated during the 1870s, but in its place enacted a series of "vagrancy laws" and contractual agreements negotiated by ladino intermediaries (*habitadores*) between planters and laborers. These laws were enforced through the use of *libritos,* booklets inscribed with debt and work records that all rural workers were required to carry at all times. These changes brought about the seasonal migration of Indians to often-distant commercial plantations that continues in a modified form to the present day. This distinction was crucial; where the *mandamiento* had permitted Indians to live on and farm their traditional lands for most of the year, the vagrancy laws were purposely designed to interrupt ancient rhythms of harvest and plantings and thereby disrupt the agricultural basis of Indian life.[8]

When Manuel Estrada Cabrera assumed office in 1898 to begin the longest term of office of any Guatemalan president to date, he underscored the spirit of the Labor Code by encouraging the sale of the misnamed *terrenos baldíos*—so-called public lands—to private individuals and corporations. Of particular value were the rich parcels of the coastal piedmont known as the *boca costa,* which German, American, and wealthy Guatemalans coveted for cultivation. In 1906, the monolithic United Fruit Company set up shop in Guatemala and quickly bought up the *terrenos baldíos* of the torrid zone along the Atlantic coast for fruit production. Although these public lands were often unoccupied, particularly on the disease-blighted coast, many of the plots, especially in the higher coffee zones, had actually been claimed and worked by Indian communities for generations. The sale of these lands severely reduced such communities' subsistence base, thereby assuring that the Indians would be not only illegally vagrant, but also unable to subsist. Forced by necessity to work in the export sector, Indians would thus be part of the solution to national development rather than part of the problem.[9]

It was in this context that Protestant missionaries fit within the discourse of development, although the missionaries themselves perhaps understood this dimension of their calling better than their Liberal mentors did. Because Protestantism emphasizes the salvation of the individual, in contrast with Catholicism, which stresses salvation through membership in the corporate "body of Christ," Protestant beliefs seemed to complement the usurpation of Indian lands and the denigration of indigenous communal forms. Although most missionaries were chary of many aspects of Liberal domestic policy toward Indians, they nonetheless applauded the idea of weakening the influence that Catholicism in any form—folk, orthodox, or otherwise, for they made no distinction—had in indigenous communities. It was the Catholic Church, as Haymaker took pains to note, that had "crushed out the middle classes," forced the Indians to live in "degradation, humiliation, and deception," and reduced them to "pauperism and illiteracy."[10]

It is worth noting that Haymaker, whose opinion on this subject seems to have been representative, adamantly believed that the Indians' poor state was due to religious and cultural oppression, and not to any innate mental, physical, or intellectual inferiority. This belief in Indian potential must have seemed absurd to most Guatemalan ladinos of the period, who measured their own status against Indian debasement, as well as to the *indigenistas*, who generally believed that the Indians' subordination rested in their innate cultural inferiority.

Despite this relative broad-mindedness, the missionaries agreed that the ultimate assimilation of the Indian population was both inevitable and desirable. The transition would be all the easier, they believed, if their charges could come to an understanding of the value of the individual over the community—a concept that was at once at odds with both traditional Catholic and non-Western indigenous beliefs. While the elevation of the individual over community was general to Protestant belief, it posed a specific challenge to indigenous communities in Guatemala, where religious *costumbre*—the body of tradition, ritual, and local government—was a primary agent of community cohesion and local ethnic identification.

It is clear from turn-of-the-century missionary accounts that the North Americans understood and endorsed the general implications of the shift from individual to corporate values. Protestant missionaries from every denomination unblushingly equated their faith with capitalism and with a moral and pragmatic "Protestant work ethic." They believed, moreover, that these things were part of a larger, normative "good": to borrow Haymaker's words once again, Protestantism could embolden Guatemalans of all ethnicities to "overcome the false idea that there is something demeaning about labor" in a highly individualized, capitalist context.[11] It is less clear that the missionaries in the first decades of the twentieth century grasped the more specific implications of the extraction of the individual from the community, or, indeed, the very real threat that religious diversity posed to existing patterns of inter-ethnic or political behavior.

On the other hand, the disruption of these patterns played such an important part in the Liberal political agenda that the missionaries' potential—if not real—influence in Indian communities could not be (and was not) underestimated by the Manuel Estrada Cabrera administration (1898–1920). This surely accounts for the proliferation of slightly baffled but triumphant anecdotes that pepper the missionary journals at the turn of the century. Typical is the tale of the regional political commissioner (*jefe político*) of Huehuetenango, who supplied mules to missionaries at his own expense for preaching trips, or the *jefe* of San Marcos, who told a CAM preacher in 1906, "I would be glad if you were able to win all the towns in San Marcos."[12]

Despite these considerations, there was great controversy among the missionaries in the early years concerning the efficacy and importance of indigenous-language ministries. Early on, there were very tentative forays by British Bible societies to assess the prospects for what was then known as "dialect ministry" in Guatemala; these missions were based on models used to disseminate religious literature on the Asian subcontinent and elsewhere in the British Empire. One survey conducted by the British and Foreign Bible Society in 1892 looked into the prospects of translating scripture into Ki'ché, Kaqchikel, and Carib, while an English philanthropist commissioned the Central American Mission to conduct a survey in 1896 to "obtain a full knowledge of the natives [of Central America] . . . with a view of giving them the Gospel."[13] Neither effort, however, ever came to fruition.

Among the established North American mission groups, there was no initial enthusiasm for "dialect ministry," in part because of the logistical nightmare of trying to adapt their work to the nearly two dozen Maya languages in use in Guatemala, but even more important because indigenous-language work seemed irreconcilable with the missionaries' assimilationist goals. This opinion was shared by their supporting denominations in the United States, partly because of a general perception abroad that indigenous idioms were simple "dialects" rather than true languages capable of conveying complex ideas and thought. From this perspective, to lend legitimacy to the unwritten indigenous vernacular through codification and use seemed, at least in the abstract, to border on the absurd.

To be sure, there were a few missionaries who disagreed with this policy from its inception. Haymaker attempted to learn enough Ki'ché to preach to his small congregation in Quetzaltenango in 1898, until the complexity of the language and the censure of his mission board forced him to stop.[14] In 1913, the Presbyterian mission board in New York so opposed the work of William McBath, who worked briefly in Quetzaltenango with a Ki'ché-speaking congregation, that McBath resigned from his post, charging that "the mission was unfriendly to the cause of the race."[15]

In the case of the Central American Mission, there was less equivocation. In 1908, the mission's bombastic patriarch, Albert E. Bishop, pronounced what he thought to be the last word on the issue: "The Indians of Guatemala cannot read their own language; they have no literature in their own tongue, schools in their own language are prohibited by the government. . . . Among the converts of different centers of missionary work there are Indians who read and speak Spanish. Through such mediums the tribes must be evangelized, if evangelized effectively."[16] To do less, he added in an ominous footnote, would doom Indians to be "two-fold more the children of hell."

The missionaries were also unwilling to segregate their congregations by ethnicity, an interesting concern, given the fact that Protestant churches were almost universally segregated by race in the United States at that time. Yet their reluctance to establish separate ladino and Indian churches perhaps reflects the fact that the missionaries, like many Guatemalans in the same period, considered "Indianness" to be less an ethnic identity than a problematic social condition for which they had a remedy. Seen in this light, to the missionaries, Guatemalan ladinos and

Indians were both equally afflicted with the common vices of Catholic sinfulness—drunkenness, poverty, sloth, and superstition.

Two looming practical considerations eventually ruled the day, however. First, at the beginning of the twentieth century, over half of Guatemala's population were Indians who spoke little or no Spanish; thus, Spanish-only ministries by definition excluded a large portion of the target audience.[17] Second, because of ancient enmity and distrust, Indians and ladinos often refused to worship in the same place at the same time. The issue came to a head in 1919, when Cameron Townsend, a renegade CAM missionary stationed in San Antonio Aguascalientes, began work on a systematic translation of the New Testament into Kaqchikel, in flagrant violation of his mission's mandate. Although initially castigated by the CAM, Townsend personally publicized his work widely in missionary circles and trumpeted the value of his indigenous ministry from the pages of the *Central American Bulletin*, the newsletter sent to mission donors in the United States. Although the translation was not completed until 1929, Townsend's promotion of the Kaqchikel New Testament generated such enthusiasm that the mission reassessed its decision on separate indigenous ministries.[18]

The turning point for dialect ministry came in 1921, when ten missionaries representing the various denominations and some thirty Indian church leaders convened in January to hold the three-day-long Conference on the Evangelization of Latin American Indians, for the lofty purpose of constructing a strategy to evangelize indigenous people all over Latin America. The conference established the bylaws for a new organization called the Protestant Indian League, which, at least in Guatemala, was designed to foster evangelization among indigenous peoples in ways that were as culturally appropriate as possible. The Indian League's mandate was, wherever possible, to have native leaders trained by missionaries do the brunt of evangelical work; otherwise, missionaries were obliged to use indigenous languages and translate scripture into the language of use. The Indian League's charter recognized women as special agents of change within indigenous culture and specifically targeted them as converts, along with children, who were good subjects for literacy training in their own languages.[19]

The goals of the Protestant Indian League placed it far ahead of its time. The Presbyterian and Central American Mission boards in the United States refused to send additional funds or personnel to support the effort, and even the missionaries in-country who supported the initiative worried that the league's broad mandate would stretch scant resources too thin.[20] Yet the Protestant Indian League's brief existence served to point up the fact that ethnic-based ministries were to be a permanent part of the missionary landscape. By the mid-1920s, the missionaries of both the CAM and the Presbyterian churches had committed themselves to learning indigenous languages and conducting services for ethnically segregated congregations, with the understanding that such methods were to serve as bridges to Spanish and future integration.

This concession on the matter of language did not mask the missionaries' assimilationist agenda, a fact that was not lost on the Indians themselves, whose reactions ranged from frosty to outright hostile. Although rebellion, *tumultos* (uprisings), and criminal violence in general decreased dramatically in the western highlands after 1880, individual and group actions against missionaries were quite common in the same area well into the twentieth century. What is striking about this indigenous resistance to Protestants and their message is that it was raucous and overt, hardly the passive resistance of the cowed and subaltern people described in contemporary accounts of the day.

A few illustrations form the missionary records bear out this point. Missionary correspondence and newsletters from every denomination recount how belligerent crowds tried to drown out Protestant services with shouts and loud music as a matter of course. In 1904, an angry mob in Quetzaltenango lit fires laced with firecrackers in the doorway of a small Presbyterian church to smoke out the congregation. In Cobán, locals refused to sell Nazarene missionaries food, in hopes that starvation would drive them away; when this tactic failed, they tainted their food with ground-up hot chiles and red ants.[21] Elsewhere, another missionary complained that people continually "spit and threw filth" on tracts that he kept in his window.[22] According to one (possibly apocryphal) account, as late as 1926, a trio of CAM missionaries faced a more direct threat in Nahualá, where members of the local *cofradía* met them as they reached the edge of town. "Maybe the government gives you license to preach that religion in the rest of the republic," the *cofrades* reputedly informed them, "but our towns are different. Get out and stay out or we will kill you."[23] This was hardly an idle threat, for the Presbyterians, the CAM, and even the peaceable Quakers regularly reported incidents in which angry mobs roughed up local converts, often injuring them seriously and occasionally mortally. In the first two decades of the new century, every denomination lost at least one local convert to community-sanctioned violence.

Internal mechanisms of resistance, including persuasion, rumor, and coercion, were also in motion. During Holy Week of 1907, a CAM missionary reported that Mam *costumbristas* (elders) in Huehuetenango had set the city in an uproar by spreading a rumor that "the image of Jesus was crying and sweating blood" in anguish over the Protestant interlopers.[24] The *CAB* reported that, in Papalhualpa, the people of the village believed that new converts had to sign their names in blood to join the Church. As late as 1930, noted anthropologist Ruth Bunzel mentioned that, during her year of fieldwork in Chichicastenango, she had lived in the house of the Roman Catholic priest and had felt no disadvantage in being associated in the villagers' minds with him. "On the contrary," she wrote, "his sponsorship prevented me from being identified, as were most North Americans, with the Evangelists . . . who were generally regarded by the Indians as an intrusive and hostile element who wanted to destroy their religion." Her words echoed those of her colleague Oliver La Farge, who bluntly noted in his field notes from his work in Santa Eulalia Huehuetenango in 1932 that "the hatred of most of the Indians for the missionaries and their converts is unbelievably intense. There was no possibility of my obtaining any information at all from any Indian until it had been fully established that I had no connection whatsoever with them."[25]

Violence and innuendo were not limited to indigenous areas. In 1904, Albert Bishop, while preaching in the Cinco Calles Church in Guatemala City, was outraged to find that "the work of Satan was manifest—mud, brickbats, etc., were thrown at us through the open door . . . sometimes striking us in the face or shirt while preaching." Perhaps the most colorful rumor circulated among the citizens of Chiquimula, who widely believed that the Friends made young children into soap, thus accounting for their cleanliness in that dusty region.[26]

To the missionaries, these episodes were evidence less of cultural resistance than of Catholicism's enduring death grip on Guatemalan hearts and minds. Launching their own counterattack, the missionaries at the turn of the century regularly assaulted Catholicism from the pages of their journals and from their pulpits, and not a single denomination stayed aloof from the fray. The most vitriolic voice was a short-lived newspaper called *El Protestante,* which an independent missionary named Charles Secord published out of Chichicastenango between 1910 and 1912. Secord proudly announced in the first edition that the journal would be "anti-roman in every sense of the word . . . it will be dedicated to the Polemic."[27] True to his word, Secord lambasted the Catholic faith weekly from the pages of *El Protestante* for two years.

Though none ever achieved *El Protestante*'s level of nastiness, all of the other denominations, including the usually peaceful Quakers, devoted substantial space in their journals to the sport of Catholic-baiting. In the second decade of the new century, ecumenical mud-slinging reached such a level that even some home mission boards saw fit to intervene. In 1910, the Presbyterian Board of Missions warned its missionaries not to be "diverted in [their] way for the purpose of attacking Romanism."[28]

Nevertheless, the use of anti-Catholic rhetoric continued to make up a major part of Protestant proselytization well into the second decade of the century. That this was an impolitic approach, given that virtually all of their potential converts considered themselves to be Catholics, seems not to have entered the equation, but the Protestants nonetheless began to tone down their fiercely anti-Catholic rhetoric in the early 1920s. In part, this was due to the missionaries' tardy realization that anti-Catholic rhetoric generated a climate of hostility that was counter to their central aim. As the ever-conscientious William McBath, who remained as an independent missionary after his break with the Presbyterians, observed in 1905:

> Among some of the missionaries . . . I have noticed a constant tendency to include in their preaching bitter attacks on the Catholic Church even to denunciations of the priests and especially the pope. I am doing all I can to prevent that here [in Quetzaltenango] and am not altogether successful. . . . I believe that the truths of the Bible properly presented will speak for themselves and the hearers can make the applications without offending themselves and it will have the force of being their own conviction and interpretation. . . .[29]

But the shift from anti-Catholic rhetoric also underscored a fundamental change that had taken place in Guatemala since the beginning of the missionary effort: due to the force and duration of Liberal anticlerical politics, the institutional Roman Catholic Church had largely disappeared from the social and geographic landscape of the country. As John Lloyd Mecham notes in his classic *Church and State in Latin America,* Guatemala was hardly unique in its anti-Catholic efforts under successive generations of Liberal rule, but it does stand out in that the nation's "anticlerical laws persisted so long without change." Throughout the late nineteenth and early twentieth centuries, the institutional Church suffered a steady loss of property, personnel, and hegemony. This was true especially in indigenous rural areas, where the Church's influence had long been proscribed by the resilience of indigenous beliefs and also by the chronic shortage of Catholic clergy, made acute by Liberal restrictions on foreign clergy and limitations placed on seminary training.[30]

By 1910, Liberal anticlerical reforms had exacerbated these conditions to the extent that indigenous communities in the western highlands and Alta and Baja Verapaz were, in Edward Cleary's words, "mostly free of direct Catholic control." Oliver La Farge, writing in 1927, noted that the organizational structure of the Catholic Church was so weak, even in the densely populated zone between Huehuetenango and Quetzaltenango, that "the Diocese of Los Altos was merged with that of Guatemala, and for a decade or more no priest was resident in these mountains." The clerical depopulation of rural Guatemala was so protracted that, even in the 1940s, newly arrived Maryknoll missionaries found not a single Catholic priest resident in rural San Marcos or Huehuetenango, despite the large populations of those departments.[31]

The power vacuum left by the institutional Church left a new space for the expansion of localized popular expression, specifically, for the expansion of what Louis Luzbetak has called "Christopaganism."[32] Although Catholicism, shamanism, and indigenous non-Christian religious beliefs had coexisted in Maya communities since the time of the Spanish conquest, orthodox Catholicism, personified by a resident or itinerant priest, had remained the dominant religious ideology. In the absence of a clerical presence, however, local religion moved into the dominant position.

The *agents moteur* for popular religion's new hegemony were the *cofradías,* the religious brotherhoods of Spanish medieval provenance introduced by the Church into indigenous communities as mechanisms of instruction and control during the colonial period. Although a powerful presence in indigenous areas since colonial times—Sandra Orellana has estimated that by 1787, some 3,153 *cofradías* and *guachibales,* a local variation on the institution, were already in place—the structure and function of the indigenous *cofradía* had undergone a slow metamorphosis.[33] From the late seventeenth through the nineteenth centuries, the *cofradía* functioned in Guatemala as a mechanism of internal control and local religiosity—two elements that were as intimately intertwined in Maya religion as in European Christianity.[34]

But as David McCreery has shown, the power and wealth of indigenous *cofradías* declined precipitously from the early to the middle years of the nineteenth century. This was due largely to land loss to ladinos and conflict within villages, often between the local priest and the brotherhoods, to the point that church officials complained that the Indians were "giving up" the *cofradías* and that "no one can be forced to serve." Yet by the final decades of the century, the *cofradías,* or more correctly, their "illegal" counterparts, the *guachibales*—brotherhoods founded without Church imprimatur—were enjoying a strong revival, the apparent free agents of Catholicism thriving in the anticlerical climate of the Liberal state. In McCreery's words, "Indian cofradías during the [late] nineteenth century were thus able to escape what had always been an imperfect church and *cura* control to become more fully Indian institutions."[35]

It is clear that Liberal reforms directly—if inadvertently—contributed to the *cofradías'* growing influence, not only because of the declining clerical presence, but also because the *cofradías* successfully grafted the republican forms of municipal government introduced by the Liberals onto the existing structure of the religious brotherhoods, thus creating a fusion of civil authority and religious hierarchy.[36] In this way, the *cofradía* emerged as the nexus of community authority, in that it served as both the autonomous basis of local government and as the arbiter of community identity, or *costumbre,* as it was called by ladinos and other outside observers. As a marker of place and identity, *costumbre* was usually centered around religious motifs that came from both orthodox Catholicism and traditional Maya cosmology and practices, including such things as life cycle rituals around birth, marriage, and death, curing procedures, rituals related to the agricultural cycles, worship of locally revered saints and spirits, and the external manifestation of community cohesion and belief in dress and language use.[37]

The *cofradía* and its incumbent civil-religious hierarchy much impressed the anthropologists who went to Guatemala and southern Mexico in the 1920s and the 1930s. Innovative and demanding scholars though they were, virtually none questioned the ancient provenance of *costumbre* and the brotherhoods; most thought them to be relics of pre-Hispanic Maya belief obscured by the accretions of centuries of poorly understood Catholicism. The ubiquity and depth given to descriptions of the *cofradía* in the early anthropological literature suggests it was a thriving and vigorous institution in the early twentieth century. But had these observations been made three quarters of a century earlier, the anthropologists might well have tagged the *cofradía* as a nearly moribund colonial institution.

The particular character of indigenous *cofradías* in the early years of the twentieth century was still evolving, largely as a response to the manner in which Liberal reforms had impinged on traditional community patterns. For example, while cash earned from wage labor made it possible to expand the accoutrements of *costumbre*—fireworks, candles, alcohol—it was also the introduction of salaries and what Sol Tax so famously dubbed "penny capitalism" that made the redistributive function of the *cofradía* so important in maintaining community integrity. Moreover, as Liberal government insinuated itself into far-flung localities, the *cofradía's* assumption of local government allowed it to function between government and community as a buffer and broker of Liberal policies. Although Jim Handy has pointed out that the strictly civil function of the civil-religious hierarchy had begun to decline somewhat by the middle of the twentieth century, its religious and cultural influence did not, as it continued to be the primary broker of ethnic, cultural, and spiritual identity well into the revolutionary period of the 1940s.[38]

In short, by the first decades of the twentieth century, the *cofradías* and the very ideology of *costumbre*, in the face of Liberal reform and the massive changes brought by land loss and migration for wages, had partially reinvented community identity in the western highlands. As such, the *cofradía* may be seen as the medium of symbolic and substantive resistance against the onslaught of Liberal hegemony, of which Protestantism was but one tiny aspect and an obvious target. As Flavio Rojas Lima has indicated, this resistance was largely cultural, but it was also economic and political. That this resistance would find religious expression was entirely in keeping with traditional Maya notions of authority, locality, and the sphere of the sacred; but it also suggests an understanding that successful political and economic resistance could be mounted only through the intentional centrifuge and diversion that have been aptly described as the "weapon of the weak."[39]

It is worth noting, however, that the resurgence of the *cofradía* was by no means the only survival strategy during this period, nor was it uniformly effective. Indeed, in rare cases, it was the Protestant missions themselves that provided a broker function, although this was fairly exceptional, given that the Protestant population nationwide at the time was negligible. The earliest reliable figures for Protestants in Guatemala date from the 1940s, when Protestants accounted for fewer than 2 percent of the population. The missionary corps, made up of fewer than fifty members in the country at a given time, was even smaller. In 1920, the overall Protestant population was almost surely under two thousand, and even the largest churches (located in Guatemala City) had fewer than three hundred members. Outside the capital, in the western highlands and elsewhere, most congregations included at most a few dozen members.[40]

Nevertheless, a modest number of conversions did take place. As Thomas Bogenschield has shown, the western departments, which fell in the Presbyterian jurisdiction, experienced relatively rapid evangelical growth between 1917 and 1925, first in the piedmont area and somewhat later in the highland zones, two "areas most negatively affected by economic change." Although Bogenschield detects no direct correlation between conversion and ethnicity, he finds that converts were most likely to be "seasonal workers on the cusp of economic viability in traditional communities, men who had been pressed into military service, and [geographically] displaced highlanders"—in short, people most likely, for one reason or another to be marginalized from their community at large.[41] He also notes that towns that, in relative terms, tended to be most receptive (or less hostile) to Protestant missions tended to be those where the introduction of wage labor and nontraditional forms of economic organization had occurred unusually early.

Some of the most striking growth took place in the town of Cantel. Presbyterian mission work there dates to the first decade of the twentieth century and was well established by 1919, when local converts established the first independent (nonmissionary) Presbyterian church. The *municipio* of Cantel, for which ethnographic data is serendipitously rich, is a predominantly indigenous community in Quetzaltenango. There, unlike most towns in the area, the establishment of a textile factory in 1876 disrupted older economic patterns early on.[42] At the time the factory was built, the traditional economy in Cantel and the surrounding area was intact. Owners could not persuade local residents to work in the factory, a situation that forced them to bring in labor from neighboring towns such as Totonicapán, San Cristóbal, and Salcajá.[43]

By 1890, however, economic displacement in Cantel was so great that residents were competing vigorously for jobs in the factory. Even so, factory work attracted the poorest of the poor, people utterly without access to land or agricultural labor, often women or children under the

age of fifteen. The factory also controlled important community resources, including a school, a clinic, some workers' housing, certain
public buildings, and the electrical public utility.[44]

Although the factory was obviously the most important outside factor in the community, other actors were at work as well, including Protestant missionaries and lay workers. In 1924, the Cantel Presbyterian
church had a regular attendance of around one hundred, a large congregation during an era when most Protestant congregations elsewhere
could easily meet in a small home. On its face, this suggests the classic
equation between Protestantism, capitalism, and a perceived opportunity for economic advancement; Protestantism in this "modernizing"
town might appear to appeal to those most affected by the influx of wage
capital. Yet two sets of data, Nash's work from the 1950s and Bogenschield's study of the 1920s, suggest a different profile of members. Nash
noted that "[factory] workers . . . turned to Protestantism with less fre-
quency than . . . farmers or artisans." This observation is borne out by
Bogenschield's analysis of congregational rosters from 1921–1930. His
examination of the occupations of Presbyterian converts—the vast majority of whom were simply classified as *agricultores* (subsistence farmers)—suggests that "many impoverished Guatemalans . . . turned to
Protestantism not for reasons of social mobility, but for basic survival."[45] But survival in what sense?

While the Presbyterians did establish charitable auxiliaries (*comités de
beneficencia*) to assist members in dire straits, the mission's own resources
were quite limited, and membership would have offered few financial
advantages, either real or perceived. Instead, the tangible attraction of
membership in the missions seems to have been their ability to adjudi-
cate and resolve conflict, a function once served by traditional community elders or the Catholic priest. As Bogenschield's study demonstrates,
an extensive body of correspondence indicates that missionaries and
mission elders functioned as adjudicators of social and moral behavior,
ruling on and meting out solutions to problems ranging from property
rights to public intoxication to, by far most common, allegations of sex-
ual misconduct (often reported to Church elders in anonymous notes
signed "unos crellentes"[*sic;* some believers]). The volume of correspondence on such matters is so substantial that Bogenschield remarks, "The
impression is left that the church's primary function was one of social
control on a local level."[46] Although Bogenschield's study examines only
Presbyterian work, the newsletters and correspondence of the Quakers,
the Central American Mission, and, especially, the Pentecostals suggest

a similar role of conflict resolution, conferred by converts and eagerly assumed, *in loco parentis,* by the missionaries.

The record does not give a clear indication of why this minority would choose the Protestant way over traditional means of mediation and discipline in civil matters; it would be reasonable to presume, however, that converts might tend to be individuals who, for one reason or another, believed themselves to be—or preferred to place themselves— outside of traditional structures of justice. It is clear, though, that, in a large number of cases, the moral stricture of Protestant belief and practice, particularly regarding the consumption of alcohol, was a key element of attraction and differentiation. In rural areas, sobriety offered the potential for improved employment and a higher salary. Moreover, in an era that long predates 12–Step programs and clinical remedies, Protestant missions and their support structures, however limited, afforded one of the few avenues for relief from the "slavery of alcohol."

There is no question that alcohol and drunkenness loomed large on the social landscape of Guatemala in the late nineteenth and twentieth centuries. The problem of excessive alcohol consumption did not escape the notice of Liberal elites, one of whom, writing in *El Diario de Centro América* in 1900, called alcohol a "slow poison that consumes the larger part of our vital elements . . . the most powerful factor in the decline of our race."[47] Alcohol, as a growing threat to public health and national development, became an important theme of public discourse in the new century, as is apparent in the number of newspaper articles and tracts published on the subject between 1910 and the mid-1920s.

Alcoholism was especially acute in Indian areas, where poverty, deprivation, and ritual drinking (a traditional element of Maya worship that dates at least to the conquest), all exacerbated the problem. The dimensions of the problem reached beyond the very fundamental realities of drunkenness and disease, for excessive alcohol use directly contributed to Indian poverty. Given the ideological constructs of the day, it is not surprising that this fact alone provided fodder to the *indigenista* intelligentsia, who proclaimed alcohol to be either the cause or the result of Indian degeneration and called for stricter enforcement of liquor laws. In Miguel Ángel Asturias's words, drink was "the factor that has most contributed to the degenerative defects of the Indian." La Farge, however, in his study of the Kanjobal of Santa Eulalia, offered a dissenting opinion: "While these people undoubtedly suffer from drunkenness, one would hesitate to remove the bottle from them until the entire pattern of their lives is changed. They are an introverted people, consumed by fires which they cannot or dare not express, eternally chafing under the yoke of conquest, and never for a moment forgetting that they are a conquered people. In occasional drunkenness . . . they find a much-needed release."[48]

To be sure, Liberal governments ostensibly tried to monitor alcohol consumption by regulating the production and distribution of liquor and prohibiting private production of alcohol; this state liquor monopoly had been sporadically enforced since 1830. The official intent of state control of the industry was to control supply and consumption; however, given the high revenues that the state garnered from liquor sales, it had little incentive to limit supply. This obvious conflict of interest was made clear in a tract on the Indian problem published by Fernando Juárez Muñoz, who later became an adviser to the Liberal strongman Jorge Ubico. Juárez Muñoz condemned the use of alcohol by Indians as a terrible vice, but he conversely reasoned that it was not in the state's interests to give up its lucrative liquor revenues simply to pander to the Indians' childlike weakness.[49]

On this point, the missionaries, however, suffered from no such ambiguity. Liberal or conservative, modernist or fundamentalist, the Protestant missionaries were unified on the question of temperance. In this respect, they mirrored the beliefs of most Protestant denominations in the United States at the time: the use of strong drink was the hallmark of Hell—"the river of fire . . . rolling through the land . . . destroying the vital air . . . and defeat[ing] the hopes of the world," in the words of Lyman Beecher, a prominent U.S. preacher and early temperance advocate.[50] In the United States, temperance became a dominant issue in evangelical Christianity in the mid- to late nineteenth century, during a period when, according to Robert Abzug, "the traditional systems of ritual and symbolic life for all sects . . . were being challenged by religious freedom and disestablishment." In this context, strict temperance—the absolute repudiation of alcohol in any form or amount—provided a fundamental marker of identity for Protestant Christians.[51]

In Guatemala, missionary advocacy of temperance was further bolstered by the influence of the North American Progressive Movement, at least in the Presbyterian mission, where mission policy after about 1915 was strongly influenced by Paul Burgess, a German American who, with his formidable wife, Dora, worked in Guatemala from 1913 until his death in 1958.[52]

One of a new breed of missionaries that the seminaries of the more "liberal" mainline denominations in the United States had begun to produce, Burgess studied at McCormick Theological Seminary in Chicago. McCormick was then closely tied to progressivism, a social and political ideology that, in the words of Herbert Croly, one of the movement's most articulate spokesmen, sought to achieve a better society "devoted to the welfare of the whole people by means of a conscious labor of individual and social improvement." Burgess's marriage in 1912 to Dora, who was more conservative in both theological and political matters, tempered "don Pablo" somewhat, but he nonetheless brought fresh social and theological perspectives to Presbyterian work in Guatemala that meshed nicely with the older Social Gospel–oriented work already laid down by Haymaker.[53]

In no area did Burgess's own social agenda dovetail with established mission concerns better than in the matter of temperance. The missionaries of every denomination waged their crusade against alcohol by example and censure. The most outward and visible sign of a person's conversion to Protestantism in Guatemala then, as now, was total abstinence from hard drink of any kind. Although even the missionaries recognized that some recidivism was inevitable, missionaries or church elders banished would-be converts after repeated offenses involving intoxication.

Under Burgess, the Presbyterians, reflecting that denomination's institutional commitment to social projects, organized a variety of temperance societies in the first decade of the century. Among these was the Anti-Alcohol Society (Sociedad Anti-Alcohólica), founded in Quetzaltenango in 1917 or 1918, which eventually became the national headquarters for the secular National Temperance League (Liga Anti-Alcohólica) with charters all over the country, including a large organization in Guatemala City. The mission later sponsored the establishment of a women's division of the Temperance League in 1926, as well as an international chapter of the U.S.-based Women's Christian Temperance Union in 1935. After the ratification of the Eighteenth Amendment brought Prohibition to the United States in 1919, the missionaries, led by Burgess, pressed for similar legislation in Guatemala. Manuel Estrada Cabrera publicly supported the missions' temperance efforts, but he declined to endorse prohibition in Guatemala, although the idea did find some support in newspaper editorials and medical reports published in the mid-teens and early 1920s.[54]

The Protestants' temperance efforts no doubt brought them a new valence with the Guatemalan government, which could add their perspicacity concerning the very modern public health menace of alcoholism to the list of their developmentalist utility. It was in this regard, too—as facilitators in addiction control and adjudicators in personal conflicts—that the missionaries gained their first real entrée with potential converts. The all-encompassing ideologies of the missions and the missionaries themselves provided a rigor and a new moral order that were clearly valued by those who did convert. It is significant that converts, though few in number, came from precisely those marginalized sectors of society where traditional mechanisms of mediation and authority, such as the village elders, the priest, or the clan, had already ceased to exercise real control.

But in general, communities like Cantel, where the forces of modernization came early and thus indirectly fed Protestant growth, were the exception rather than the rule. It is true that the decades of Estrada Cabrera's rule, which straddled the nineteenth and twentieth centuries, brought dramatic economic and social changes that signaled Guatemala's full-scale commitment to agrarian capitalism. But the impact of these changes in indigenous villages was in some respects mitigated by forces within the communities that helped insulate their members against hostile outside forces. Most notable was the *cofradía*, which became not weaker but significantly stronger in the early twentieth century as a locus of local authority, power, and identity. It did so by rigidly codifying the rules and definitions that uniquely distinguished what John Watanabe has called "the way of being," at a time when economic and social change made these kinds of distinctions increasingly important.[55]

Because the discourse of identity was thus cast primarily in religious terms, it is little wonder that Protestant missionaries and native workers met with almost universal hostility in Indian communities. Although missionaries specifically did not endorse the false science of *indigenismo*, they did share secular Liberals' belief that assimilation and ladinoization were desirable ends, a sentiment that is obliquely borne out by the controversy over indigenous-language ministry. But even in native languages, their message could not permeate the protective membrane of communities as long as the "way of being" remained intact and resilient.

CHAPTER 4

PROTESTANTS AND POLITICS

At one time it was said that the evangelical missions were the instruments of the North Americans for the pacific conquest of Central and South America. Along these lines, someone wrote that the United States would make Guatemala its colony within six months after the fall of Cabrera. Now such things are not said. . . . No one can say that the evangelical missions do more than heed the law of the country and obey the authorities. . . . They preach salvation for the faith and Christ, not to procure loyalty for Hitler or Mussolini or Roosevelt.

—Paul Burgess, in *El Noticiero Evangélico,* 1937

IN APRIL 1920, a popular uprising in the capital led by the Unionist Party forced the resignation of Manuel Estrada Cabrera and brought a chaotic close to Guatemala's longest period of one-man rule. During the first hours of the siege, a pro-Unionist mob killed a native pastor of the Central American Mission because a rumor was circulating that the Liberals were storing ammunition in the mission's building.[1] For the Protestants, this was an inauspicious beginning to an era that for them and the nation at large was to be characterized by both transition and ambiguity.

Outright recrimination for the missions' association with the discredited regime, however, proved to be even more short-lived than the brief tenure of the Unionist Party. The new government demonstrated early on that it would cautiously follow the Liberals' precedent, at least regarding its relations with the Protestants. Shortly after the new government headed by the Unionist Party took power, an article appeared in the national party organ, *El Unionista,* that reaffirmed Guatemala's commitment to freedom of religion. The article warned, nonetheless, that the state reserved for itself "the preeminent and absolute authority over all political and religious institutions."[2]

The 1920s were an anomalous decade in Guatemala's history, in some ways, little more than a transitional period between caudillos, but in others, the prelude to Guatemala's flirtation with reform that began in 1944. Politically, it was a tumultuous and bracing decade. The overthrow of Estrada Cabrera in 1920 by the Unionists, a group that espoused political opening and, perhaps anachronistically, the cause of Central American unification, was followed in quick succession by the ouster of the Unionists themselves by the Liberal Party, which reclaimed the presidency in 1921. Throughout the 1920s, Liberal presidents broke precedent by following one another in what was, for the most part, peaceful electoral succession and by attempting to implement a type of Liberal developmentalist policy that was less dogmatic or authoritarian than that of either of the strongmen whose rule bracketed the era.[3]

It was during this extraordinary decade of experimentation and relative political openness that Guatemala became a haven for new kinds of political organization. Nowhere was this more evident than in the case of urban labor, perhaps because of that sector's endorsement of the anti–Estrada Cabrera movement—a small but significant base of support that had proved critical in April 1920, when mobilized workers defeated forces loyal to the caudillo in the streets of Guatemala City. In return, a small radical group with Mexican labor associations established Central America's first official Communist Party, which the Guatemalan government discouraged but did not expressly suppress. In 1925, this group spearheaded the establishment of the Central America Labor Council (COCA), which encouraged trade union organization and surreptitiously helped disseminate Communist literature throughout the region until around 1930. Although the government during this period periodically prevented these groups from actively recruiting and dispensing their publications, it nonetheless did ratify the International Labor Organization's code of worldwide minimum labor standards in 1926. Despite Liberal president José María Orellana's executive decree in 1923 that prohibited strikes in the public services, the administration tolerated nineteen strikes by workers associated with United Fruit Company between 1920 and 1926.[4]

This relative open-mindedness toward urban labor organization, however, did not translate into a reassessment of policies or attitudes toward rural populations by either the Unionists or the Liberal presidents of the 1920s. Both continued to regard the rural labor force in conventional liberal terms: as unproletarianized and still largely unassimilated *"indios brutos"* (brutish Indians) to be utilized as a commodity in the project of national development. Indeed, it was during this period that the *indigenista* discourse took on new, well-defined contours that would persist into the revolutionary period two decades in the future; they were articulated best by men who would be influential during that later era, the so-called Generation of 1920—graduates of San Carlos University, including Miguel Ángel Asturias and Jorge García Granados, a respected statesman of the later revolutionary era, who came of age around the time of Estrada Cabrera's overthrow.[5] The defining elements of this "reformed" *indigenismo* were twofold: first, that the Indian was "a child that from the night to the morning [could be] turned into an adult," and second, that this transformation might be realized through improved education, nutrition and medicine, and, ultimately, the cultural and even physical absorption of Indians into ladino society at large.[6]

Thus, it was not surprising that missionaries—still valued for their promise of wholesome, civilizing values and modernizing projects—continued to enjoy the support of the national government, even during the experimental period of the 1920s. Relations were especially rosy in the early years of the decade, particularly during the presidency of José María Orellana, who missionaries claimed once expressed an interest in seeing a Protestant mission in "every town."[7] The request was not hyperbolic, even given the general public distaste for evangelicals, for the social expedience in supporting missionary expansion was clear. By the mid-1920s, during the presidencies of Orellana (1921–1926) and his successor, Lázaro Chacón (1926–1931), Protestant missions were actively expanding their many programs in education, medicine, and translation projects, and each such project relieved the government—which was committed ideologically, if not fiscally, to such developmentalist projects—of further responsibility in those areas.

By the waning years of the decade, however, for reasons that are not entirely clear, the symbiotic relationship between the missions and the national government began to fray. Internal domestic politics may well have been one factor, for by mid-decade, the relatively moderate Liberal government began to face growing internal opposition from both the political Left and the Right. The government adopted increasingly nationalistic rhetoric, some directed toward the missions, which were easy political targets because of their strong foreign connection and their overall marginality in Guatemalan society. In 1926, rumors began to circulate that members of the still-powerful Unionist Party were trying to ban the entry of evangelical pastors into the country; at the same time, missionaries complained that Catholic confidants of powerful men in the government had tried to implicate evangelicals in antigovernment plots. By 1929, relations between the Protestants and the national political parties had reached a low ebb, as evidenced by an article in *El Unio-nista* that denounced the evangelicals as "new *conquistadores*" who plot-ted "intrigues and deceptions" against the Guatemalan people.[8]

The conspiratorial tone of this renunciation reflects the growing am-biguity with which government officials had come to regard Protestant efforts, particularly in indigenous-language work, which had grown to be the most dynamic area of mission work by the late 1920s. Although, as we have seen, the missionaries themselves in the early years were du-bious of so-called dialect ministry, the enthusiasm of both the few Gua-temalan faithful and, especially, donors to the mission in the United States for the 1929 publication of the CAM's Cameron Townsend's Kaq-chikel translation of the New Testament ended debate. By the early 1930s, the Central American Mission, the Presbyterians, and even the poorly staffed and underfunded Nazarene missions had launched trans-lation projects among the Kaqchikel, the Kanjobal, the Chuj, the Ki'ché, the Mam, and the Kek'chi, respectively.

Even in this matter, the objectives of mission-sponsored indigenous-language projects broke down along moderate and protofundamentalist lines. Of all the missions, the CAM devoted the most resources to trans-lation projects—although evidently not enough to suit Cameron Townsend, who left the mission in 1934 and eventually founded the Wycliffe Bible Translators, a group whose sole intended purpose was to translate the Scriptures for "unreached peoples."[9] For the CAM, as for the Nazarenes, whose *modus operandi* and purpose were like those of the CAM, the generation of usable native texts was a multistage process that involved eliciting grammars and dictionaries of local languages from in-formants, creating appropriate orthographies, and, finally, actually translating the twenty-seven books of the New Testament into usable texts. Compounding the difficulty of the task was the fact that linguis-tics as a social science was still in its infancy; even those few missionar-ies who came to Guatemala with some background in anthropology or foreign languages (many had some background in the classical lan-guages and Hebrew) were generally ill prepared for the complex mor-phology and decidedly non-Western syntax of the Maya languages. A missionary might labor for years on a single project—Townsend, for example, spent a full decade working on his Kaqchikel New Testa-ment—only to find that the rapid change of unwritten language and re-gional dialectical differences among native speakers had rendered the freshly published translation unreadable, even to the few Indians who were literate in their own language.[10]

The Presbyterians, typically, took a broader approach to indigenous-language work, believing that missionary-generated grammars and transcriptions should be used to develop secular texts as well as to translate the Holy Scriptures. In 1922, Paul Burgess established the Indian League (Liga Indígena) in Quetzaltenango to publish and disseminate religious tracts and informative pamphlets in Ki'ché on matters such as health and hygiene.[11] Quickly realizing that such efforts put the cart before the horse, Burgess, in open defiance of legal restrictions on the use of indigenous languages in schools, shortly thereafter began an ad hoc program to teach Ki'ché speakers to read in their own language. The mission school, despite this illegality, attracted no government censure. In 1941, the Burgesses established a school in Quetzaltenango where Kik'ché was formally taught along with Spanish.[12]

Conceding the obvious logic of this approach, the Central American Mission rushed to establish its own indigenous language schools. In 1925, the CAM founded the Robinson Bible Institute in Panajachel to train indigenous pastors to evangelize and translate Christian sacred texts into their own languages; however, instruction was in Spanish, the only common language of the Maya student body. In 1931, the CAM launched a Kaqchikel literacy program in San Antonio Aguascalientes. Most ambitious of all was the CAM's 1934 announcement of a five-year plan to evangelize and teach the Mam in that language, using a phonology and orthography of the language prepared by two Presbyterian missionaries working in San Juan Ostuncalco.[13]

This grand plan of generating texts in Maya languages and of using indigenous languages for literacy instruction plainly flew in the face of liberal and *indigenista* assimilation goals. While the missionaries insisted that language work was a necessary bridge to "true" literacy and *castellanización*—arguing, quite reasonably, that it was easier to learn to read one's own language than an alien tongue—the written codification of what liberal and *indigenista* elites considered to be primitive, anachronistic "dialects" seemed a dangerous precedent. For this reason, beginning at the end of the nineteenth century, Maya languages were proscribed in any sort of public discourse; no legal documents, contracts, or books could legally be published in indigenous languages, nor could Mayan be spoken in any school or at any official public gathering. Yet, probably because of the larger ideological implications of the Protestant work, the government turned a blind eye on mission schools and literacy projects, thus granting them a unique position in popular education.

Despite these somewhat anomalous advancements in indigenous education, mission work faltered slightly in Guatemala during the 1920s, in part because missionary boards in the United States were hesitant to fund new work in the climate of perceived political instability that characterized the country during the decade of civil rule.[14] The problem of support worsened significantly after the United States' economy collapsed on 29 October 1929; North American mission boards in the United States attempted to downsize the missions by reducing staffing and external financing to a bare minimum.

The globalization of the U.S. stock market crash from national economic crisis to world depression coincided—not by accident—with the political ascendancy of Gen. Jorge Ubico, who assumed office in February 1931, after a presidential election in which he was the sole candidate. A prominent landowner and former departmental governor educated at the Escuela Politécnica and the godson of Justo Rufino Barrios himself, Ubico had what Handy calls a well-deserved "reputation for efficiency and cruelty."[15] To rich landowners and powerful army officers, both of these elements provided the ideal résumé for the leader of a newly bankrupt country, ripe for class and ethnic unrest.

Although fashioning himself as a "republican dictator" in the traditional liberal mold, Ubico's policies differed significantly from those of his predecessors. Paranoid and idiosyncratic, Ubico refused to surround himself with a coterie of advisers or ideologues ("I have no friends," he once famously declared, "only domesticated enemies. . . . Beware! I am a tiger and you are monkeys") and ruled largely by intuition and fiat, tempered with steel-cold pragmatism. His was an administration defined by contradiction. Ubico desired and successfully courted foreign investment, but disliked the influence of foreigners. An army general, he distrusted the military. And, although he considered the Maya "rude and brutish," he believed they made good soldiers, farmers, and laborers, even without the paternalistic "regeneration" still called for by the *indigenistas*.[16]

Ubico's personalistic brand of liberalism was evident in his dealings with Protestant missionaries, whose benefits to the development of the country, he believed, did not outweigh their presence. During his second year in office, Ubico defied liberal precedent by inaugurating legislation that specifically discouraged mission work. In November 1932, the president issued a decree that established quotas for the number of missionaries that each denomination could sponsor within the country. The law froze each mission's quota at the number of missionaries that it had in the country at that time and allowed for personnel changes only if a missionary left Guatemala. The law also specified that all missionaries be certified by the government and affiliated with an established mission organization, which in turn had to guarantee in writing that each missionary had a salary paid from the United States. Last, the law stipulated that every missionary carry written certification that he or she had enough cash on hand to leave the country at any time. In 1933, Ubico tightened the reins on the missions even further by requiring that all Protestant missionaries register regularly with the Ministry of Foreign Relations and demanding that they regularly give a full accounting of all their projects, both secular and religious, to the Ministry of Interior. In a final symbolic snub, Ubico refused to send his children to the Presbyterian La Patria School in Guatemala City, making him the first president since Barrios not to do so.[17]

Ubico justified these measures as a contribution to his larger program of fiscal conservatism, which otherwise included clamping down on corruption in government, renegotiating foreign trade agreements and alliances, and managing the five-million-dollar debt that he had inherited as president. Although it is true that Ubico was clearly serious in his concern about Guatemala's fiscal integrity—and his efforts to rescue the nation from bankruptcy were so genuinely successful that Handy has called them "near miracles"[18]—as a justification for restrictions on the missions, which were entirely self-supporting, his claims rang hollow. Nonetheless, in keeping with this rationale, the Ministry of Foreign Relations throughout the 1930s consistently rejected visa applications for missionaries with the phrases "There is no place" or "Rejected because of the economic crisis."[19] The excuse was transparent, since Ubico's earlier decree had mandated that missions be entirely funded from abroad.

While personal taste and preference may have had something to do with these decisions—Ubico, a hard-living *machista*, surely had little tolerance for the teetotaler, sanctimonious missionaries—Ubico's decisions more likely had to do with his unique approach to the old liberal task of building nationalism and the elusive goal of progress. Though schooled in liberalism and the aging precepts of positivism, Ubico's vision of nation building was profoundly influenced by an event that occurred in neighboring El Salvador in January 1932, only months after he took office. There, as the world depression exacerbated already bleak conditions, ladino and Indian peasants, loosely organized by communist leaders in the western departments of Ahuachapán and Sonsonate, rose up in rebellion. The Salvadoran army put down the rebellion (known as the Matanza, the Massacre) with great brutality: while possibly fewer than one thousand people actively participated in the rebellion, estimates of those killed by the army range as high as thirty-five thousand, the majority targeted because they were Indians.[20] The Salvadoran government did nothing to hide the massacre, and instead touted the repression as an object lesson for communists and future agitators, particularly if they happened to be Indian.

The lesson was not lost on Jorge Ubico, who, governing a population that was more than 60 percent indigenous—as compared with El Salvador, where the Indian population was probably closer to 20 percent in 1932—sat on a powder keg.[21] Although the political rhetoric of the day regarding El Salvador's Matanza was defined exclusively in class and political terms, Ubico clearly understood that the real implications of the rebellion in Guatemala were fundamentally ethnic. This may be why the Guatemalan government falsified the census figures for 1940, which reported that Indians made up less than half the population, although they actually made up close to two thirds.[22] It also accounts for the dual preoccupations of the Ubico administration from 1932 on: communism, and the desire to stabilize and control the Maya population so that it would not be moved to rebel.

To this latter end, Ubico launched a carefully balanced program of maintaining indigenous community autonomy, which he believed to be a base of both Maya pride and stability, and pulling political and economic power toward his own vortex of power. As Richard N. Adams has noted, "[Ubico's] view of Guatemala was as a well-ordered family, in which the Maya [were] irrevocably allocated the roles of agricultural farmer and laborer, and of soldier." Ubico's task, as he saw it, was to assert his power of *pater potestas* and absolute authority over this essential but potentially unruly sector of the population. One of the most important steps in this process included the preemption of local *alcaldes* (mayors) with *intendentes* (managers) who answered to the president alone. The impact of this change was immediate and reverberating, for it challenged the traditional patterns of authority and power that governed many indigenous communities by introducing new contenders for power and eroding the authority of the civil-religious hierarchy.[23]

A second strategy in Ubico's careful renegotiation with Mayan communities was the abolition of the older practices of *mandamiento* and debt peonage; he replaced them in 1934 with a national vagrancy law that placed control of labor more directly under the control of the state instead of with powerful *finqueros*.[24] Although these sorts of changes did virtually nothing to better the plight of indigenous peoples—indeed, the hemorrhage of labor, land, and community autonomy from indigenous villages was so steady and unabating from the 1870s until the mid-1940s that George Lovell has called it a "second conquest"—Ubico's policies did much to effectively shift the economic and political center of gravity toward the state. In this regard, Ubico was the first national leader since Rafael Carrera to consider the Maya to be a "personal [political] clientele" rather than an inchoate economic commodity, an attitude not shared by most of his successors in the twentieth century.[25]

This sense of the Maya as his personal clientele may well account for Ubico's distrust of missionaries, who clearly had their own agendas, and who fell, for the most part, outside the leader's suasion and control. That they were working largely among the indigenous population in such dubious fields as language and literacy made them all the more suspect— for, as Gleijeses has noted—Ubico feared that "people who read might fall prey to subversive ideas."[26]

Yet the missionaries were not entirely outside the jurisdiction of the president, as illustrated clearly by an incident in 1933 over a small almanac that Paul Burgess of the Presbyterian Mission in Quetzaltenango produced. Burgess's *Almanaque de Tío Perucho* was an innocuous secular publication that usually contained such things as farming advice, epigrams, weather predictions, and pithy, instructive lessons. In mid-1933, Ubico, perhaps aware of Burgess's youthful flirtation with socialism and suspicious of his work among the Ki'ché, issued orders for his arrest on the grounds that one of the articles in the almanac was seditious. Burgess dashed off a letter of apology to the president and prudently headed for the coast, but the president's men apprehended him on the way. The missionary remained imprisoned in the capital for several perilous days, until prominent members of the American community interceded on his behalf.[27]

Burgess's arrest marked the nadir of the relationship between Ubico and the North American Protestants. By 1934, relations between the missionaries and the government began to improve slightly, almost certainly because of external political considerations. By the middle 1930s, new global conditions and the expansion of North American political hegemony demanded that Guatemala and the other Central American nations work in concert with U.S. foreign policy and institutions abroad. The first of these was the Good Neighbor policy, which Franklin D. Roosevelt presented to Latin America in 1933 in the depths of the Great

Depression; it was designed to make the countries of the region self-supporting and, in theory, equal allies of the United States.[28]

The Good Neighbor policy, though fundamentally a plan for a re-structuring of the economic and political relationships between the United States and Guatemala, did not lie entirely outside religious controversy in Guatemala. Applying the logic of the good neighbor to domestic religious politics, the conservative Roman Catholic hierarchy argued that the new policy of coequal status meant that Guatemala was entitled to its religious patrimony. Specifically, the bishops argued, all foreign missionaries, at least of the Protestant variety, should be immediately and categorically expelled from the country. Although this argument had the potential to bolster Ubico's established policies toward the missions, the specter of the political expansion of the Catholic clergy loomed large for the caudillo, and he rejected it.[29]

By 1934, in response to Hitler's rise in Europe, the focus of the Good Neighbor policy shifted from the economic to the political, as the United States began a forceful policy drive to assure that the nations of Latin America would be loyal allies in case of war. In Guatemala, the situation was unusually tenuous because of the nation's large and influential German community and Ubico's open admiration for Franco and Mussolini.[30] By mid-decade, however, the United States' Latin American envoy, Sumner Welles, the strong-willed forger of hemispheric alliances under Roosevelt, had cajoled and pressured Ubico into making Guatemala a "good neighbor." In narrow, practical terms, this meant that Ubico needed to demonstrate support for American efforts abroad and in his own country, for example, by expanding U.S. investment, appointing a U.S. military man to head the national military academy (the Escuela Politécnica — a post traditionally held by German officers), and encouraging the expansion of various U.S. agencies in the country — which, by extension, included the work of missionaries from the United States.[31]

Ubico's new conciliatory posture became evident when he permitted two new American denominations, the Church of God and the Assemblies of God, to send their missionaries into Guatemala in 1934 and 1935, respectively. He also gave permission to ten thousand Mennonites who were fleeing from Germany to settle in the Petén. Finally, Ubico ordered local authorities to end the casual harassment of Protestants and began to make annual personal visits to some of the more prominent missions. By 1937, so willing was Ubico to advertise his reconciliation with the missionaries that he requested that the "bishop of the Protestant

Church" accompany him and the Roman Catholic archbishop to the annual Independence Day parade. The pastor of the Central Presbyterian Church in Guatemala City attended the event, tactfully ignoring the misplaced nomenclature.[32]

The gathering storm clouds of war in Europe in the second half of the 1930s helped restore Protestant ties to the government in other ways as well. It was in these years that North American missionaries, provoked by the suppression of religion in Russia and Mexico and influenced by the hegemonic symbolism of the Spanish Civil War, launched a major and united crusade against world communism. On this topic as on no other, the missionaries and the caudillo found themselves in complete harmony, although enough latent suspicion remained on both sides to prevent a concerted convergence of interests.[33]

It was, however, the home mission boards in the United States that aggressively initiated the missionary thrust against communism in the late 1930s. In large measure, this reflected the sentiments of a North America that had been buffeted by economic depression, displacement, labor unrest, and the threat of war in the East and the West. As a rule, American missionaries in Guatemala were ideologically fairly independent from their mission boards, but the call to arms against communism—coming as it did on the heels of the Salvadoran uprising—fell on receptive ears. By the late 1930s, American missionaries, particularly the fundamentalists, expressed increasing concern that Guatemala would descend into the chaos of revolt and tumult that had engulfed the neighboring countries of Mexico and El Salvador unless there was immediate political or moral intervention. As Americans and as Protestants, and with the backing of their mission boards, they believed it their responsibility to warn their charges against political peril, which, in the case of Guatemala, seemed most likely to come from the political Left. Thus, in the late 1930s, Protestant missionaries for the first time began intentionally to politicize their message by equating Protestant religion with the absolute rejection of godless communism.

The missionaries' anticommunist crusade cut across all denominational lines, though the fundamentalists led the way when Cameron Townsend published a sensationalistic novel that offered up horrific depictions of El Salvador's struggle against communism. The journals of every mission began to publish articles that described the atrocities that the communists had visited on believers in other parts of the world; they highlighted China as a special point of interest, perhaps because there were so many missions there.[34]

But the fight against communism was not confined to the pages of evangelical journals. A bulletin from the Central Presbyterian Church from the late 1930s pointed out that congregation's concern with the communist peril by including a prayer for the forgiveness of "bolshevism." Another issue addressed the congregation's young people. "Communism, socialism, and fascism can all destroy the world," the paper exhorted. "What an opportunity young Christians have to work under the direction of their Savior to help solve the economic problems of the day!"[35]

To many missionaries, an important corollary to the battle against communism was to instill in their readers and listeners support for the present anticommunist regime. This in itself was a marked departure from precedent, as the missions had heretofore tended to avoided mention of Ubico altogether in their papers and journals. Seizing on the biblical injunction to respect authority, however, the missionary journals of the late 1930s strove to drive home the time-honored theme that good Christians were also good citizens. Many articles in the evangelical journals from around 1937 to 1944 characterized civil loyalty as an allegory for Christian behavior, although few sank to the sycophantic depths of the Nazarene journal, which claimed in 1937 that Ubico was "provided to Guatemala by God."[36]

Nonetheless, in spite of their latter-day support for his regime, Ubico never developed any genuine trust of the Protestant missions. Evidence of this lay in the fact that, even though he permitted the two new denominations to come into the republic during his term of office, Ubico continued to rigorously enforce the quota system for missions for the entire duration of his rule. Even after World War II began to alleviate the economic crisis, Ubico continued to enforce the law with vigor, which further undermined his assertion that the quotas were merely an economic necessity.[37]

The *modus vivendi* between government and the Protestant missions remained in cautious balance until Ubico, conceding to pressure from students, mid-level professionals, and labor for reform and elections, relinquished power to a hand-picked junta on 1 July 1944.[38] The earlier effusiveness in mission journals about the caudillo notwithstanding, missionaries shared fully in the national exultation at Ubico's departure and anticipated a return to the status they had enjoyed under earlier Liberal regimes.

Ubico's successor was quickly, if not bloodlessly, expelled by real reformers. In 1944, a new junta formed to oversee the writing of a new constitution and the democratic election of a new president. A civilian regime under Pres. Juan José Arévalo was installed in early 1945. Arévalo's election heralded the beginning of Guatemala's "ten years of spring," an era of social reform and political opening unprecedented in that nation's history. For the missions, this new era was to bring both opportunity and crisis; what it did not bring was a return to the government patronage and favor they had enjoyed under the Liberals before Ubico.

The relationship that existed between Protestant missions and Jorge Ubico sheds some light on a man whose administration has never been underestimated but has perhaps been somewhat misunderstood in Guatemalan historiography. As a caudillo and a Liberal, albeit an idiosyncratic one, Ubico single-handedly shifted power and authority toward the center, thus doing more to further the creation of the centralized nation-state than had any of his predecessors. In so doing, he was unique in recognizing that Indians could be utilized politically precisely as such, and that the construction of statehood did not demand the price of their complete cultural elimination. For Ubico, it was more realistic and politically useful to construct an identity for the Maya as personal clientele than to pursue a long-range goal of assimilating them into a general proletarianized but ethnically undifferentiated working class. But he also recognized that this clientage could be cultivated only with great prescience and care, a point driven home even more acutely by the 1932 uprising and its aftermath in El Salvador.

This, above all, may account for Ubico's disdain for mission work. In many respects, mission projects such as translation work unintentionally valorized indigenous language and culture by codifying and disseminating languages that were not encouraged by any other formal means. But mission work operated entirely outside of Ubico's dominion and control, and this he could not tolerate, for it represented a threat (if only potential) to his own carefully calculated manipulation of indigenous interests and loyalties. By asserting his own mandate of control over mission activities through legislation, occasional arrest, and, eventually, uneasy alliance, Ubico was thus able to subordinate even the missionaries into the grand scheme of *ubiquismo.*

CHAPTER 5

THE REVOLUTIONARY YEARS

We confess that there is much truth in the charge: "the measure of the success of the Communists in the modern world is the measure of the failure of the Christian Church to practice what it has been preaching."

—Paul Burgess, Presbyterian mission, 1954

As the nation's first freely elected civilian president, Juan José Arévalo promised to create a new Guatemala based on the principles of what he called "spiritual socialism," a loose ideology of reform that borrowed from many traditions and incorporated the efforts of diverse groups, including Protestant missions. Arévalo's spiritual socialism consisted of a bold nationalism combined with a concern for the working class and aimed to build up Guatemala's economic resources without foreign capital and to provide what he called a "square deal" for the common man. Specifically, this program translated into a number of pieces of innovative, if short of outright revolutionary, legislation. Between 1945 and 1950, Arévalo initiated a progressive labor code that allowed for the unionization of urban workers and of laborers on large agricultural plantations and for the establishment of the national Social Security Institute. His administration made overtures toward reforms in land tenure, although these were tentative and stymied by controversy.[1]

But Arévalo also believed that "man [was not] primarily stomach" and that spiritual socialism meant more than simple economic reform. During most of the Ubico years, Arévalo had lived in self-imposed exile as a university professor in Argentina, where he was influenced by the work of the Uruguayan writer José Enrique Rodó. In his 1900 treatise *Ariel,* Rodó argued that, unlike the materially driven societies of the

North Atlantic, Latin people were grounded in spiritual motives; this, he suggested, ultimately promised a type of higher development that fused practical Yankee know-how with sublime principles. Arévalo grafted Rodó's ideas onto his own liberalism to create a basic belief that it was the metaphysical transformation of society that would ultimately lead to its economic and political maturation. For him, true revolution had less to do with the redistribution of economic goods and services than with making "each worker a man in the absolute fullness of his psychological and moral being."[2]

In reality, the "spiritual" element of Arévalo's socialism was grounded almost entirely in traditionally liberal, secular ideas of what constituted metaphysical enrichment. In particular, spiritual socialism sought to "restore to the moral and civil personality all its grandeur." This was to be ensured through such measures as increasing voter participation by expanding the franchise for the first time to literate women and illiterate men, and, critically, opening a national debate on the place of Indians and the poor rural in general within the national culture.[3]

Above all, however, the basic mechanism for the spiritual redemption of the nation was to be universal, basic education. This, for Arévalo, would serve the nation on two levels. First, education would create dignity and opportunity for all through the acquisition of basic skills and knowledge. Second, education would create a loyal citizen of the new state by "dispers[ing] to the farthest corners of the republic the cult of patriotic symbols and historic values of the nation," along with the "moral origin and social sentiment" of the revolution."[4]

As a secular political philosophy, spiritual socialism had no place for the missions' theological offerings, but the Protestants' expertise in languages and teaching had great potential value for the new national education program. Arévalo may have become familiar with mission education projects when he briefly served at a mid-level post in the Ministry of Education under Ubico from 1934 to 1936. The Presbyterian La Patria School had regularly supplied graduates to work in the Ministry of Education since the waning days of the Estrada Cabrera administration and continued to do so throughout the 1940s. It was one of these graduates, Antonio Guerra, a prominent Presbyterian layman, whom Arévalo named to head the Ministry of Education's national literacy project in 1945. He also designated Guerra to act as a liaison to coordinate activities between the government and the Protestant churches.[5]

Guerra's appointment to this important post served notice that Protestants were to play a critical role in the education project of the new regime. Although Protestants were still in 1945 a minuscule group, their leadership in education assured that their impact during the Arévalo years would far exceed what could be expected of their numbers.[6] Because of their belief that the ability to read the Bible was essential to salvation, Protestants had championed the cause of universal literacy in Guatemala since the 1890s. The missions exclusively had imported and tested literacy curricula. They had been among the first since colonial Spanish friars to transcribe and translate texts into indigenous languages, although one important Indian scholar, Adrián Inés Chávez, had also worked independently to create a new alphabet for Mayan languages.[7] Even more important, because of past government restrictions on official use of indigenous languages, mission schools in 1945 were the only private or public agencies with prior experience in monolingual or even bilingual indigenous education.

Although Arévalo was solidly committed to the broad concept of Indian education, the form that education should take provoked considerable debate in the editorial pages and within the halls of the Palacio Nacional itself. Guatemala's official subscription to certain "pro-Indian" bodies like the Mexico-based Instituto Indigenista Interamericano, and the establishment of national indigenous organizations such as the Instituto Indigenista Nacional and community-based Misiones Ambulantes de Cultura, both of which were based on their Mexican counterparts, suggested—with unrealistic optimism—that Indian language, culture, and lifeways were to be treated with unprecedented equality and respect under the new regime. But when the Instituto Indigenista Nacional proposed in June 1945 that primary schools in Cobán offer bilingual education through the second grade, both the logistics and the theory behind such a program came under sharp attack.[8]

Echoing both of the arguments that the Protestant missionaries had voiced on the subject two decades earlier, the Ministry of Education reluctantly conceded that bilingual instruction was a necessary, though temporary, means to the larger goal of national literacy and education. Yet this conclusion hardly solved the problem. Given the long-standing legal prohibition on the printing and official use of indigenous languages, there were virtually no secular dictionaries, grammars, or pedagogical aids available to government teachers in 1945. (The exception to this was the Chávez alphabet for Ki'ché, which utilized original symbols rather than Spanish-based orthography.)[9] Moreover, although the national teachers' union (Sindicato de Trabajadores de Educación Guatemalteco, STEG) was one of the largest unions in the country, relatively few well-trained teachers were willing to volunteer to teach Indians in remote areas. Fewer still had the linguistic training to do so effectively.[10]

It was here that the missions' quarter century of experience in grass-roots education filled an obvious void, for their arsenal of experienced teachers, schools, and established pedagogy was a resource that could hardly be ignored. At the government's behest, the Evangelical Synod, an interdenominational committee made up of representatives of the five major denominations, created a joint literacy campaign to coordinate the denominations' disparate and sometimes overlapping programs. The Evangelical Synod established the Literacy Committee (Comité de Alfabetización), made up of representatives of each denomination, to oversee the campaign and assessed each denomination money and personnel to support the campaign; the project was subsidized by a small grant of ten thousand dollars from the Presbyterian Church in the United States. The project's goal was to teach four hundred people functional literacy every six months.[11]

The Central American Mission, the Friends, the Nazarenes, and even the Primitive Methodist Church all contributed to the literacy campaign, but the Presbyterians dominated the effort. In early 1945, the synod named Presbyterian Paul Winn to coordinate the campaign. With the synod's backing, Winn started up a number of rural schools for children and adults in isolated parts of the country, specifically in the altiplano. These schools, some taught by uncertified teachers trained hurriedly by the missions, were ungraded and designed for students of all ages. The mission schools were run in close conjunction with government-sponsored literacy programs, and, to prevent redundancy, were established only where a government-run reading program did not exist. The evangelical schools taught reading using the "Laubach method," designed by and named for an American missionary in the Orient; the government eventually adopted it for use in its own literacy campaign.[12]

The evangelical literacy campaign also worked in tandem with the government to provide reading materials for the newly literate. Missionaries who worked among the Ki'ché and Mam published syllabic reading charts in those languages—the products of two decades of linguistic work—while the government printed most of the literature in Spanish and oversaw the content of reading materials in both Spanish and Mayan languages. To complement the formal primers used in the schools, from 1946 until 1951, Winn published a monthly magazine for new readers called *Publicación Pro-Alfabetización*, or simply *PAN*. Utilizing a colorful, large-print format, a typical issue of *PAN* included short stories, anecdotes, Bible passages, brief lessons in health and hygiene, all lightly peppered with political slogans.[13]

By late 1946, the evangelical literacy campaign and the government reading programs articulated closely with one other. The synod campaign coined the slogan, "For God and Country—That Which I Have, I Give to You."[14] The Presbyterians helped coordinate a national literacy census among the Mam in the summer of 1946. The government also adopted the Presbyterians' Mam alphabet as the basis for the creation of a single alphabet for the transcription of all of Guatemala's indigenous languages. The CAM, which by this time had the most extensive linguistic program of all the missions, was active not only in synod-run schools, but also in the government literacy projects. Substantial numbers of CAM converts served as teachers in rural government schools, where they were frequently the only personnel trained to both read and write in local languages.[15]

The mission-run rural schools proliferated in the western highlands, in Huehuetenango, Quetzaltenango, San Marcos, Chimaltenango, Totonicapán, Sololá, El Quiché, and Suchitepéquez, while active programs also operated in Jutiapa and in Alta and Baja Verapaz. The project also thrived on the large *fincas* on Guatemala's Pacific coast, where the synod sold *PAN* and other reading materials to local *finqueros* to distribute among their workers.[16]

Although the primary point of conjuncture between the missions and the government was education, the former also lent open support to other "revolutionary" ventures, particularly in the area of labor organization. Breaking with the precedent set by the Ubico government, the Arévalo administration actively supported the development of labor organizations from its first days in power. In 1947, the government's concern for the rights of labor culminated in a progressive labor code that permitted urban workers to form unions, to strike, and to bargain collectively—rights that also extended to rural laborers on the larger plantations.[17]

Despite their earlier preoccupation with communism—for the missions' "Red scare" of the 1930s all but vanished with Ubico—the missionaries endorsed unionism, as long as it did not smack of Marxism, as part of the process of democratization. The Presbyterians, under Burgess's guidance, were most vociferous in their support. In a letter written in 1944 to a national gathering in New York, a Presbyterian missionary explained the situation:

> We are in the midst of a peaceable (to date) social revolution. Labor unions that have been suppressed for more than a decade are suddenly coming to life and are making demands that would have been unthinkable under the former administration. In almost all walks of life, railroad employees, schoolteachers, public officials, carpenters, buss [*sic*] drivers, masons, shoemakers, etc. [are involved]. In our estimation not enough attention has been given to the calamitous lot of the peon as yet but we hope and pray he will not be forgotten in the grand scramble.[18]

The missions lent more than passive support to the labor movement, as evidenced by the president's allowing a Lutheran pastor, a representative of the small, predominantly German Evangelisch-Lutheranische Landeskirche congregation based in Guatemala City, to present him with a copy of the Lutheran catechism at a public labor rally.[19] In 1944, after soliciting support from its National Assembly back in the United States, the Presbyterian Church officially went on record to advise its blue-collar members to join a union and to support the government's collective bargaining policy. Nor was Protestant support merely symbolic. In 1945, the Evangelical Synod began an active literacy campaign among banana workers on United Fruit Company's (UFCO) plantations in Tiquisate.[20] In 1947, the Tiquisate literacy campaign began to focus specifically on members of the new banana workers' union, which had formed after the promulgation of the new labor code.[21] The Friends mission, too, actively proselytized the banana workers' union while pragmatically noting that "the higher economic level of believers among the company employees was another asset to the spread of the Gospel, because churches . . . could rapidly become self-supporting."[22] As late as 1950, a nondenominational missionary from the United States began a ministry of what he called "industrial evangelism," a program with a specific orientation toward labor on commercial agricultural enterprises. The missionary, whose name (perhaps intentionally) does not appear in the records, concentrated his ministry among UFCO workers and the newly unionized workers on large coffee plantations in Alta and Baja Verapaz; his efforts earned him the distrust of commercial producers, particularly the U.S.-owned United Fruit Company. Shortly after Jacobo Arbenz took power in 1950, this "industrial evangelist" left Guatemala at the forceful urging of UFCO.[23]

In effect, the collusion between the Protestant missions and the government seems to have insulated the American missionaries at least temporarily against the rising tide of nationalism—most clearly demonstrated in workers' strikes led by radicals and communists—that began to take hold in Guatemala during the late 1940s. In 1949, one missionary reported to his home board: "The Government has welcomed the collaboration of the Mission in the Literacy Campaign and even when anti-American feeling was at its height [a reference to the Guatemalan government's request in 1949 that the United States withdraw its ambassador] . . . the Government maintained a sympathetic attitude toward our missions and missionaries."[24]

So sympathetic was the Arévalo administration toward the missions' work that two new denominations came into the country during this period, the first in over a decade. The Missouri Synod Lutherans and the Southern Baptists occupied opposite ends of the theological spectrum but, at least for the time being, shared a lack of interest in either politics or active proselytization. Both denominations moved into the abandoned work of earlier evangelists, and both catered to a fairly circumscribed constituency. In 1947, the Missouri Synod Lutherans pieced together a single large congregation out of the remnants of the old German Evangelisch-Lutheranische Landeskirche in Guatemala City, though they prudently held services in English (though, perhaps tellingly, not in Spanish) out of fear of anti-German sentiments.[25] They also established two small parishes in the countryside, a Spanish-language church in Zacapa and an English-language church, built from an old Anglican mission, for West Indian banana workers in Puerto Barrios.[26]

The work in Zacapa put the Lutherans in direct confrontation with the Quakers, who still claimed Zacapa as their territory under the old Comity Agreement. The aged matriarch of the Friends Mission, Ruth Esther Smith, spent the last months of her life trying to prevent the Lutherans from moving into Quaker territory. In a fury of letters, she informed the Lutheran Mission Board that the congregation was violating the time-honored terms of the Comity Agreement and tried to convince the board that a heretical splinter group of the Friends was falsely calling themselves Lutherans.[27] The Lutheran Mission Board tried to reassure Smith that it was against mission policy to proselytize among other Protestant denominations; further, they did "not want to disturb the work of another Church." Privately, however, Lutheran board members noted that the number of Protestants in Zacapa was so small—only around a hundred—that a new denomination would probably not make any difference one way or the other to the Friends' work. The Lutheran congregation remained in Zacapa, and a short time later the CAM opened a small mission there.[28] The old Comity Agreement was, for all intents and purposes, dead.

In 1946, the Southern Baptist Convention began making tentative forays into Guatemala at the request of several small independent churches that had splintered off from the Cinco Calles Church in 1928 over a financial controversy.[29] These groups had grown slightly during the 1930s and early 1940s, but they suffered from a lack of leadership and direction. In 1945, the independents decided that they lacked a "definite physiognomy" and petitioned to join the Southern Baptists, with whom they agreed on questions of doctrine and baptism. The Baptists agreed and, in 1947, independent evangelicals in three churches—in Guatemala City, Escuintla, and Tecpán—became Southern Baptists.[30]

The stepped-up mission activity during the Arévalo years had its critics, especially in religious sectors. The established missions' close relationship with the Arévalo government served to exacerbate the existing hostility between the Protestants and the Roman Catholic Church, as well as to further aggravate the already poor relations between the Catholic Church and the state. The Catholic hierarchy, under the leadership of conservative archbishop Mariano Rossell y Arellano, had initially hoped that Arévalo would look to the Church for the "spiritual" component of his socialism and reverse the anticlerical tone of the Liberal period. It soon became clear, however, that the new Constitution of 1945 retained the same anticlerical religious legislation as the one that had preceded it, including a new proviso that "no religious groups or their members . . . or clergy may intervene in politics or in questions of organized labor."[31] It was equally evident that Arévalo himself—whose own mother, rumor had it, had become a Protestant after listening to a CAM radio broadcast—was as anti-Catholic as any of the old Liberal leaders.[32]

Such factors convinced the Roman Catholic hierarchy that the new regime was virtually indistinguishable from any since that of Justo Rufino Barrios in matters of church and state. Indeed, in the 1940s, the potential for conflict between the state and the Church, even in the Church's debilitated condition, was every bit as great as it had been at the start of the Liberal era. This was because the institutional Catholic Church in Guatemala at the time was substantially influenced by internal conservative movements that flourished in Spain under Francisco Franco. One such movement was Opus Dei, founded in 1928 to restore traditional dogma and values to lay Catholics. Another, Catholic Action (Acción Católica), was more overtly political, seeking to channel the energies of volatile sectors such as labor and youth into church-sanctioned activities.[33]

Both Opus Dei and, to a lesser extent, Catholic Action flourished in Spain in the 1930s and 1940s, where they became a part of the profoundly conservative pro-Franco movement known as National Catholicism. In the wake of the Spanish Civil War, this movement became an integral element of Franco's political ideology of *hispanidad:* the repudiation of communism, secularism, and other ills of modernism through the elevation of traditional Spanish heritage, the Church, ardent nationalism, and corporatism.[34]

In Guatemala, key members of the Church hierarchy, including the archbishop, were drawn to National Catholicism and *hispanidad,* though few dared subscribe to Franco's falangism outright.[35] Compounding the tension was the fact that, while Arévalo's government was essentially liberal in its treatment of the Church—indeed, the government's willingness to quietly permit the entry of Sacred Heart, Maryknoll, and missionaries of other Catholic orders to work in the country indicated a somewhat more tolerant attitude—the administration continued to use a vituperative public rhetoric toward the Church.

In this context, it is not surprising that the battle lines between the Catholic Church and the spiritual socialism government were drawn early and publicly. The Church made the first offensive move in the pages of a caustic and widely read Catholic weekly called *Acción Social Cristiana,* only a month after Arévalo took office. An anonymous front page editorial denounced the new government as being made up of "Liberals, Masons, and communists," as an enemy of the Church, and as hostile to the Guatemalan people. The journal, which was modeled after the Spanish falangist *Cristianidad,* was not an official voice of the Church, but it did reflect the opinions of the most reactionary elements in the local hierarchy, who were forbidden by the Constitution to express any overt political sentiments in a public forum. Despite this prohibition, through such journals as *Acción Social Cristiana* and pastoral letters, the Catholic Church would become a symbolic leader in mobilizing internal opposition to the revolutionary governments of Arévalo and, later, Jacobo Arbenz.[36]

Particularly distasteful to the ultraconservative Catholics were the Protestants, whom they opposed not only on religious but also on political and nationalistic grounds. Using the model provided by Spain's National Catholicism, Guatemala's Catholics identified Protestantism and socialism as parallel heterodoxies and attacked them accordingly. As early as 1944, *Acción Social Cristiana* accused the Protestants of being "the opening wedge of communism" in Guatemala. An October 1945 article entitled "Protestantism: Fountainhead of Communism?" linked American missionaries and the "dean of Canterbury" to Moscow and Vicente Lombardo Toledano, the Marxist head of the national labor union in Mexico. An article published in May, 1947, raised the hackles of nationalists by claiming to expose an "accord or allegiance between Protestantism and communism" and proposing that "the avalanche of missionaries could be communists taking advantage of excessive freedom of religion" to take over the country.

Although these attitudes were by no means universal, *Acción Social Cristiana* did have some impact outside of the Catholic hierarchy. In 1945, a series of articles that unfavorably equated radical social change with Protestant infiltration and written by Catholic laymen appeared in local newspapers. A 1945 article written for the daily newspaper *La Hora* argued that "only Catholicism can withstand communism" and used Franco's Church-backed triumph over the Spanish Republicans to illustrate the point. Another reiterated the right to hold private property as a tenet of the Catholic faith.[37] This polemic thus recast the Protestant missions in their familiar role as a counterweight to the Catholic Church's political influence.

By the last two years of Arévalo's four-year term, however, the cordial ties between the government and the missions had begun to fray. By 1948, Arévalo's reforms had alienated the traditional bases of power in the country—landowners, businessmen, key factions of the army, and, obviously, the Church—to such an extent that the president was forced to rely increasingly on other sectors, including leftists within his administration, for support. The 1949 Presbyterian annual report to New York could still note, perhaps with false bravado, that "the Government maintains a sympathetic attitude toward our missions and missionaries." Privately, however, missionaries had begun to worry that the government's shift to the left would soon threaten the missions and their own physical presence in the country.[38]

In 1950, these fears proved to be well founded, when the election of Jacobo Arbenz to the presidency brought the transitory alliance of the

Protestant missionaries and the revolutionary government to a close. Although Paul Burgess himself had baptized the infant Arbenz, politics prevailed in adulthood, and the new president found the idea of foreign missionaries to be utterly at odds with his fiery brand of nationalism. In his inaugural address, Arbenz vowed to channel the nationalistic spirit of reform kindled during the Arévalo administration into a wholesale restructuring of Guatemalan society. His stated objectives were lofty and ambitious: to convert Guatemala into an economically independent nation; to end the country's feudal patterns of labor relations and landownership; and to raise the standard of living for Guatemala's poor workers and campesinos.[39]

The historical postmortem of the Arbenz regime has devoted considerable attention to whether Arbenz was a communist, an issue of inestimable importance during the cold war 1950s, an era that permitted little political nuance.[40] Arbenz did rely heavily on the advice of Communists in his cabinet, but in the context of that era, this subtle distinction was utterly lost. Under their guidance, Arbenz's chief policy aim was to reclaim the wealth of Guatemala for the working class. His administration introduced unprecedented legislation to divest the nation's largest landholders of their vast plots of unused lands and redistributed it to the tillers of the soil. Since the largest landowner in the country by far was the mammoth United Fruit Company, Arbenz's demands for land reform and his overall agenda for social change carried strongly nationalistic overtones.

It was not surprising, then, that shortly after taking office, Arbenz began to slow the tide of Americans coming into the country. Under the new administration, the Ministry of Foreign Relations began to tighten up requirements for entry and residence visas for foreigners, including missionaries. Not long before Arbenz's inauguration, Paul Burgess wrote to the Presbyterian board in New York that missionaries of all denominations were having considerable difficulty obtaining residence visas from the Ministry of Foreign Relations. Burgess, however, was sanguine. "This is not necessarily an anti-missionary attitude on the part of the Government," he reassured his board, "for employees of the UFCO and other commercial enterprises find it even harder to secure these visas. It may be the part of the 'Red' influence in the present government or just the inferiority complex of a little country expressing itself before the great United States."[41]

For the short haul, Burgess was correct. Nationalistic rhetoric notwithstanding, the Arbenz administration permitted two new mission agencies to enter the country between 1950 and 1952. One, a small independent group called Spanish American Inland Mission, sent a handful of missionaries to Guatemala in 1953, but the group's minuscule size and Canadian origin may have neutralized its impact.[42] The other group admitted under Arbenz, however, the Wycliffe Bible Translators/Summer Institute of Linguistics (SIL), founded by former CAM missionary Cameron Townsend, was a much larger and better funded organization, with nascent ties to conservative Christian groups in the United States. One can only presume that Arbenz was unaware of this latter connection, for he allowed two Wycliffe missionaries into the country in 1952 under contract to the Ministry of Education's National Indigenous Institute (Instituto Indigenista Nacional) to supply textbooks, train teachers, and continue work in developing orthographies for the Mayan languages.[43]

These admissions aside, it became apparent as time went on that foreign missionaries were indeed a target for the Arbenz administration. The government set into action a series of new regulations that made it increasingly difficult for foreign Protestant missionaries to work in Guatemala. The Ministry of Foreign Relations tightened the criteria for entry visas by demanding that the missionaries be able to "pay expenses during the time [they remained in the country] and pledge not to molest the state in any way." Some applicants for missionary work visas were required to undergo review by the National Police.[44]

Applicants from the Central American Mission fell under the particular scrutiny of the Ministry of Foreign Relations, perhaps because the government did not believe the CAM's claims to "apoliticism."[45] Successful completion of the visa application process, however, was no guarantee of success, and by 1952, the Ministry of Foreign Relations routinely denied admission to North American missionaries without explanation. By 1953, the Arbenz government made the visa application process for missionaries such a labyrinthine process that the immigration of Protestant missionaries slowed to fewer than a dozen per year, a fraction of what it had been during the Arévalo years.[46]

Even had the government not created these obstacles, however, the Protestant work would have slowed on its own after 1950. Still smarting from the forced closure of their missions in newly communist Asia, mission boards in the United States watched with growing concern as Guatemala inched to the left under Arbenz; they withheld funds from their projects and made plans to evacuate their personnel from the country. Their fears deepened in June 1952, when the government announced its watershed Agrarian Reform Law (Decree 900), which authorized the compensated expropriation of private properties two *caballerías* or larger and on which two thirds or more of the land was unused.[47] While the law could be applied to relatively small municipal holdings, the most obvious effect was on large commercial plantations, particularly the holdings of the U.S.-owned United Fruit Company, which kept hundreds of thousands of *manzanas* of land in fallow reserve to save the product from rapidly spreading disease and to keep its profit margin relatively high.

The expropriation of UFCO lands began almost immediately, over the protests of the U.S. government, which in the context of the cold war, simultaneously began to build a case that communists controlled Guatemala. At the same time, violence in the countryside began to mount, as peasants, hungry for land and unwilling to wait for the formal redistribution process, began to take over plots of land by force.[48]

The government's increasingly radical agenda created a growing obstacle to Protestant work by the early 1950s. The problem with the expropriation of UFCO's land had caused hostilities between the United States and Guatemala, the immediate burden of which fell on foreigners who worked in the country. After the passage of Decree 900, Arbenz mandated additional legislation designed to lessen the institutional strength of the American missions and thereby rid Guatemala of unnecessary foreign influence. In 1953, the president backed an antiforeigner law requiring that 40 percent of the faculty at all private schools be assigned by the government. Congress vetoed the law, but had it passed, it would have cut at the heart of the Protestants' educational program.[49]

In early 1954, the Protestant missionaries had lost their only tie to the government, the rural schools. In an effort to end the foreigners' prominence in the national literacy program, the Arbenz government had enacted a law requiring that all reading teachers have a national title of credentials or a certificate of aptitude. Though this new legislation sounded innocent enough, the missionaries complained that titles were issued in a capricious manner, and that the certification process was rigged so that foreigners were cheated out of passing scores. They reported that officials enforced the new laws rigorously in the Protestant schools, even though by one missionary's reckoning, "not even one" teacher in the government schools had such a certificate.[50] To the missionaries, the arbitrary—or even malicious—enforcement of this law was clear indication of the government's nationalistic antagonism.

By the end of Arbenz's first year in office, American missionaries, reflecting the opinion of their compatriot policy makers and business-men in the country, were nearly united in their opposition to the regime. Although they had initially hoped that the Arbenz regime would in-crease social justice in Guatemala, many missionaries were convinced by 1951 that it was communist and, as such, was both a religious and a political threat to their work. Although few missionaries shared the opinion expressed in *Verbum,* the official mouthpiece of the Catholic archbishop, that land distribution was unnecessary and was merely a po-litical lure for ignorant, illiterate voters, most agreed that the govern-ment's means of land reform were unacceptable.[51] For the missionaries, moreover, the apparent national sympathy for "communism" was a spe-cial source of anguish, for it seemed an outright rejection of the package of North American values and Protestant beliefs that they had disbursed so freely from their schools and churches for so many years.

This is not to suggest that the missionaries took the challenge pas-sively. The CAM issued a battle cry to "answer the barrage of Commu-nist literature with Christ-centered propaganda produced in quantity and quality." The Presbyterians initially took a more temperate view, advising their missionaries to "remember that the idealistic Communist is very close to us in his zeal to serve others. Treat him as a friend and not an enemy and show that only methods of love and sacrifice, not vio-lence and coercion, will win." As relations between their churches and the state became more icy under Arbenz, however, the Presbyterians grew more wary, and in 1951 they sponsored a session on recognizing communism at the annual conference of the Evangelical Synod. After that, missionaries of all denominations thundered thinly veiled de-nunciations of communism from their pulpits and reasoned that all true and just governments must come from God, rather than from god-less ideologues. A few even dared attack government programs directly, as when the pastor of the Central Presbyterian Church, located across the street from the National Palace, preached a sermon on the God-given right to private property the Sunday before Decree 900 went into effect.[52]

Below the level of institutions and national politics, a more immedi-ate threat to mission work lay with the local congregations, where bitter schisms arose between those who supported the government's revolu-tionary programs and those who did not. While the foreign missionar-ies almost all opposed the ambitious government programs, many of their local parishioners were among the most avid supporters of the agrarian and political reform. The greatest advocates of reform were quite obviously those who benefited the most from it—the poor, the landless, and the dispossessed. Since the lower classes made up the largest proportion of the Protestant membership, it was not surprising that the reform found considerable support in the Protestant churches. Moreover, the fact that church members had already greatly deviated from accepted social norms by joining a Protestant church in the first place meant that, often, Protestants were more personally predisposed to change than were their Catholic brethren.

From every structural standpoint, Protestant Guatemalans were in a better position to become involved in revolutionary politics than were Catholics. Articles appearing in the Catholic journals *Verbum* and *Acción Social Cristiana* warned against communism in all its guises and threatened excommunication for voters who cast their ballots in local elections for "communist candidates"; such articles influenced the thinking of many Catholics.[53] Protestants, on the other hand, who lacked the direction of a single authority, could and did interpret their local churches' more ambiguous positions on political involvement to their individual satisfaction.

Rural Protestants' economic differentiation from their communities at large also made them more open to reform, land reform in particular. Incremental savings earned from abstinence from alcohol and other vices notwithstanding, indigenous Protestants in the early 1950s tended to have fewer material vested interests than their Catholic counterparts. By definition, Protestants were outside traditional economic systems that centered on the duties of the *cofradías* and the ritual expenses of *costumbre;* however, neither could they take advantage of commodities or income derived from *comunidades indígenas*, communal lands managed through the structure of the civil-religious hierarchy. Under the Agrarian Reform Law, municipal lands could be subject to expropriation and, over protests, sometimes were.[54] Protestants, on the other hand, who had no *cofradía* interests at stake, obviously stood to benefit from such reforms.

It was in the predominantly Indian sections of the country where the indigenous Protestants became most actively involved in the radical reform. Although this type of political activism was unusual, it was not unprecedented, as evidenced by Protestants' participation in the Patzicía uprising of October 1944, which took place in the wake of Ubico's ouster. This was a minor revolt by a small number of Kaqchikels in which fourteen ladinos were killed. The security forces put down the uprising quickly and brutally, but the episode was seen in Guatemala

City as a "horrifying massacre and pillage" and a prelude to ethnic unrest. Three members of the CAM church in Patzicía were among the
thirty-four rebels who were either executed or, as in the CAM members'
case, imprisoned for instigating the rebellion.[55]

During the Arbenz years, it was the members of the Central American Mission and the Presbyterian Church, the denominations that had
the greatest presence in the highlands, who tended to be most active in
the revolutionary reforms. In Chinaulta, in the Presbyterian-dominated
Department of Guatemala, Protestant laymen formed the leadership of
the Unión Campesina, which managed the distribution of lands under
the terms of the Agrarian Reform Law. Indigenous Protestants also
figured prominently in the agrarian reform movement in the Indian villages around Lake Atitlán, which lay in CAM territory, and Protestants
formed the core of leadership of local agrarian committees and peasant
leagues in a disproportionate number of highland villages. In several
lake villages and in San Juan Ostuncalco, local elections placed Protestant leaders in public office for the first time.[56]

Protestants, however, were by no means united in their support of the
radical reform. Churches were like microcosms of their communities at
large: political controversy shattered the fellowship of congregations,
causing permanent rifts between congregations and fratricidal division
among the members of churches. Nowhere was this more evident than
in the Presbyterian mission in Cantel, which, as previously noted, was
atypical in its size and particular rootedness in the community, but
which nonetheless provides a useful and unusually detailed illustration
of this process.[57]

As we have seen, the construction of a textile factory in 1876 meant
that the *municipio* of Cantel felt the impact of modernization early on.
In Cantel, a fairly large sector of the population had already moved from
agriculture into the wage economy, and traditional avenues of authority
had already begun to erode before the Revolution, but revolutionary
programs hastened the process. In 1944, immediately following the Arévalo victory, a new *alcalde*, a member of Arévalo's political party (PAR)
and the only candidate on the ballot, was elected. He was a factory
worker and Arévalo follower, but he nonetheless followed Cantel's traditional patterns of authority in consulting the traditional elders and
members of the civil religious hierarchy in all important matters. Between 1944 and 1946, however, the political landscape in the community
changed dramatically. The factory workers' union (the Sindicato de
Trabajadores Fábrica de Cantel, STFC) gained strength, and eventually

the government-sponsored Unión Campesina (Campesino Union) was established. In reaction, traditionalists established an anticommunist party, the Partido Independiente Anti-Comunista del Occidente (Independent Anti-Communist Party of the West, PIACO); this was counteracted by the establishment of a second prorevolutionary and pro-union party, the Partido Revolucionario Guatemalteco (Guatemalan Revolutionary Party, PRG).[58] By 1946, then, municipal elections offered something unprecedented: a slate of candidates with differing agendas, backed by nontraditional groups, in a meaningful and contested general election.

Biennial elections to *alcalde* and town council posts in the 1946–1954 period yielded a variety of shifting alliances and strange political configurations, but the upshot was that during this period the traditional lines of authority in local political officeholding were broken forever. The union-affiliated PRG, which captured important posts in almost every election, ceased to consult and then ignored the local *cofradía*. Political party membership and union activity became decisive considerations for elected office, and men who had never served in the religious hierarchy took public office for the first time. Observing these new configurations of power, Manning Nash, who did his ethnographic fieldwork in Cantel in 1953–1954 concluded, "the entry of the local union into politics, the control of the election mechanism, the ignoring of *principales,* the overriding of the principles of age and public service as criteria for high office and bases of respect, resulted in a civil-religious hierarchy that was badly undermined. . . . I do not think it will ever return to the integral structure it used to be."[59]

The disintegration of traditional authority provided obvious new political opportunities for Cantel's Protestants, who numbered around five hundred at the time, most belonging to the Presbyterian mission. Many Protestants worked at the textile factory, where they became active members of the STFC and, through the union, the PAR. In 1946, some of Cantel's Presbyterians joined the Unión Campesina, where they became active and vociferous members. By 1953, several had moved into leadership positions.[60]

The Presbyterian residents of Cantel, however, were by no means unified in support of the PAR. Some members of the congregation subscribed to the notion that evangelicals should play no role in local politics, while others heard a different call and joined the PIACO. As the political stakes in Cantel grew, fed by leaflets, soundtrucks, rumor, and innuendo, so did the polarization of the congregation. In the last months of 1953, the union, in which a number of Presbyterians were active, allegedly began to harass some PIACO members of the congregation with death threats. The conservative Presbyterians responded with a blistering public campaign against the Presbyterian unionists. They posted printed placards around the town denouncing the "Protestant scoundrels" (*politicastros evangélicos*), upbraided them for the moral shame they had brought to the Church, and exhorted them "not to use the smoke screen of religion for their vile politics." In the first months of 1954, the Cantel Presbyterian mission split at the seams, dividing into two separate churches. The reformers formed a new mission called Getsemaní, while the conservatives remained part of the old congregation and continued to meet in the church building.[61]

It is worth noting that the American missionaries usually stood by their radicalized congregations, even though growing nationalistic sentiment in the country posed a specific threat to their work and the new programs were often contrary to their personal political views. Indeed, Paul Burgess wrote a singularly sympathetic report about activists in the Cantel church to readers in the United States in 1953. "We thot [*sic*] it only fair," he explained, "to share some of the experiences of the brethren in Christ who have chosen to remain Presbyterians while being enthusiastic agrarians." Even as late as 1954, the Presbyterians urged congregations in the United States to "pray for the Government of Guatemala. Many are sincerely seeking to remedy age old evil in our society. Finding sympathy and help in Communist circles, they naturally think the beast is not as evil as he is pictured." Even the more conservative CAM missionaries tried to explain to their dubious mission board: "A number of people in Guatemala, including university students and some Protestants, have been exposed to Communism and attracted by it . . . especially with its basic appeal for social justice."[62]

Nevertheless, mission boards in the United States watched the situation in Guatemala with rising anxiety. In anticipation of political unpleasantness, they began to make plans to reduce or withdraw their mission projects from the country. The Presbyterian Board of Missions sent the Guatemala mission a packet of materials labeled "Confidential Crisis Strategy. Information Concerning the Experiences of Christians under Communist Pressure," which detailed the trials of missionaries in Europe, China, and Korea. It also refused, out of fear that "a communist uprising might prevent paying it back," to lend the Guatemala mission money to celebrate its diamond jubilee in 1953.[63] At the home office in Dallas, CAM officers began drafting documents that outlined their theological reaction to the political crisis, some of which later became the basis for a new wave of missionary activity promoting a "spiritual alternative to communism."

Back in Guatemala, the missionaries tried to reassure their sponsors. "Those of us who have lived through revolution in Latin America," a missionary wrote, "realize that the newspapers often give the impression of greater danger than actually exists." But the Presbyterian mission board for one was not convinced, and in 1954, it issued a standing order for its missionaries to evacuate the country if the political situation worsened.[64]

In fact, most missionaries were determined to maintain or even expand their work during the Arbenz years, even as the political climate became increasingly threatening. The Evangelical Synod literacy campaign continued to operate on the United Fruit Company's plantations around Tiquisate, despite large-scale strikes that paralyzed the area in 1948 and 1949 and even after the plantations became the focus of the expropriation issue in 1952. As late as 1954, the interdenominational journal *Guatemala News* reported "a great campaign to put the Word into the hands of the new settlers [of the expropriated lands] in the Tiquisate region. [These will be given both] to the settlers and workers of the United Fruit Company."[65]

Indeed, at least one mission was openly sympathetic to the radical government, even at the height of the Arbenz reforms—the Lutheran Church, which, as a newcomer to Guatemala, was oblivious to the traditional political orientation of the Protestant churches. Between 1950 and 1953, the Missouri Synod Lutheran Church in the United States sent at least five seminarians to Guatemala specifically to work in conjunction with several government-sponsored development programs. Their most ambitious program began in the summer of 1951 in Zacapa, where seminarians worked alongside the Ministry of Agriculture's Instituto Agropecuario Nacional (National Agricultural Institute) to try to improve agricultural production in a ten-*aldea* area; this program was later expanded to include classes in agricultural techniques and social welfare. The Lutherans also organized several social services projects in Guatemala City, the largest of which was a social welfare agency opened in 1952 to serve one of the capital's poorest barrios.[66] Though apparently not tied directly to any specific government agencies, these projects clearly did operate with official sanction and informal support.

Because of these programs, the relationship between the Lutheran Church and the Arbenz administration seems to have been reasonably close. Evidence of a special relationship lies in the fact that Lutheran missionaries during the revolutionary period experienced none of the problems with visas and immigration that plagued the missionaries of the other Protestant denominations. To the contrary, the papers of Lutheran applicants generally passed through the bureaucratic maze of the Ministry of Foreign Relations during the Arbenz years with remarkable dispatch.[67]

Yet the Arbenz government remained somewhat distrustful of the Lutherans, who were, after all, not only Americans, but also mostly of German descent. Although the Ministry of Foreign Relations did not demand the same stringent visa qualifications that it asked of other mission groups, it did require other kinds of certification from the Lutheran mission. It insisted that the Lutheran missionaries agree to the stipulation that they keep 250 quetzales (then worth the equivalent amount in dollars) on hand to pay for return to the United States at any time the government might judge that they had acted "to the detriment of the country."[68]

The evidence suggests that the Arbenz administration was suspicious of all Protestant missions, including the one denomination that actively supported the regime's projects. The hostility and uncertainty took its toll on the Protestant work, and few missionaries mourned when Carlos Castillo Armas, backed by the CIA and most of the Guatemalan army, forced Arbenz to step down in June 1954. Most missionaries, however, backed the Castillo Armas coup only passively. Although relieved to have the leftist government out of power, they were unsure how the new regime would regard mission work, especially since so many indigenous converts had been actively involved in revolutionary programs. Paul Burgess of the Presbyterian mission, now seventy-two years old, summed up his concern for the future of the work in his annual Christmas letter in 1954 by invoking a particularly apt metaphor. "The Communists are out now," he wrote, "but they left the yarn in such a snarl that we can hardly continue the old pattern of weaving."[69]

Burgess was more correct than he realized, for Protestant work would never be the same in Guatemala. Although on an institutional level, relations between missions and the postrevolutionary government continued to wax and wane, what is more important is that, by 1954, the word "mission" was no longer synonymous with "Protestant church," for the word had ceased to be adequate to embrace the totality of evangelical experience. It was during the "ten years of spring" that converts made their first break with their missionary mentors. In so doing, they served notice that, at least on some small scale, Protestant identity had gained, for the first time, a kind of local valence, value, and meaning that lay outside the ideology of foreign missions.

CHAPTER 6

THE POSTREVOLUTIONARY YEARS

We have received from Americans not only the imperishable legacy of the Gospel message, but with it a body of attitudes, ethical stances, political postures, economic ideas and relational loyalties that are more substantially linked to . . . American manifest destiny . . . than to the Gospel of Christ.

—Rubén Lores (1976)

ON 18 JUNE 1954, Carlos Castillo Armas led a U.S.-backed invasion force into Guatemala. They entered the country from Honduras and began fighting in Chiquimula. There, mistaking uniformed schoolboys at play for soldiers, the "liberation force" bombed the playground of the Friends' Berea school.[1] From Chiquimula, Castillo's invasion army moved on toward the capital. On 27 June, Jacobo Arbenz resigned, and he and his supporters fled the country. Eleven days later, Castillo Armas became the head of the national governing junta.[2]

Castillo Armas's victory was a matter of urgent concern to Protestant missionaries in Guatemala. Of primary consideration was the fact that Castillo enjoyed the strong backing of conservative Catholics. From the Liberation Army's battle cry, "Por Dios, la Patria, y Libertad" (For God, Country, and Freedom), to its banner displaying the sword and cross, the missionaries feared that the entire "reconquest" of Guatemala from the leftists had taken on the air of a Catholic crusade.[3]

Their fears were not unjustified, for Castillo Armas made it clear from the beginning that he would reward the Catholic Church for its political support in the ouster of Arbenz. The Plan of Tegucigalpa, the manifesto that laid out the agenda for counterrevolutionary political reform, offered significant concessions to the Catholic Church. The plan gave lip service to the principle of freedom of worship, but it strongly implied that the Roman Catholic Church should regain its former position as the preeminent religious body in the republic. It pledged to restore the juridical personality of the Catholic Church and to encourage the growth of parochial education, on the grounds that "the constraints on the Church's educational work [under Arbenz] favored the penetration of communism." But to the Protestant mind, the most ominous phrase in the Plan of Tegucigalpa was the one that promised that "the word and social action of the Church [should] be the most valuable [weapon] against communism."[4]

So apprehensive were the missionaries about the pro-Catholic bias of the new government that they sent an ecumenical delegation to the American embassy in Guatemala City to brief the ambassador. Representatives from the three largest denominations expressed their fears that the new administration might take some sort of political action against the foreign Protestant missions. They also asked that the ambassador, who along with the papal nuncio was one of two advisers to the committee that was overseeing the creation of a new national constitution, "jealously guard religious freedom."[5]

Despite the missionaries' plea, the resulting Constitution of 1955 rewarded the Roman Catholic Church for its efforts in the Arbenz overthrow with some of the most proclerical legislation to appear since before the Liberal era. The new Constitution granted the Catholic Church a juridical personality and abrogated a nearly century-old prohibition on its right to acquire and possess real property (two privileges that were reinforced in the second postrevolutionary constitution, which went into effect in 1966). It permitted the establishment of new convents and the clergy's right to perform civil marriages.[6]

Despite this, the 1955 Constitution fell far short of resolving the conflicts between the interests of church and state. An unreconstructed liberal at heart, Castillo Armas ignored Archbishop Rossell y Arellano's demand that the government declare Catholicism the exclusive religion of the state. He also rejected the archbishop's request that all schools include mandatory courses in Catholic religious instruction, although the Constitution did state that it was "in the national interest that religion be taught in schools," thereby opening a space for parochial teaching in the national curriculum. The archbishop was equally ambivalent, for even as he sought concessions from the government he remained dubious of politics as a force that restricted the independent power of the

Church and made the poor receptive to irreligious policies.[7] Despite these differences, the 1955 Constitution was easily the most pro-Catholic document to come from the government in nearly a century.

In large measure, the pro-Catholic tone of the new Constitution was attributable to the powerful ultraconservative Catholic lay factions, which did not share the archbishop's suspicions and operated openly within the Movimiento de Liberación Nacional (National Liberation Movement, MLN), the former Liberation Army and the base of support for Castillo Armas's formal political party, the Movimiento Democrático Nacional (National Democratic Movement). Seeking to reassert the Catholic Church's traditional hegemony, this faction of lay Catholic conservatives sought to sever all ties between Protestant missions and earlier governments. Emphasizing the participation of Protestants in revolutionary reforms, the MLN encouraged the new government to place the missions under careful surveillance, lest the missionaries or native converts exhibit signs of subversive political activity.

Official scrutiny of missionary activities fell to the Comité Nacional Pro Defensa contra el Comunismo (National Committee for Defense against Communism) of the Ministry of the Interior, which monitored missionaries' activities closely between 1954 and 1955. During this time, at least one missionary from the Presbyterian Church refused to write reports to his home board and instead sent back only newspaper clippings, out of fear of "the eyes and ears of the Committee of Defense against Communism." In other cases, new missionaries entering the country, particularly those associated with the Central American Mission, had to meet the committee's stringent clearance requirements before the government would grant them entry visas.[8]

At least from a Protestant perspective, the issues of politics and the new Catholic resurgence were clearly linked. In November 1954, a Nazarene writer complained in an open letter that appeared in *El Imparcial:* "We will know that the politics of the Vatican are against the Protestant missions, and the defamation of Protestants and the restrictions on freedom of worship are conducted with the sympathy and the goodwill of the government, predisposing the attitude of the anticommunists against the evangelicals, and seeking the physical elimination of our . . . works."[9]

It was not the missionaries, however, who bore the brunt of suspicion for the Protestants' relationship with the discredited regime, but indigenous converts in the western highlands who suffered the most for their flirtation with revolutionary organizations. Within a matter of weeks after Castillo Armas took power, hostile villagers all over the highlands, apparently acting with official approval, began to bait the local Protestants, accusing them of being "communists, tricksters, and terrorists."[10] The evidence from newspaper and church records (from both Protestant and Catholic sources) of fairly systematic repression of Protestants is ample, if sometimes frustratingly vague. In one account, angry Mam locals were accused of dousing a CAM splinter group with *aguardiente* and dirt during a church service. When the worshipers evacuated the building, local police arrested members, who had allegedly participated in radical activities. In another, villagers in El Quiché were said to have run local Presbyterians out of town, warning that, if they returned, they would be cut to pieces. In the lake village of Santiago Atitlán, the level of violence against Protestants was especially high. There, townspeople, whipped into a frenzy by local *cofrades*, brutally beat Protestant villagers and pummeled them with stones. The Protestants were denounced as "communists" and, perhaps more to the point, malcontents who did not "participate in the world of Maximón," the town's patron saint.[11]

As the pace of the counterrevolution quickened, public violence against Protestants escalated. In September 1956, in a particularly vicious attack on a Nazarene congregation in San Pedro Charcá, Alta Verapaz, angry Kek'chí villagers shot rockets into the church during a service, burning many of the worshipers, some quite severely. This attack prompted the Evangelical Synod—now renamed the Alianza Evangélica (Evangelical Alliance)—to issue a statement in the daily newspaper *El Imparcial* condemning the "acts of intolerance" against Protestants that had taken place over the previous two years. Noting that local authorities had not attempted to control the vigilantelike activities of traditionalist Catholic villagers, the statement cited one example in which the local *alcalde* had told some Nazarene pastors that, "since it was difficult to stop the difficulties, it would be better if the Protestants did not meet publicly at all." In a strongly worded request, the alliance demanded that the government provide "energetic protection for ALL its citizens" (original emphasis) so that Guatemala could "go forward to join the civilized nations."[12]

On the face of it, the actions against Protestants in the postrevolutionary decade seem fairly clear-cut: Protestants were targeted for recrimination because they had actively participated in the agrarian and municipal reforms; because of their standing as "outsiders," they could easily be singled out for punishment without damaging the structure of community coherence and authority. Yet the evidence suggests that this explanation masks much larger issues concerning community division and fractured authority, of which Protestants were among the most obvious symptoms, but rarely the primary cause. Nor was national politics necessarily the central issue, although the fallout from the political opening of the "ten years of spring" would continue to reverberate at the community level for some time. What was at stake was *costumbre* itself: the traditional patterns of authority, status, identity, social exchange, and belief that were now threatened not only by politics (and, to a minor extent, by missions), but also by economic transition and, perhaps most important, by religious pluralism originating within the Catholic Church itself.

The catalyst for this was the Catholic Action movement. As we have seen, Catholic Action originated in Europe as a Church-based political movement in the late 1920s to channel the energies of politically volatile sectors of the population into church organizations. In Europe, Catholic Action targeted groups deemed most likely to be attracted to radical politics, especially students and urban workers; by the early 1940s, Catholic Action was among the largest and most influential lay organizations in the Church.

Catholic Action first came to Guatemala in 1935, but its activities were confined at that time primarily to the city. During this early period, members involved themselves exclusively in activities that promoted "religious and moral education," and Catholic Action operated mainly as a lay organization largely outside of episcopal control or concern. This narrow focus changed abruptly in 1944, however, when a tally of clergy revealed that the institutional Church had disintegrated to such an appalling state that only 120 full-time ordained priests served the entire country. To rally forces in this institutional emergency, Bishop Mariano Rossell y Arellano took Catholic Action under diocesan control and deployed it around the country. In so doing, he hoped to infuse vigorous, new Catholic lay organizations into the countryside to revitalize the presence of the Church and to help offset the secular temptations of the revolution.[13]

Catholic Action's *modus operandi* was to train lay leaders (*catequistas*, or catechists) in conventional Catholic orthodoxy, which they could then use to combat "humanism, Protestantism, rationalism, auto-revelation, historical materialism, and laicism."[14] But the subtextual purpose of introducing new lay groups, highly decentralized and tied to a parish and diocese rather than to traditional community structures, was to further erode the power of heterodox traditionalist belief and the authority of the local religious technicians. In a very real sense, the introduction of Catholic Action was both a preemptive strike against the Church's own marginalization and an attempt to provide an alternative ideology to the siren call of politics and the "modern world" at large.

In Guatemala, the vanguard action of Catholic Action came with the entry of two priests of the Maryknoll Order, a Catholic missionary order based in the United States. Fleeing the Maoist revolution, they came to Guatemala from postings in China. These priests arrived in 1943, and were soon followed by other Maryknolls, who shortly became identified with Catholic Action. In addition to the Maryknolls, clergy of the predominantly Belgian Sacred Heart brothers, the Salesians, and the Marian brothers also gained permission to work in the country. In doing so, the foreign clergy greatly augmented the number of priests serving in Guatemala; but they also introduced a reformist and progressive agenda that turned traditional concepts of church work in ladino and indigenous communities alike on their head.[15]

For the Maryknolls, the largest of the Catholic missionary orders in Guatemala, this reformist agenda called for a plan of action that, perhaps not coincidentally, bore some resemblance to that of the Protestants in the late 1940s and the 1950s. As Bruce Calder notes, the Maryknoll program in this period consisted of four elements: (1) a core of catechists' instruction in orthodox Catholic doctrine; (2) the combating of traditionalist religion by distributing medicine to draw people away from shamans; (3) the denunciation of ritual drinking and excessive public ritual as immoral and wasteful; and (4) an increase in missionary-directed education to help the Maya "defend themselves against ladino exploitation."[16]

Only this first element is integral to the general principles of Catholic Action universally; the last three are specific only to Guatemala, but it was in these very matters that Catholic missionaries quickly ran afoul of their flocks. The Catholic Church was in no way prepared for the bitter resistance Catholic Action encountered in indigenous communities in the 1940s and the 1950s, perhaps because the Church itself had assumed that the Guatemalan government's modernizing programs had already defused the intense religiosity of indigenous society. While traditionalists might initially have been delighted to have a priest in close proximity and welcomed his efforts to improve their community's secular welfare, they did not hesitate to react with hostility or even outright violence if he attempted to encroach on community religious autonomy.

Although community responses to Catholic reformism obviously differed with location and circumstance, the ethnographic record is replete with evidence that Catholic Action changed forever the social reality of many altiplano communities. This it did by introducing new factional alignments and by calling into question—through external agents (foreign priests) and internal players (local catechists)—the canon of *costumbre* and social relationships that had heretofore defined the community and its members. Kay Warren, for example, notes that in 1952 traditionalists in the town of San Andrés refused to allow local chapels to be used by priests affiliated with Catholic Action. Ricardo Falla, himself a young priest in the field at the time, details the sometimes violent conflict between Catholic Action adherents and the Zanhorines (the traditionalists) in San Antonio Illotenango. John Watanabe's informants in Santiago Chimaltenango marked religious change and dissension in their community not from the visits of CAM missionaries in the 1920s, but from the arrival of Maryknoll priests in 1945: "When the *padres* came," one said simply, "many *costumbres* died." [17]

Given that Catholic Action came to Guatemala in the turmoil of the revolutionary period, it is difficult to assess which changes were brought about by Catholic Action and which by other factors, such as the formation of new political organizations and land reform. It is perhaps because of this that community conflicts are not generally described by outside observers along religious lines until after 1954. It is clear, however, that by the early 1950s, traditional structures of authority and community cohesion in many locations were severely undermined, at least in a symbolic sense, and the culpability lay at the feet of Catholic Action. Catechists, in Douglas Britnall's phrase, having "revolted against the dead," against the traditional beliefs and authority of their elders, had shattered the local hegemony of *costumbre* and created a new type of identity. In dividing indigenous communities into catechist and traditionalist factions, to paraphrase Peter Berger, the "sacred canopy" was rent, thus creating an opening for new religious and political ideologies. [18]

Where Protestants fit into this picture is that they, along with "communists," were the most easily identifiable as the sources of the crisis of community division. As such, they also provided a much less ambiguous target for recriminations than did the catechists. The process of redefinition and identification among traditionalists and "Catholics" was fairly attenuated. As Warren has shown, traditionalists in San Andrés at first considered catechists to be "neither devils nor ancestors," but something in between. [19] In general terms, Protestants, on the other hand, though few in number and ineffectually organized, were unequivocally the Other, and as such, made ideal scapegoats to blame for community division.

This may account for one of the reasons why the Presbyterian mission in 1959 took the unusual step of permitting a congregational referendum on the status of indigenous churches. The result was the formation of an ethnic-based presbytery (an administrative jurisdiction much like a Catholic diocese) called the Presbiterio Maya-Quiché. The Presbiterio Maya-Quiché was distinctive in that it was based on ethnicity rather than geography, and it used a trained indigenous pastorate specifically to encourage the propagation of indigenous congregations. So successful was this effort that in 1965 the Presbyterians established a second ethnic presbytery, the Presbiterio Kek'chi, for indigenous congregants living primarily in the Departments of Alta Verapaz, Baja Verapaz, and Izabal.[20]

All of this had dramatic implications for the future, but for the most part, the indigenous communities' internal struggle for identity remained largely invisible to the outside world. So it was that, despite indigenous Protestants' continued castigation, U.S. missionaries continued to come into Guatemala in a small but steady trickle. Between 1954 and 1963, two fundamentalist denominations, the Church of the Four Square Gospel, and the Source of Light Mission, three smaller fundamentalist organizations, and a handful of short-term "thrust groups" all initiated work in the country. Unlike the established denominations, which bore the stigma of association with the ousted regime during this period, these new missions went into Guatemala riding the very crest of the counterrevolution.[21]

There were several reasons for the renewal of missionary interest in Guatemala in the late 1950s. First, the Arbenz affair had brought Guatemala to the attention of the general American public, and the dramatic events of the past few years had caught the eye of politically conservative American fundamentalists, who had previously had little interest in the region. Second, political events in Asia during this same time period had effectively closed off the Far East to foreign missionaries, forcing American mission boards to funnel virtually all of their resources into the Western Hemisphere.[22]

The most important reason for renewed missionary interest in Guatemala, however, was ideological, and it reflected the conservative attitudes in the United States as much as it complemented the current political climate in Guatemala. This new ideological focus was the product of Guatemala's well-publicized flirtation with socialism and Fidel Castro's victory in Cuba in 1959. These two events in Latin America, a region much nearer in geography and spirit than Asia, bore nearly apocalyptic significance for the North American evangelical movement, which interpreted them to be a final indictment of Catholicism. By 1960, conservative Christians in the United States had devised their own strategy to prevent the fall of any more Latin American dominoes: the promotion of evangelical Christianity as an ideological alternative to communism. The political implications of this definition of faith tied it closely to the United States, as a model for spiritual, social, and political values.[23]

The new faith missions, which heralded this fresh approach, were a breed apart from the established Protestant churches in Guatemala and differed from the traditional denominations in structure, purpose, and methodology. Where the original churches were sectarian, the new groups were interdenominational; where the traditional denominations engaged in a wide range of projects such as schools, clinics, and translation projects, the new groups—with the exception of the Wycliffe Bible Translators—concentrated entirely on evangelization. Above all, where the established churches had been divided on the question of politics, the new organizations were staunchly and unequivocally anticommunist.

This is not to imply, however, that there was necessarily any overt antipathy between the old groups and the new. By 1955, the established denominations, anxious to shake off any remaining association with the discredited revolution, welcomed the new groups and quickly adopted their anticommunist stance. The new political attitudes were so pervasive that in 1955 one CAM missionary requested of his home board that they "pray for the leaders of the . . . government. . . . They are maintaining a strict anti-communist attitude which is unmistakable and for which we praise the Lord." In 1963, a Presbyterian bulletin urged its congregation to support the national government by exhorting, "Spiritual and political salvation depends on evangelicals."[24]

The greatest initiative for the new and active evangelical crusade came not from any specific denominations, however, but from a new interdenominational group, the fundamentalist faith mission called the Latin American Mission (LAM). One of the key founders of the LAM was Harry Strachan, a North American missionary who, along with his wife, had briefly served the CAM in Guatemala in the 1920s. The LAM received much of its support from the United States, but for reasons of logistics and credibility, the organization operated out of San José, Costa Rica. Unlike other mission groups, the LAM was an authentically *inter*denominational organization that sought to convert people to evangelical Christianity, in the English sense of the word, that is, by stressing personal salvation and spiritual transformation, characterized by the spreading of the gospel. The LAM, however, did not seek to affiliate converts with any particular denomination or dogma.

The LAM launched its first crusade in Guatemala in 1962. Attempting to end the schisms that divided the major denominations and mission agencies, the LAM urged the churches to set aside doctrinal differences for the sake of greater outreach, with the goal of implementing a coordinated, nationwide conversion campaign. Although the most traditional denominations—the Presbyterians, the Quakers, the Lutherans, and the Nazarenes—accepted this idea with some reluctance, the nonliturgical evangelical churches embraced the broad approach eagerly, resulting in a strong fundamentalist emphasis within the LAM program.[25]

In November 1962, the LAM unleashed a massive evangelization crusade known as Evangelism in Depth (Instituto Internacional de Evangelización a Fondo, IINDEF) in Guatemala. IINDEF was a comprehensive outreach program that combined door-to-door evangelism with media campaigns, revivals, radio programming, and church programs. The LAM campaign also departed radically from earlier proselytization methods by introducing business planning and marketing techniques into its conversion approach. The LAM methodology included massive advertising campaigns, radio sermons, elaborate parades, advertising jingles, seminars, and weeklong retreats, as well as door-to-door evangelism delivered by believers trained in sales merchandising. In 1962, IINDEF distributed half a million Gospels and one million mission tracts, and native evangelists visited almost a quarter of a million homes.[26]

The Latin American Mission was not the first Protestant organization to use modern communication methods for proselytization in Guatemala, but it was easily the most influential. As early as 1946, the Central American Mission had bought airtime on local radio stations for religious broadcasts. In 1948, the mission had opened its own station, TGQA, which was devoted entirely to religious programming such as Bible readings, hymns, and sermons. The Quakers, too, had tried their hand at broadcasting in 1952, when the mission mounted speakers on the roof of their church in Chiquimula and played religious broadcasts so loudly, as the *Harvester* cheerily reported, that "people heard it in the village across the Motagua River." Eventually, the police received so many complaints about the Friends' broadcasts that they were forced to stop.[27]

It was the LAM evangelization program, however, that was most successful in integrating old evangelization methods, such as revivals and preaching meetings, with new sales techniques and media exposure methods. The combination was dynamic, and the IINDEF campaign in Guatemala was enormously fruitful. In 1950, after nearly seventy-five years of missionary activity in Guatemala, the national census showed that Protestants made up less than one percent of the nation's population; a study in 1954 showed that only thirty thousand people called themselves evangelicals. During the LAM crusade in 1962 alone, however, fifteen thousand Guatemalans converted to Protestant Christianity.[28] In the next few years, Protestant membership continued to grow prodigiously, although not at the pace established during the 1962 campaign.

The Guatemalan crusade was by far the LAM's most successful effort, although the organization launched similar programs in all the other Central American nations during the early 1960s. In general, growth came from new churches rather than within the established denominations; of the mainline groups, only the Central American Mission, which supported the LAM from the beginning, took a noticeable jolt from the crusade, when its annual growth rate more than doubled between 1960 and 1965. The LAM attributed its success to the fact that the crusade was united rather than sectarian and to the strategy of door-to-door evangelization, efficient planning, and, above all, divine favor. But sociopolitical factors were at work as well.[29]

One important factor in the LAM's success in Guatemala was the country's climate of growing political instability. The great LAM crusade coincided precisely with the first guerrilla mobilization, to which Pres. Miguel Ydígoras Fuentes responded with such measures as the imposition of martial law, curfews, and the pronouncement of a state of siege. A program of military retaliation was led by Col. Enrique Peralta Azurdía, the powerful defense minister, who deposed Ydígoras in a coup in 1963. As the counterinsurgency campaign heated up, the evangelicals seized the opportunity to emphasize their message of a spiritual alternative to communism and an offer of haven in a climate of increasing repression and political uncertainty.[30]

There was indeed something fortuitous about the timing of the LAM campaign, because from the very beginning to the bitter end of the 1960s, Guatemala was buffeted from all sides by profound socioeconomic and political change. The most visible change was the militarization of national politics, as Guatemala became a state governed not by military caudillos, as in the past, but by a sophisticated and highly praetorianized martial institution. In the wake of Castillo Armas's "liberation," the military gradually assumed power to the extent that its primary goal became one of maintaining a type of political stability that would prevent reform-minded political parties from taking power. This goal necessitated the cynical manipulation of civilian elections, the occasional elimination of uncooperative political actors (as illustrated by Castillo Armas's own assassination in 1957), and collaboration with corrupt administrations. After 1963, this translated into direct intervention in national politics through coups d'état, and, by the mid-1960s, the increasing use of violence to counteract political protest or attempts at reform.[31]

For the *alto mando*, the seemingly impenetrable and monolithic army high command, the rationale for such action was fed by the political crisis that began in 1961 with the formation of Guatemala's first modern armed insurgency, the Frente Armada Revolucionaria (FAR). This guerrilla cell, the first of several armed popular movements that would eventually operate in the eastern provinces and later in the altiplano, was formed by a group of disaffected army officers and former Arbenz supporters who established the front in the Oriente.

Although at no time did the armed opposition pose a credible threat to actually take power, it would be this struggle between leftist guerrillas and the military-controlled government that would define Guatemala's political reality for the next quarter century. Twice in the 1960s, the guerrillas gained a measure of popular and strategic support only to be put down decisively by the army each time. It was during these times that the human price of the political struggle was especially high, corresponding to specific counterinsurgency campaigns. These periods were from 1962 to 1963, during the administration of President Miguel Ydígoras Fuentes, and from 1966 to 1967, when Col. Carlos Arana Osorio, the "jackal of Zacapa," conducted a sweeping, bitter, scorched-earth counterinsurgency campaign in the eastern departments that nearly obliterated the insurgency, but at the cost of the lives of thousands of peasants.[32]

By the end of the decade, the violence, displacement, and human loss inherent in the government's cyclical efforts to purge the country of leftists and their supporters had had a profound impact on the nation's collective psyche. Nevertheless, it is too facile to ascribe the crisis of the

1960s solely to what Guatemalans euphemistically referred to as "*la política*" (politics). The crisis that began in the 1960s, accelerated in the 1970s, and erupted in the early 1980s was at heart based on the transition to the long-coveted goal of "modernization." So profound and traumatic has this process been in Guatemala that Sheldon Annis has referred to it as a "bombardment of twentieth-century forces."[33]

It is outside the scope of this chapter to offer more than some statistical mile markers. During the 1960s, Guatemala experienced a "green revolution," wherein foreign aid agencies such as the U.S. Agency for International Development (USAID) and, frequently, Catholic missionary workers, introduced the large-scale use of pesticides and fertilizers into commercial and small-scale agricultural enterprises. This resulted in crop diversification away from a nearly monocultural dependence on coffee and pushed the nation's annual economic growth rate up to an impressive 6.8 percent; by 1970, Guatemala had one of the most dynamic economies in all of Latin America. Second, improvements in medicine and public health services, many of them provided by private and governmental foreign aid, promoted a significant population boom. Between 1950 and 1975, less than a generation, the national population doubled, increasing from just under three million to six million. By far, the most rapid population growth was in the indigenous sector.[34]

The combined effects of dramatic population increase coupled with the diversion of additional lands for export crops precipitated an acute land shortage for indigenous and ladino peasants. The government attempted to mollify these sectors by opening up government lands in the remote rain forests of the Petén, Alta Verapaz, and the Ixcán, along the Mexican border, for colonization in the mid-1960s in a development project that was codified in 1965. Although the thin soil and isolation of these zones made them unsuitable for large-scale settlement, the colonization projects were nonetheless attractive to immigrants from the land-pressed altiplano and Oriente. This new kind of migration, combined with political violence and other pressures of modernization, conspired to put additional stresses on traditional patterns of landownership, community and kinship obligations and loyalties, and even religious identity by the end of the 1960s.[35]

Reformist Catholic clergy, now backed by the moral mandate of the recently convened Second Vatican Council (1962–1965), if not by the local episcopate, were in the vanguard of some of these changes, particularly in the colonization projects. These generally also enjoyed government support after Julio César Méndez Montenegro became president in 1966, in part because of the government's hope that a strong national presence would stop Mexico's plan to dam the Ucumacinta River, which bordered the two countries. Sacred Heart and Maryknoll fathers were among the first to organize migrants who had spontaneously moved into the near-vacant lands of the Ixcán and along the Ucumacinta River in the Petén by collecting them into cooperatives and helping them win legal title to their lands. These examples of Catholic social activism spawned parallel, if more modest, Protestant measures, at least from the traditional denominations that had some history of social action. In 1965, the Presbyterian Church, urged along by a more activist Church in the United States, joined forces with the Ministry of Agriculture and the national institute of public health to train agricultural promoters to teach new agricultural techniques in highland villages. More ambitious was a Quaker project in 1968 that oversaw the relocation of Chortí Indians from their marginal lands along the Honduras border to a Friends-run cooperative farm in the Petén. Although the government provided land for the project, the Quaker mission, heavily subsidized by donors in the United States, contributed farm machinery, free dental and medical care, child care, and agricultural training for the cooperative's members.[36]

Positioned in the vortex of these many changes, Protestant work expanded rapidly from the mid-1960s into the early 1970s. IINDEF continued as the method of conversion, but the LAM itself diminished in importance, as churches—particularly the mainline denominations—began to reject its emphasis on growth over doctrine. The most important reason, however, for the LAM's decline in the late 1960s and the early 1970s was the growth of native churches. These churches were, in many respects, the spiritual offspring of the IINDEF crusades, but with the difference that, as they matured, these missions began to reject certain aspects of the American missionaries' evangelization package. In particular, the new native-church movement objected to the way that the LAM and other American fundamentalist groups promoted American values, lifestyles, and politics along with the gospel. One Latin American evangelist tried to explain this attitude in an essay that appeared in a missionary journal in 1976:

> Americans should understand the ambiguities of their calling and the way in which consciously or unconsciously this pervasive ideology of "manifest destiny" has made them more the ambassadors of an Anglo-Saxon Christianity and the American way of life than of the Gospel. . . . We have received from

Americans not only the imperishable legacy of the Gospel message, but with it a body of attitudes, ethical stances, political postures, economic forces, and relational loyalties that are more substantially linked to . . . American manifest destiny than the gospel of Christ.[37]

To be sure, the growing nationalism of the Guatemalan churches was not entirely the product of the LAM crusade, nor was it entirely unexpected. Beginning in 1945, the Presbyterian mission board had begun to train local pastors and to reduce American aid to native churches by 10 percent each year to encourage self-sufficiency. The effort came not a moment too soon, for in 1946, a nationalistic group broke off from the Central Presbyterian Church to form a separate native Presbyterian church in the capital. During the heyday of the Arbenz reform, the Presbyterian mission had concluded that the time had come to remove all its foreign missionaries from the country. "The evangelism of any country must be completed by the nationals," wrote the pastor of the Central Presbyterian Church in the capital in 1952. "The task of the alien missionary is to introduce Christianity, but once an adequate national church is established, [the nationals] must take over the major responsibility."[38]

The specter of nationalism rushed the weaning process, and in 1961, the Presbyterian Guatemalan mission became the independent, self-supporting, and self-staffed Iglesia Evangélica Nacional Presbiteriana de Guatemala. The severing of the relationship with the American mission board, however, proved so premature that the denomination nearly collapsed within months. Local pastors and church administrators found themselves ill-prepared to cope without the missionaries, and by 1962 the Church was nearly bankrupt. As a result, the first years of the Iglesia Evangélica Nacional Presbiteriana de Guatemala were so precarious that the denomination suffered a precipitous decline in membership from which it has never fully recovered. Moreover, during the early 1960s, the Presbyterian Church was forced to abandon some of the secular projects it had sponsored for decades. The greatest loss came in 1963, when, because of lack of funds and staffing, the Church was forced to sell off the American Hospital, which the mission had run for more than half a century.[39]

The Presbyterian Church was not the only denomination to heed the signs that the time was drawing near to turn mission work over to the nationals, for the political implications of both the Arbenz program and the CIA-backed Castillo Armas coup weighed heavily on the missions.

As an article in the *Christian Century,* an interdenominational magazine, charged in 1954, "Failure [to relinquish control to native clergy] can only serve to strengthen the belief among Latin Americans that the Protestant missions are branch offices of materially interested groups such as United Fruit Company."[40]

Nevertheless, the conservative backlash and the success of the LAM campaign of the early 1960s momentarily lulled the missionaries into believing that there was no pressing need to nationalize their missions, an impression that was underscored by the Presbyterian Church's miserable circumstances. The one exception was the Nazarene mission, which followed through with long-standing plans to nationalize in 1962, but only with the caveat that the new national Church, the Iglesia Nacional Nazareno, continue to receive staff and funds from the United States. The missionaries' complacency, however, soon proved to be unwarranted, as "nationalism," in the guise of national reconciliation, became one of the catchwords in the consolidation of military hegemony in the early and mid-1960s.[41]

Thus it was that the forces of nationalism, doctrinal differences, and the divergent beliefs of large numbers of newly converted Protestants combined to make Guatemalan Protestantism a centrifuge. During the 1960s, tens of small indigenous sects began to spin off the older established churches to form new congregations that, by design, bore no overt ties to American-sponsored denominations.

The proximate causes for church schisms were varied. In some cases, the issue at hand was a clash of personalities or doctrine involving the pastor of a church and the members of his congregation; in others, members refused to accept church discipline and left the Church to found new congregations. But in almost all instances, there was a single common denominator: whatever the underlying sources of friction within a congregation, the dissenting faction characteristically cited nationalistic reasons for leaving the Church. In the lexicon of schism, the mother Church—regardless of denomination—represented the old traditional Protestant Church in Guatemala, with a paternalistic missionary and close ties to American politics and lifestyle. The new splinter church, on the other hand, was *pura guatemalteca*—pure Guatemalan. It was, in theory, at least, completely autonomous and not tainted by association with foreign personnel or agencies.

One of the most dramatic examples of this kind of nationalistic fractionalization took place in the Assemblies of God. The Assemblies of God was a Pentecostal denomination and had never had the respectability or the close relationship with the government of most of the other "historical" denominations. Nonetheless, a large Assembly of God church had thrived in the capital, and by the mid-1950s had a congregation of several hundred people under the leadership of an American missionary who had served the congregation for more than a decade.

In 1954, the congregation of the Assembly of God broke into warring factions over an issue that is now shrouded by decorum and time. At issue was the behavior of one José María Muñoz, who refused to accept church discipline (by his account) and atone for his protest of the American missionary's imperious ways. (In the church's rendering of the episode, Muñoz was expelled for adultery.)[42] In either event, Muñoz personally spearheaded an attempt to expel the American missionary and replace him with a native pastor. When his effort failed, Muñoz left the church, taking a large faction with him. He established a new church a few doors down from the old Assembly of God and christened it the Iglesia Evangélica Príncipe de Paz. Príncipe de Paz mirrored the doctrine and practice of the Assemblies of God in every way but one: it was, by Muñoz's design, "pure Guatemalan." It had no foreign pastors or staff, was self-consciously patriotic, and refused to accept financial support from any source outside of Guatemala.[43]

The appeal of a nationalistic Church was infectious, and Príncipe de Paz grew meteorically. The Church attracted many defectors from the Assembly of God and later from other denominations. By 1970, the congregation numbered several thousand members and had established more than half a dozen churches outside of the capital.[44]

The centrifugal effects of nationalism were not limited to the Assemblies of God or even specifically to the Pentecostal churches. Generally, there was a rough correlation between the liturgical rigidity of a denomination and its potential for fractionalization; the more formal churches seem to have been less likely to produce splinter groups than were churches that had loosely organized liturgies and administrative structures. But even the most hidebound denominations suffered from some internal divisions.

The Central American Mission, which is not technically a denomination and therefore does not have a rigid church structure, was particularly balkanized. Even before the evangelical boom of the 1960s, the CAM was the most schismatic of the traditional missions; between 1926 and 1962, at least five new denominations spun off it.[45] None of these early splinter groups developed into denominations of any size or influence.

In 1961, however, a group broke off of the Cinco Calles Church in

Guatemala City that was to have a lasting impact on the course that Protestantism would take over the next few years in Guatemala. This was a group of dissidents under the leadership of Moisés and Antonio Ríos, who had fallen out with the pastor of the Cinco Calles Church. Following Muñoz's example, they credited the difficulties to nationalistic and doctrinal difference and left the mission to form their own congregation, called Misión Cristiana Elim.

The Elim Mission initially followed the doctrine of the Central American Mission, but in 1965, the entire congregation became Pentecostal. The change galvanized the congregation, and it grew exponentially. By 1970, the original Elim church had nearly a thousand members and had opened several auxiliary congregations in the capital and in neighboring departments.[46]

The conversion of the Elim Mission illustrates the second salient factor in the development of the indigenous churches in the late 1960s: although many of the new sects splintered off from non-Pentecostal churches, virtually all of the new denominations became Pentecostal churches within a few years of their establishment. All of the major indigenous churches that emerged after 1954 either were founded as or eventually became Pentecostal churches. Some, like Príncipe de Paz or Puerto del Cielo, which broke off from the Church of God, were Pentecostal; others, like Elim or El Calvario, a splinter from the Baptist and Nazarene churches, became Pentecostal churches during the mid-1960s.

The sudden popularity of Pentecostalism stemmed from both theological and sociological factors. Theologically, the growth of Pentecostalism in Guatemala in the 1960s was part of a larger movement called "neo-Pentecostalism" that originated in California around 1960. The neo-Pentecostal movement differed from the older type of Pentecostalism exemplified by what were now mainline denominations such as the Assemblies of God in that it was considered an international and ecumenical movement that extended even to the Roman Catholic Church. In theory, the neo-Pentecostal (sometimes known as charismatic) movement sought to renovate Christians by "baptism in the Holy Spirit" within the framework of traditional denominations. In practice, however, charismatic members usually left their old churches—often, even established Pentecostal churches—to form new congregations.[47] Such was the case in Guatemala, although frequently the neo-Pentecostal transformation did not occur until the congregation had already separated from its mother Church.

The international ecumenical movement of the 1960s enhanced the

growth of Pentecostalism. One of the precepts of Vatican II was to pro-
mote ecumenical fellowship among the Roman, Orthodox, and Protestant churches, and during the mid-1960s, mainline Protestant churches
worldwide began to make overtures in this direction. To Guatemalans
who had risked ridicule and social ostracism to convert to Protestantism, however, the idea of rekindling any sort of relationship with Rome
was heretical, and they abandoned the mainline denominations in protest. The Pentecostal churches, however, reaffirmed a defiantly anti-
Catholic stance and refused to participate in the ecumenical movement,
as did the CAM, thereby giving them an added attraction over the traditional denominations.[48]

Additional factors drew Guatemalans to the Pentecostal churches
as well. The form of worship in the Pentecostal churches—with an
emphasis on the gifts of the Holy Spirit and highly emotional and spontaneous worship services and the ecstatic practice of speaking in
tongues—appealed to Guatemalans on an innate level. The practice
held a special resonance for Indians, in that speaking in *lengua*—that is,
in native languages rather than the Latin or Spanish of Catholic worship—had traditionally played an integral part in the traditional religious practices of the Maya, with glossolalia substituting for the indigenous utterances that signaled contact with the divine.[49] Moreover, the
Pentecostal churches offered a provocative style of worship; unlike the
mainline denominations, which usually offered liturgical predictability
in worship, the Pentecostal services provided entertainment in its purest
form. Services included live musical groups, impromptu and frequently
tantalizing testimonials from other members of the congregation, punc-
tuated by spontaneous displays of "receiving the Spirit," when members
might speak in tongues or go into ecstatic convulsions. To the poor in
urban and rural areas alike, the Pentecostal services provided free entertainment and emotional outlets with which neither soccer games,
movies, nor other churches could compete.[50]

This explanation, however, trivializes the spiritual allure of Pentecostalism, which to outsiders tends to be obscured by the visual and
aural spectacle of Pentecostal worship. As theologian Harvey Cox has
pointed out, Pentecostalism is not form without substance, and it em-
bodies a complex body of religious ideas and insights. As Cox observes,
what is unique to Pentecostalism is that, "while the beliefs of . . . many
other religious groups are enshrined in formal theological systems, those
of Pentecostalism are embedded in testimonies, ecstatic speech and
bodily movement. But it *is* a theology, a full-blown religious cosmos, an

intricate system of symbols that respond to perennial questions of human meaning and value."[51]

The proliferation of indigenous Pentecostalism in the late 1960s and the early 1970s was only a prelude to church growth in the future. Indeed, although the number of denominations in Guatemala increased significantly between 1954 and 1975, the aggregate number of converts to Protestantism was not nearly as great as one might expect. The reason for the discrepancy was that almost all of the new denominations had won most of their members at the expense of the mainline Protestant churches. The shift in affiliation was clear; by 1970, 60 percent of the entire evangelical population of the country was Pentecostal.[52] By 1980, this figure exceeded 80 percent.

The new popularity of Pentecostalism and of Protestantism in general was above all indicative of the tectonic social shifts that were taking place in Guatemala during the 1960s. These included the acceleration and institutionalization of political violence, the increased militarization of the state, unprecedented population stresses, and changes that brought both increased prosperity and added economic disequilibrium to rural communities. All these factors converged to push conventional agencies to their limits, but they also opened a social space for new kinds of players, including, among many others, pluralistic religious groups.

One conventional agency under particular stress during this period was the Catholic Church, which also had to cope with internal challenges posed by reformist but divisive groups like Catholic Action. The demise of Catholic spiritual hegemony became more or less complete in the 1960s, the victim of the hundred-year war of attrition waged by the state, the corrosive forces of modernization, and acrimonious internal division. Not surprisingly, the end of this long-held hegemony paralleled the dramatic expansion of Protestant churches—not of "missions," fed and directed from abroad, but of domestic, autochthonous congregations that promised to restore order and belonging from the confusion and anomie of the counterrevolutionary decade.

CHAPTER 7

THE EARTHQUAKE AND
THE CULTURE OF VIOLENCE

I will display portents in heaven above and signs on earth below. The sun
will be turned into darkness and the moon into blood before the Day of
the Lord dawns. All who call on the name of the Lord will be saved.

—Joel 3:1–5

WHILE human actions abetted Protestant growth in the 1960s, it
was a cataclysmic "act of God" that did so in the 1970s. In the
early morning hours of 4 February 1976, a massive earthquake ravaged
Guatemala, killing close to twenty thousand people. Over three times
that number were injured, and more than one million Guatemalans were
left homeless. Hardest hit were the villages near the epicenter at Chimaltenango, but damage and loss affected every region.[1]

Church response to the tragedy was prompt, if somewhat limited, as
the Central American Mission, the Nazarenes, the Presbyterians, and
the independent Pentecostals rallied together to provide supplies and
funds to help rebuild members' homes and churches.[2] The rationale for
this narrow approach was that congregational rebuilding was the most
inexpensive form of relief aid, an important consideration given that the
earthquake had destroyed a substantial amount of church infrastructure
and killed many parishioners. The internal logic of rebuilding basic community structures such as churches and homes was that the replacement
of these essential symbols of family and identity would help heal the
psychological wounds the earthquake had inflicted, a belief that was
borne out by the observations of outside relief agents. The correlation
between Church-orchestrated relief and community reconstruction was
so clear that the government's Comité para Reconstrucción Nacional

(National Reconstruction Committee) in mid-1976 authorized the Nazarene churches in Alta and Baja Verapaz to receive special priority for construction materials to rebuild their churches.[3] Only three local denominations—the Lutheran Church, the Episcopal Church (two denominations that still maintained a strong foreign affiliation), and the Friends Mission—initiated relief work on a broad, nondenominational level.[4]

Although the Alianza Evangélica formed an interdenominational emergency relief committee (CEPA) within days of the quake to coordinate emergency relief locally, interchurch rivalry so plagued the organization that most of the denominations abandoned it to run their own relief programs.[5] It was largely left to foreign interdenominational agencies, then, to conduct the large, broad-based programs of disaster relief.

At the vanguard of these organizations were Protestant aid agencies from the United States, which saw in the tragedy the opportunity to help rebuild Guatemala physically and retrofit it spiritually. In all, just over a dozen large Protestant relief agencies, most affiliated with mainline U.S. denominations and nondenominational church-related organizations like World Vision, came to Guatemala in the weeks that followed the disaster. Their efforts were coordinated under an umbrella board begun by the National Council of Church and Church World Service—the Consejo Cristiano de Agencias de Desarrollo (Christian Council of Development Agencies, CONCAD). A handful of smaller church-related groups, several of which were sponsored by conservative and fundamentalist groups in the United States, also joined the relief effort, but declined to join the CONCAD because of its affiliation with the liberal National and World Council of Churches. Though their primary object at this point was to provide physical relief to the stricken, their long-term objective was to "saturate with Scripture," winning converts by word and example.[6]

Within a few months of the earthquake, evangelical church membership jumped by 14 percent. Critics quipped that such timely conversion was "lámina por ánima" (a soul for tin roofing), for the evangelicals' material largesse clearly enhanced their appeal considerably. This clever bit of wordplay did not tell the whole story, however, for in general, Guatemalans in the postearthquake period appeared to be more than "rice Christians." There is no question that some "converts" lapsed as soon as the Protestant agencies ran out of concrete blocks and potted meat, but this explanation fails to account for the continued meteoric growth of Protestant churches after the immediate emergency passed.

By 1982, the annual growth rate of Protestant conversion in Guatemala had risen to 23.6 percent, nearly four times what it had been a decade earlier.[7]

All denominations enjoyed a surge in membership immediately after the earthquake, but by far the greatest growth took place within the Pentecostal groups. In the days immediately following the earthquake, this was attributable in part to the activities of El Calvario Church, a Guatemala-based church that had broken off from an independent Canadian Baptist group during the 1960s. El Calvario underwent a group conversion to Pentecostalism in 1965, after one member of a small charismatic prayer group within the Church had a terrifying prophetic vision that Guatemala would be destroyed by a major earthquake in the near future. This specter so horrified the prayer circle that they persuaded the entire congregation to convert to Pentecostalism en masse and stockpile supplies for the impending disaster.

When the earthquake did strike, El Calvario was fully prepared. Within days of the disaster, the congregation began to proselytize and distribute supplies in the worst-hit parts of the country, particularly in the densely populated region around Chimaltenango, where the earthquake's destruction was so vast that people continued to die from shock and despair weeks after the actual event. Cynics scoffed that anyone with even a limited knowledge of Guatemala's history could predict an earthquake with a fair degree of confidence, but to the many quake victims who began to rebuild their lives with provisions from El Calvario's well-stocked warehouses, the evidence spoke for itself. The church seemed to have a direct line to a higher power that could not be ignored, prompting whole extended families and even *aldeas* to join El Calvario and other Pentecostal churches like it.[8]

Beyond the drama of El Calvario's experience, however, purely secular side effects of the earthquake contributed to the growth of evangelical churches. One factor was urbanization, in part the result of increasing population pressures that worsened significantly when the earthquake pushed rural people into the city in search of jobs and sustenance. In the city, immigrants joined evangelical churches in substantial numbers, as religious organizations became one of the few forms of urban voluntary associations accessible to low-income families.[9] Of particular importance were small Protestant-run neighborhood organizations, such as women's support groups, youth fellowships, and Alcoholics Anonymous, which often met in church buildings or members' homes. These types of associations provided important supportive relationships, which helped newcomers to the city avoid the kinds of social ills most commonly associated with low-income urban migration, such as family disintegration, alcoholism, and petty crime.

At one time, immigrants to the city would have looked to the Catholic Church to provide these kinds of services, and, given the fact that the vast majority of urban immigrants in the 1970s were at least nominally Catholic, one might have expected the Church to play a significant role in their resettlement. But the Catholic Church did not, in part because Mario Casariego, Guatemala's archbishop from December 1964 until his death in June 1983, generally did not support humanitarian work beyond the most traditional sorts of Catholic charities.[10] But it also stemmed from the fact that the Catholic Church's cumbersome institutional structure made it a poor competitor with the mobile and highly decentralized Protestant churches. For example, the Catholic Church also sponsored small-group programs, but the size and formality of large urban Catholic parishes did not allow for the kind of intimacy that smaller Protestant congregations engendered.

An even greater problem was a shortage of priests, the sine qua non of the faith. Despite the influx of fairly large numbers of Catholic clergy during the 1950s and the early 1960s—mainly Maryknoll, Sacred Heart, and Salesian fathers—one legacy of the state's long tradition of anticlericalism was that the Guatemalan Church was still severely understaffed. Richard N. Adams reports that, in 1966, for example, there were only around 530 priests and regular clergy to minister to a nation of more than 4 million Catholics; of these, some 434 were foreign clergy. Ironically, the shortage was particularly acute in Guatemala City, since the majority of new clergy had gone to serve parishes in the long-neglected countryside. By 1978, the ratio of Catholic priests to congregants in low-income areas of Guatemala City was 1:30,000.[11] In this context, and given the Protestants' belief in the "priesthood of all believers," the aggressive evangelism of even a small congregation could put Catholic work at a significant comparative disadvantage.

But not all Protestant gains came vis-à-vis Catholic institutional weakness. In purely temporal terms, one draw was economic, for the Protestant churches actively encouraged the economic improvement of their members by conflating notions of material and spiritual well-being. In the postearthquake period, evangelical churches often provided food and temporary housing for newly arrived migrants, and many initiated short-term loan programs to help rural transplants cope in the city. In more general terms, the evangelical churches' taboos on smoking and drinking, offering apparent testimony to a modern-day "Gospel of Wealth," encouraged members to keep more of their marginal savings. Yet even here, the advantages were not purely economic, especially regarding alcohol; not only money was saved by not drinking, but also marriages and families, as men who no longer drank were demonstrably less likely to batter wives and children. Even for women whose husbands did not convert, the wife could find solace and support within her congregation.[12]

From the missionary standpoint, the surge in conversions was the rightful fruition of decades of work in the "fields ripe for the harvest" planted by missionaries long ago. As the volumes of letters by Presbyterians, CAM missionaries, and Friends from the first part of the century attest, the early missionaries had envisioned many of their efforts, particularly the Bible translation projects, as long-term projects that would pay off in the future, perhaps well after their own ministries in Guatemala had ended. Seen in this light, the rapid growth of Protestantism in the 1960s and the acceleration of that growth after the earthquake seemed the natural culmination of the long pursuit of missionary virtues: hard work, diligence, faithfulness, and, above all, patience.

Through the cold prism of social science, however, the equation is not nearly so clear, for there appears to be no discernible pattern that links long-standing mission work to rapid church growth, at least not of the missionary denominations. The evidence lies in a survey of Protestant churches and their members taken in 1980 (which tallied up the number and variety of Protestant denominations present in each department and *municipio* in Guatemala). The Proyecto Centroamericano de Estudios Socio-Religiosos (Central American Project for Socioreligious Studies, PROCADES), the organization that conducted the census, relied primarily on the national denominations or local pastors for their information, so the survey instrument is indeed imperfect. Given the political and social conditions of the time, the census was especially unlikely to measure church growth accurately in the zones of conflict. The methodology also made it more likely to pick up churches that were part of well-organized national denominations than the small, house-sized congregations that then and now compose so much of Guatemalan Protestantism.

Yet even given these limitations, the survey opens a window into Protestantism in the late 1970s and demonstrates quite decisively that the growth of churches in Guatemala was almost entirely outside the traditional denominations, even in locations in which the missions were long established (see Table 3). In all but one case, the mission denomination is outnumbered by Pentecostal congregations, often dramatically. The church survey also suggests that, although the Comity Agreement had ceased to dictate the parameters of mission work half a century earlier, it still cast a shadow, for it was still unusual in 1980 for traditional denominations to coexist in the same location.

In some respects, this sort of categorization of church membership had become fairly meaningless, for even in churches that retained strong ties to traditional denominations, the congregations had often developed their own local variety of theology and ritual, which, though solidly "evangelical" from the participants' perspective, might be quite heterodox from a traditional Protestant viewpoint.

Evidence of this is found in the work of David Scotchmer, a Presbyterian missionary and anthropologist who worked in the 1970s in San Juan Ostuncalco, where the Presbyterians had maintained a mission and translation project among the Mam since the 1920s. In a systematic study of linguistic classifications of terms for the deity, Scotchmer was surprised to learn that, even among second-generation Mam Presbyterians, basic Christian concepts were framed in a decidedly traditional context. For example, they conceptualized God in a manner that was quite different from the orthodox Trinity of Western Christianity: the deity was vested in an unanthropomorphized Tyol, Dios/God's Word, and a second, more-accessible figure, Kman, Dios/Our Lord Christ, who sent sun and rain, embodied love and forgiveness, and protected the body and soul. For some Mam Presbyterians, these two aspects of the Christian God were more powerful than the traditional deities, and more portable, since they did not reside in mountains or shrines; but they did not necessarily negate the existence of the others.[13]

If this kind of fluid interpretation was present in the Presbyterian Church, where doctrine and liturgy are closely prescribed, it must have been more prevalent in the unaffiliated churches headed by pastors whose essential qualification was divine revelation. By 1980, there were more than two hundred denominations in Guatemala, three quarters of which were classified as "independent." These tiny sects, often numbering no more than a dozen people, met in houses or storefronts. Most were led by male pastors who were highly authoritarian and who enforced strict, dogmatic, and sometimes idiosyncratic church rules.[14]

The appeal of such churches is that members feel they give structure to what would otherwise by a chaotic and evil world; they also recall the authority of traditional elders, the *patrón*, or the priest of pre-Protestant

TABLE 3
Denominational Distribution in 1980 in Missionary Zones
Designated by the Comity Agreement of 1902

Locations of Early Presbyterian Missions

MUNICIPIO	TOTAL	PRES	CAM	NAZ	QU	PM	PENT	OTHER
Almolonga	11	1	—	1	—	—	9	—
Cantel	31	3	—	—	—	—	28	—
San J Ostu	36	16*	—	—	—	—	17	3
Quetzal	53	3	2	1	—	—	38	9
Retal	58	12	1	2	—	—	43	—

Locations of Early CAM Missions

MUNICIPIO	TOTAL	PRES	CAM	NAZ	QU	PM	PENT	OTHER
Chimal	26	—	3	1	—	—	17	5
Chinaultla	23	3	2	2	—	—	14	2
Huehue	44	2	14	1	—	—	22	5
La DemSM	28	—	21	—	—	—	6	1
Nahualá	16	3	3	—	—	—	10	—
Patzicía	8	—	2	—	—	—	6	—
Patzún	16	—	10†	—	—	—	6	—

Locations of Early Primitive Methodist Missions

MUNICIPIO	TOTAL	PRES	CAM	NAZ	QU	PM	PENT	OTHER
SnCruzQ	33	—	—	1	—	5	26	1
Chichicast	33	—	—	—	—	21	11	1

Locations of Early Nazarene Missions

MUNICIPIO	TOTAL	PRES	CAM	NAZ	QU	PM	PENT	OTHER
Cobán	13	—	—	—	—	—	9	4

TABLE 3 (*continued*)
Denominational Distribution in 1980 in Missionary Zones
Designated by the Comity Agreement of 1902

Locations of Early Friends Missions

MUNICIPIO	TOTAL	PRES	CAM	NAZ	QU	PM	PENT	OTHER
Chiquimula	30	—	1	1	7	—	13	8
Livingston	28	—	—	—	4	—	22	2

*6 of the Presbyterian congregations were served by one pastor.

†5 of these CAM congregations were served by one pastor. In both cases, this would suggest small "congregations" rather than established "churches."

SOURCE: Proyecto Centroamericano de Estudios Socio-Religiosos, *Directorio de Iglesias, Organizaciones, y ministerios del movimiento protestante: Guatemala* (San Francisco de Dos Ríos: Instituto Internacional de Evangelización a Fondo, 1981).

days. Yet there is a schismatic quality to these congregations, and when a dispute arises or authority is breached, dissidents can and do start new congregations elsewhere.

As all of this implies, the earthquake was a major catalyst for social change in Guatemala, of which Protestant growth was only one aspect. The earthquake forced into the open the many fundamental social ills that had long lurked beneath the nation's surface: unemployment and gross inequities in income distribution; the vast chasm that separated the nation's poor, largely indigenous majority from the wealthy and cosmopolitan elite; and the societal stresses of increased urban migration by the poor. The earthquake magnified these problems and catapulted Guatemala into social and political crisis.

Within a year, the nation's decade-old guerrilla movement had gained unprecedented momentum, and the military clamped off what small political openings had existed in the prequake years. In the months after the disaster, a small armed group calling itself the Ejército Guerrillero de los Pobres (Guerrilla Army of the Poor, EGP), based in the zone between the Quiché highlands and the lowlands of the Mexican border, actively began to try to organize among Indians in a backward area, where, as Stoll has noted, "state authority was weak." In 1979, another group, the Organización del Pueblo en Armas (Organization of the People in Arms, ORPA), also began to try to mobilize the population in the Sierra Madre ringing Lake Atitlán to the south and west. Other types of popular organization not associated with the armed opposition became more visible as well, although this distinction was largely lost on the Guatemalan military, as evidenced in May 1978, when the army fired on and killed over one hundred Kek'chí Indians who had gathered in the plaza of Panzós, Alta Verapaz, to discuss land issues. The most visible of these popular organizations were the Comité de Unidad Campesino (Campesino Unity Committee, CUC), formed in 1977–1978; urban trade unions, which organized a united front around a strike of Coca-Cola workers that started in 1978; and, finally, student and faculty activists from San Carlos University, especially those who belonged to the University Students' Association.[15]

In August 1978, General Fernando Romeo Lucas García took the office of president, thereby inaugurating one of the darkest periods in Guatemala's recent history. Corruption and moral malaise emanating from the military government and, to a lesser extent, the armed opposition bred what Sheldon H. Davis has called a national "culture of fear." Political assassination was commonplace, while personal vendettas and common crime were regularly played out in the guise of political provocation. From 1978 until 1982, according to Jim Handy, students, teachers, professionals, trade unionists, journalists, and opposition politicians were assassinated at a rate of at least five per day.[16] Increased guerrilla activity in the altiplano provoked a downward spiral of attacks and counterattacks, with the civilian population either pulled into the struggle or caught in the crossfire.

In 1982, the armed resistance joined forces in a confederacy known as the Unidad Revolucionaria Nacional Guatemalteca (Guatemalan National Revolutionary Unit, URNG) and began to occupy territory stretching from the Ixcán, the stretch of lowland jungle north of the Cuchumatanes Mountains near the Mexican border, to as far south as the indigenous Ixil towns in El Quiché; it also began to conduct regular actions in nine of Guatemala's twenty-two departments.[17] The guerrilla occupation of national territory, though spotty, often coercive, and, to some extent, ineffective, goaded the military into taking brutal offensive action.

Church people, both Catholic and Protestant, found themselves in the heat of this crucible, but it was Catholic activists who bore the real brunt of political violence. In one sense, this was unusual, for the great swell of change that took place in the Catholic Church after the Vatican II Council (1962–1965) and the Latin American Church's articulation of its position regarding the "preferential option for the poor" at the Medellín meeting in 1968 played out rather wanly in Guatemala.[18] Unlike in neighboring El Salvador, in Guatemala, the Catholic Church at large, led by a conservative archbishop, never endorsed Liberation Theology. And, unlike in Nicaragua, Liberation Theology attracted few influential members of the native clergy in Guatemala.

On the other hand, many foreign priests, who made up the great majority of Guatemala's clergy, embraced Liberation Theology with enthusiasm. As early as the mid-1960s, Catholic "pastoral teams" of predominantly foreign clergy and lay workers began to establish Christian base communities and propagate *"concientización"* (consciousness raising) among ladinos working in and around the Atlantic coast, near the lands once owned by United Fruit. In 1967, even before the Medellín conference, the Guatemalan government accused three Maryknoll missionaries of collaborating with the guerrillas, then operating in Zacapa, and expelled them from the country. This action effectively served notice of how the government would deal with such "subversion" in the future.[19]

Nevertheless, in the late 1960s, American and Spanish members of the Maryknoll and Sacred Heart Orders, working primarily in the predominantly indigenous Departments of El Quiché, Quetzaltenango, Huehuetenango, and Alta and Baja Verapaz, began to organize Christian base communities and local development projects involving such things as literacy and health care. They also drew from the pool of catechists already mobilized through their participation in Catholic Action to train lay leaders and "Delegates of the Word." Around the same time, beginning in 1965, Catholic clergy began a dramatic experiment in applied praxis by initiating colonization and cooperative projects in the isolated regions of the Petén and in the Ixcán, which at that time was nearly uninhabited.[20]

Several factors, then, conspired to put rural, and particularly indigenous, Catholics in the line of fire by the time Lucas García took power. One of the most important was that in the three decades since Catholic Action had come to Guatemala, Catholic catechists had replaced traditional figures of authority in many communities. Compared with traditional elders, catechists were outwardly focused leaders informed by contemporary ideas of development and, more recently, by concepts of social justice as defined by liberationist Catholicism as introduced by the foreign priests. The second factor was a matter of simple geography, as Catholic activism was greatest in the parts of the country in which the armed opposition was also most visible, although the two were not nec-essarily as related to one another as proximity might suggest. Finally, given the highly charged political climate of Central America in the late 1970s, the Guatemalan army feared that Guatemalan Catholics, like their counterparts in Nicaragua and El Salvador, would assume the roles of activist leaders.

The long list of Catholic clergy and lay activists who were killed or who vanished in the 1978–1983 period forms a sad litany that echoes through this dark, violent period. Catholic activists from El Quiché were involved in an event—the burning of the Spanish embassy in Guatemala City in January 1980—that many consider to be a defining moment of the era. A group of labor activists, students, and campesinos from El Quiché took over and occupied the Spanish embassy in Guate-mala City to protest army abuses in their communities. The police stormed the embassy and refused to allow firefighters to put out a fire that broke out during the mêlée. Thirty-nine people inside burned to death, many of them Catholic activists.[21]

This was the first, but by no means the last, episode directly involv-ing church people. Between 1978 and 1984, at least fourteen Catholic priests, most of them foreign, were killed outright by gunmen associated directly or indirectly with the security forces; more were kidnapped or otherwise "disappeared." The number of indigenous catechists and other lay church activists killed during the period was exponentially higher, although the grim details of their stories are only now being documented by scholars such as Jesuit anthropologist Ricardo Falla and through the Catholic Church's Recuperación de la Memoria Histórica (Recovery of Historical Memory, REHMI); the latter effort to recover the public memory of the era is an oral history project begun in 1996. According to these and other accounts, in the first three years of the Lucas years alone, at least six thousand died from political violence, many of them church people who had been mobilized into action by their beliefs.[22]

In 1980, after narrowly escaping death by ambush, the bishop of El Quiché, Juan Gerardi, requested that all clergy leave the diocese, both to protest the repression and to protect their lives. Despite only luke-warm support from the Vatican for this unusual act and outright hostil-ity from Archbishop Casariego and the government (which responded by threatening to expel any remaining priest who did not limit himself to "guiding souls"), the institutional Catholic Church in El Quiché remained shut down for more than two years. While this action did save the lives of Catholic clergy—many of whom left the country to form a group called the Iglesia Guatemalteca en el Exilio (Guatemalan Church in Exile, IGE), based in Managua and Mexico City—it also left lay Catholic activists standing alone in harm's way, without benefit of clergy, the sacraments, or strategic support to maintain the "church in the catacombs" alone.[23]

There are a variety of reasons, then, why Protestant congregations rushed in to fill the void left by the Catholic Church in El Quiché, as well as in other places in the conflict zones where the Church hierarchy failed to offer support to its endangered flock. Political expediency obviously accounted for some of this; if a strong Catholic identity was conflated with political radicalism, then it made sense for those who were not politicized to jettison the identity over which they still had some control. One alternative was to become Protestant, which even in the late 1970s may still have had a political valence of neutrality (i.e., "not Catholic") rather than one of outright political complicity with the government. It is worth noting that potential converts may have perceived this as an acceptable option partly as a result of *conscientización*, for it was only after Vatican II that the Catholic Church categorized Protestants as "separated brethren" within the Kingdom of God, rather than as heretics damned to perdition.

It is too facile, however, to credit the growth of the Protestant churches in the late 1970s and the early 1980s to simple political prudence. To the contrary, if their own interpretation of the experience is taken into account, the evangelicals' message seems to have offered authentic spiritual conciliation to victims of violence, a solace that the Catholic Church was in a poor position to offer, given the absence of priests in El Quiché and the repression of Catholics elsewhere. This was especially true in the highlands and along the Franja Transversal del Norte, the belt of land on the Mexican border wrapping from the Atlantic coast westward across the northern regions of the Departments of Izabal, Alta Verapaz, El Quiché, and into Huehuetenango. It was in this region where the fiercest fighting between the army and the guerrillas and where the most egregious army reprisals occurred. One theologian, Richard Foulkes, has called this correlation between church growth and civil strife "trench faith," when stricken people find refuge from hopelessness and rootlessness through a personal and vertical relationship with God. As Itzmar Rivera, an indigenous pastor in the stricken department of El Quiché, explained his understanding of this causality, "When people began to really suffer and feel the pressure, they found God."[24]

Without question, the growth in Protestantism had also to do with Protestants' apocalyptic message of salvation, a rendering of truth that emphasized the time of tribulation to presage the Second Coming of Christ, the rapture of the faithful, and the punishment of the wicked. This is evidenced by the type of church growth that occurred during this period in the altiplano and reflects the rapid expansion of established Pentecostal and often premillenarianist churches, independent "house churches," and even charismatic Catholic congregations whose services mimic Pentecostal ones and do not always require a priest.

Of the old missionary mainline denominations, only the Church of the Nazarene grew substantially during this period, and only under anomalous circumstances. In 1983, when the EGP abandoned territory it had held in the Transversal del Norte, the denomination's superintendent in Guatemala City learned that indigenous members had started twenty-four new congregations while the area had been out of contact with the capital.[25] The attraction of such churches was plain: not only did their message of a violent, chaotic, unjust, and sinful world reflect believers' reality, but it also rendered a larger meaning and cosmic plan from nearly incomprehensible terror. For believers, the promise of redemption in the hereafter was not simply deferred gratification, or "pie in the sky," but a time for vindication, justice, empowerment, and reunion for the poor and oppressed, the inheritors of the earth entitled by Jesus Himself on the Sermon on the Mount.

The growth of evangelical churches in the areas of conflict was not lost on the officers of the Guatemalan army, who saw in the Protestant surge an opportunity to create a new political base; the Lucas government began to court their support. By 1980, Lucas opened most public functions with a prayer from a Protestant pastor. That same year, the minister of education converted to one of the large Pentecostal churches in Guatemala City to great public fanfare.[26]

The primary thrust of Lucas's attempt to tap the evangelicals for political support came from the countryside. The army, hoping to capitalize on the evangelicals' adherence to a literal interpretation of the biblical admonition to "submit to the authority in power" (Romans 13:1), encouraged the evangelicals to settle in the tumultuous Transversal del Norte.[27] It was on the basis of this teaching that some indigenous evangelicals became informants (*orejas*, or "ears") for the army in conflict zones, although there are no records available to show whether evangelicals were systematically chosen (or auto-selected) for this task.[28]

It was symptomatic of the Lucas years, however, that, as political violence metastasized, the evangelical churches were not immune from internal political division. Although the subsequent government of born-again general José Efraín Ríos Montt convinced many people retrospectively that the evangelicals were a politically conservative monolith, this was actually not the case in the Guatemalan highlands during the Lucas years. Indeed, some evangelicals, who had already undergone a major life change through conversion, were especially receptive to the idea of political revolutionary change, just as indigenous converts had been during the Arbenz years. As June Nash notes, "The promotion of speculation about . . . doctrine starts a process of inquiry which does not [necessarily] end with questioning Catholic dogma."[29]

In the war-torn departments of the highlands, several evangelical churches splintered over politics; some congregations or parts of congregations became evident in both the traditional and the indigenous churches. At least five indigenous evangelical pastors disappeared in the early 1980s, for example, and a number of church leaders escaped into exile.[30] Virtually every case, however, involved individuals or factions that became involved with radical politics, and not the institutional Church itself.

The Presbyterian Church was the only denomination in which members (but not entire congregations) became fairly openly associated with the popular organizations. The liberal thrust of the Presbyterian Church was attributable to at least three factors. One was the division of the Church into ethnic presbyteries that operated with relative autonomy within the Church at large; it was these ranks that produced most of the activists. Second, the Presbyterian Church is the only major Protestant denomination in Guatemala that is not fundamentalist, premillenarianist, or Pentecostal; it was therefore the only large denomination outside of the Catholic Church that did not find ideas of social justice on earth to be at odds with church doctrine of the imminent Second Coming of Christ. Moreover, the Presbyterians had a long history of activism, or at least of reformism, dating back to Haymaker and Burgess. This impulse gained new life during the mid-1960s, when influential sectors of the Church in the United States came to embrace some of the basic precepts of Catholic Liberation Theology at the juncture where those beliefs converged with the Presbyterian tradition of social outreach. Although the Guatemalan Presbyterian Church was a more conservative body than its U.S. counterpart in almost every way, these ideas did permeate the Church at an institutional level. The arrival of liberal missionaries from the United States to help after the earthquake only served to encourage the latent liberalism—and, in a few cases, radicalism—of some sectors of the Guatemalan Presbyterian Church.[31]

The other traditional denomination that became deeply embroiled in politics from both the Left and the Right was the Primitive Methodist Church. It had been the weakest link in the chain of traditional Protestant churches for virtually its entire existence and had only a few small congregations in Guatemala until 1976. With the emergency of the earthquake and the increased tragedy of civil violence, however, the Primitive Methodist Church—which was located almost exclusively in the war-ravaged Department of El Quiché and in Totonicapán, where military action was minimal but social and economic disruption was high—grew prodigiously. By 1980, there were over fifty Primitive Methodist churches in the Department of Quiché alone, almost all of which were predominantly Indian congregations.[32]

That same year, a two-man feud of long standing ripped the Primitive Methodist Church in Santa Cruz del Quiché in half. The feud, like that which had splintered the Príncipe de Paz from the Assembly of God and the Elim from the CAM, started in the 1960s, when a faction of members of the church led by a local pharmacist opposed the paternalistic leadership of an American missionary who had served the congregation for many years. Unlike in the other denominations, however, the dissident group did not form a new church, and the feud smoldered for the next fifteen years.[33] The cruel excesses of violence in and around Santa Cruz del Quiché brought the feud to a head in 1980, when a large faction of the congregation left the Primitive Methodist Church to form a new denomination called the Iglesia Nacional.

The Iglesia Nacional mirrored the doctrine and dogma of the Primitive Methodist Church in all ways but one: it was fiercely anti-American in its rhetoric and quietly radical in its political stance. The Iglesia Nacional attracted members like a magnet, as pastors and believers defected from the Primitive Methodist Church and other denominations in the area. The church was reputed to actively support the region's main guerrilla organization, the EGP, though evidence of this was never overt. The Iglesia Nacional was most active in the guerrilla-controlled areas around the so-called Ixil Triangle and had its largest congregations in the ravaged towns of Nebaj, Chajul, Arredor, and Ilom de Chajul.

Moreover, the size of its congregations tended to fluctuate with the successes and defeats of the guerrilla forces in the area.[34]

Yet the Primitive Methodist Church was the only denomination that openly fractured over the issue of politics during the years of civil violence under the Lucas and Ríos Montt governments. Throughout this period, however, members and sometimes whole factions actively or passively supported the guerrillas, at times out of fear but also because they believed the insurgents shared a concern for others. The result was what one participant called the development of a "parallel church" within the structure of the larger evangelical denominations.[35]

The evolution of parallel congregations or factions was fairly common among the indigenous churches for the simple reason that they were most prevalent in the areas where the war was fiercest. In Chichicastenango, for example, the Príncipe de Paz congregations divided into two political factions that eventually became two separate and hostile churches, both retaining, with no apparent irony, the name of "Príncipe de Paz" (Prince of Peace). In 1982, the military command in the area suspected the liberal faction of the church, which met in the *aldea* of Semeja II, just outside of Chichicastenango, of being guerrillas and of using church services for planning covert activities. Shortly thereafter, the army massacred several dozen civilians in Semeja II, including a number of evangelicals from this group.[36]

Some evangelicals did formally join the guerrilla fronts, although their numbers were probably never large. In the late 1970s, inspired by the participation of churchmen in the Nicaraguan insurrection, the leadership of at least one revolutionary organization, the EGP, actively sought recruits from church activists, including evangelicals. Again, the evidence indicates that even at this point the common wisdom did not confer reactionary status on Protestants; indeed, one EGP document noted that evangelicals were good recruits because they were "more zealous and emotional" than their Catholic counterparts. In 1980, the EGP issued an open invitation to all religious, both Catholic and Protestant. "There is a place for each of us on this path of hope, for all the poor of Guatemala," the EGP announced in a communiqué. "In our country one cannot be a Christian and not be a revolutionary. . . . In any of the work taken up by true and committed Christians, they can count on our fullest revolutionary solidarity."[37]

To emphasize the involvement of Protestants in the popular movements during this period, however, is to overemphasize the exception at the expense of the rule. The more general case was of congregations that sought to provide sanctuary and neutrality for their members by offering a belief structure that extracted them from the political discourse altogether. In some of the most stricken areas, Protestant leaders did indeed take part in the army's program, but the evidence suggests that they did so out of intimidation, fear, and a desperate hope for survival rather than from any positive identification or conflation of ideology with the government's cause.

David Stoll describes such a case in the Ixil town of Cotzal, a town in northern Quiché that suffered the violence of the late 1970s and the early 1980s to a degree only slightly less severe than the other two towns of the infamous Ixil Triangle. Here, the indigenous evangelical pastor and the congregation of the Full Gospel Church of God, a denomination based in Ohio and the largest non-Catholic church in the *municipio*, engaged in a variety of activities, such as informing on guerrilla locations, that at first blush seemed to identify them clearly as the allies of the army and the proxies of imperialist designs. But Stoll concludes that this image is misleading. The congregation's collaboration with the army was entirely the product of coercion, not an ideological strategy but a last-gasp survival strategy. In order to impose order, the military commander in the area had, in Stoll's words, "push[ed] through a shattered political structure to a more basic form of social organization, the congregation," which, given the disarray of the Catholic Church in the area, was Protestant. Moreover, the Protestant congregations at the time were one of the few community organizations still to retain some semblance of a structure of leadership, albeit one that, in Stoll's assessment, "could still be intimidated into collaborating."[38]

This portrayal of Protestants in Ixil country during this period as victims matches that of Ricardo Falla in the Ixcán. "The army . . . killed catechists and massacred religious groups, surrounding them during church services and burning them in their temples, particularly in Evangelical chapels," writes Falla in a book documenting the atrocities committed by the army in the Ixcán during the early 1980s. "The army considered the religious activities deceitful, not so much a front for nonbelievers as an authentic religious screen that fomented subversion while attempting to project the false image of innocuous prayers and singing. . . . Only later, after the Ríos Montt coup d'état, did the army make a distinction between the churches in an attempt to manipulate them, using religion to curtail the force of liberating faith."[39]

In the last years of the 1970s and the early 1980s, then, Protestants as well as Catholics found themselves in the downward spiral of violence and fear. While it is true that Catholic activists were more likely to find themselves in harm's way during this period, religious affiliation did not reflect a dichotomy of political behavior; nor did membership in a Protestant congregation provide an outright political haven for believers. But in a larger sense, the growth of evangelical churches during this period was a direct response to the crisis. For the corpus of Protestant belief, specifically, locally constructed Pentecostal theologies did offer less quantifiable but nonetheless real refuge for many whose lives might otherwise have broken apart on the rocky shoals of social dislocation, urbanization, loss of friends and family members, the breakdown of traditional lifestyles, economic recession, and increasing political repression.

CHAPTER 8

THE PROTESTANT PRESIDENT

When you see Jerusalem surrounded by armies, you must realize that she will soon be laid desolate. Those in Judaea must escape to the mountains, those inside the city must leave it, and those in country districts must not take refuge in it. For this is the time of vengeance, when all that scripture says must be fulfilled. Alas for those with child, or with babies at the breast, when those days come!

—Luke 21:20–23

O N 23 MARCH 1982, a coup led by young military officers deposed Romeo Lucas García during the last days of his presidency, announced the nullification of the rigged presidential elections that had named General Ángel Aníbal Guevara to office, and put a military junta at the head of government. The junta was made of three officers: Brigadier General Horacio Egberto Maldonado Schaad, commander of the Honor Guard Brigade; Colonel Francisco Luis Gordillo Martínez, commander of army general headquarters; and a retired general by the name of José Efraín Ríos Montt, who assumed leadership of the junta and later declared himself chief of state. As the leader of the coup and very much more than first among equals, Ríos Montt immediately made it clear that Guatemalans could expect something very different from his tenure in office. On the night of the coup, he addressed the world on national television. "I am trusting my Lord and King, that He shall guide me," Ríos Montt, a born-again Pentecostal, proclaimed, "because only He gives and takes away authority."[1] This statement would set the tone for the programs, the criticism, and the retrospective analysis of the presidency of Efraín Ríos Montt.

Ríos Montt was born in Huehuetenango in 1926 to a conventional middle-class family. He joined the army at age sixteen and graduated from the Escuela Politécnica at age twenty-three. His military career advanced steadily and he moved into the top ranks while still in his early forties. He taught at the Escuela Politécnica and served for a time as its director. After studying counterinsurgency tactics at Fort Bragg, North Carolina, he became President Arana's army chief of staff in 1970 and was promoted to general two years later. In 1974, the same year that his brother Mario Enrique was consecrated a Catholic bishop, Ríos Montt made his first foray into politics as the presidential candidate of the UNO (United National Opposition) coalition led by the Christian Democratic Party. The candidate of the Movimiento de Liberación Nacional (National Liberation Movement, MLN) and the Partido Democrático Institucional (Democratic Institutional Party, PID) and the army's man, General Kjell Laugerud won this election, but under most suspicious circumstances. Shortly thereafter, Ríos Montt, realizing that his military career was derailed, agreed to take a post in "diplomatic exile" in Spain, and in 1977 he went on inactive status with the army.[2]

It was in the wake of this defeat that Ríos Montt, by his own account despondent and at loose ends, became a born-again Christian and joined a Pentecostal church called the Church of the Word. The Church of the Word, or "Verbo," as it was known to its members, was a mission of a California-based organization called Gospel Outreach, itself the product of the "Jesus freak" movement of the early 1970s. Gospel Outreach originated as an experiment in communal living, but it had evolved over the years into a rigorous and conservative Pentecostal denomination. The denomination was a small one in the United States, but after its arrival in Guatemala following the earthquake, it had attracted a large following, particularly among the wealthy of Guatemala City. They were drawn to its particular variety of Pentecostalism, which stressed morality and the rewards of right living.

According to Verbo biographers, Ríos Montt had taken to the church teachings and discipline with alacrity, even accepting the church's admonitions to "humble thyself" by doing custodial work and teaching in the church's primary school. By Verbo's account of events, the general was acting in this very capacity on 12 March, the day of the coup, when, without prior knowledge, he was summoned directly from the school to lead the coup. (The fact that Ríos Montt was wearing battle fatigues during the coup, however, might bring this assertion into question.)

Ríos Montt's membership in the church would overshadow his entire tenure in office, both in terms of his policies and in the outside world's perception of his administration. "We feel a great door has been opened," said one elder of the Church of the Word on the afternoon that

Ríos Montt assumed office. "We don't understand what is going to happen, but he will be operating with a power that is not like men's corrupting power. He is going to have an anointing from God."[3]

Ironically, Ríos Montt's religious affiliation seems to have had virtually nothing to do with his political ascendancy, which was the product of his 1974 presidential bid when he had run as a Christian Democrat—and a Roman Catholic. In March 1982, the military officers who supported him in the coup against the Lucas/Guevara regime were for the most part oblivious to their general's new religious identity. They should have been aware of his moralistic temperament from his days as director of the Escuela Politécnica, when, even before his conversion, Ríos Montt had required cadets to carry pocket-sized New Testaments and copies of the Army Code of Conduct with them at all times.[4] In any event, it quickly became clear that for Ríos Montt, all other affiliations—particularly that of *militar* (military man)—were at least rhetorically subordinate to his evangelical identity. This was brought to the fore when he dismissed the other two members of the junta on 9 June 1982 and declared himself chief of state.

One of Ríos Montt's first acts as president was to evoke his church's teaching that "in a multitude of counselors there is safety." He appointed two fellow parishioners from Verbo to specially created ad hoc positions as "secretary to the private affairs of the president" and "secretary of the president of the republic." He referred to these advisers as "my conscience," thereby setting off alarms within the army that its influence might be co-opted by Verbo members.[5]

The appointment of these advisers from his church and the Verbo's American provenance, particularly during the Reagan administration, when conservative Christians in the United States enjoyed influence even in Central American affairs, would seem to imply the administration's subordination to interests outside of the Guatemalan Army. Certainly, the general did little to allay the army's fears when he appeared on the U.S. conservative Christian talk show *The 700 Club* a week after taking office, where host Pat Robertson urged viewers to "pray around the clock for Ríos Montt" and pledged one billion dollars toward Guatemala's reconstruction.[6]

Yet the congruence of these factors belied the complexity of Ríos Montt's vision of the "New Guatemala" (La Nueva Guatemala), in which military aggressiveness articulated disquietingly with evangelical reformation. As fellow Pentecostal Jorge Serrano Elías, the head of the Council of State under Ríos Montt and himself president from 1992 to

1993 explains: "Ríos Montt has two [parallel] theories in his mind. First, he is a military man. Second, he is a moral fighter. . . . It is only in these two separate perspectives that you can understand his government." In the general's way of thinking, however, these two motives conflated neatly: La Nueva Guatemala required a return to security and the defeat of the guerrillas, but, at the same time, the government, which had been so long associated with repression and corruption, had to reestablish its own legitimacy. On a superficial level, Ríos Montt hoped that his own religious profile might help the public improve its perception of government. But at a more integral level, he sought to fundamentally redefine the nature of the Guatemalan state and base it on a trinity of essential principles: morality, order and discipline, and national unity. These three elements had been a part of the Protestant discourse in Guatemala for one hundred years.[7]

At the start of the rainy season in 1982, Ríos Montt set out the parameters of La Nueva Guatemala in a series of television speeches broadcast on every television and radio station in the country on Sunday nights at 9:00 PM. The broadcasts were popularly known as "sermons," and for good reason. The general, dressed in civilian clothes with a Bible near at hand, addressed his audience on a variety of political, economic, and social topics, but always with a religious or moral subtext that was solidly embedded in an evangelical context. In his Sunday night sermons, Ríos Montt explicated the moral roots of Guatemala's many problems. The nation's economic poverty was rooted in the national poverty of values, especially in rampant materialism and selfishness. Past governments had been corrupt and wicked, he admitted, but he urged Guatemalans to change their own attitudes and to take some responsibility for the country's failings. Ríos Montt even blamed the guerrilla movement on a lack of moral structure in families and on parents' failure to teach their children to revile communism, which he believed explicitly set out to destroy Christian culture. His demand for a national moral reckoning extended all the way to the conduct of everyday life: husbands should be faithful to their wives; children obey their parents; parents should keep their families at a responsible size; men should control their alcohol use or "drink nothing stronger than hibiscus tea." For Ríos Montt, La Nueva Guatemala meant not only "changing or improving institutions, but changing and redeeming the hearts of men."[8] The mandate was vertical and horizontal moral accountability, from mother to child to the governed and the government.

The Sunday sermons reached a wide audience, in no small part because they monopolized the airways of radio and television networks during broadcast times. But even allowing for this, the sermons gave Ríos Montt a notoriety and specific identity that his predecessors had not enjoyed. In the sermons, Ríos Montt constructed a conceptual framework for understanding Guatemala's many problems, and posed a concrete plan for their solution. While his particular and idiosyncratic agenda obviously drew many detractors, many others were drawn to the decisiveness and clarity of his vision of La Nueva Guatemala. *Newsweek* captured this ambiguity in a 13 December 1982 article that noted, "Not all Guatemalans appreciate the righteous exhortations. The largely Catholic upper-middle class ridicules Ríos Montt's religious fervor and even some of his own officers refer to him as 'the ayatolla.' But Ríos Montt has won popularity among his workers, businessmen and women, who welcome his frequent appeals for sobriety and fidelity."

In an effort to instate moral accountability in government and help restore some of its lost credibility, in December 1982, Ríos Montt initiated a plan to end the widespread corruption and graft that pervaded the national bureaucracy. The plan, privately dubbed Project David after the righteous Old Testament king, demanded that government employees from office workers to judges and congressional representatives take a pledge not to take bribes, steal, or engage in any other unscrupulous activities. The president promised that, in return for living honest lives, workers who lived up to the vow would have job security, advance in their positions, and receive special benefits. Material evidence of these mutual promises took the form of ubiquitous blue and white posters, which appeared prominently displayed in every public office around the country and declared, "No robo, no miento, no abuso"—I don't steal, lie, or take unfair advantage.[9] The government encouraged civilians to file complaints against public employees, including police, who did not obey the law.

It is doubtful that many citizens were bold enough to do so, even after Ríos Montt set up a legal forum to prosecute those who violated their pledges or who had committed human rights violations under previous administrations (though, significantly, not under his own).[10] Under these new statutes, the government arrested and tried more than 265 National Police officers and 50 members of the army for abuses committed during the Lucas regime as well as for violations of the anticorruption regulations. Although the honesty campaign could only make a dent in the enormity of government corruption, it did cut down on enough graft to infuriate the many who considered pilfering to be a privilege of officeholding.

Spreading the cloak of accountability even further, Ríos Montt also attacked private businesses and political parties for their role in Guatemala's moral crisis. He criticized private business for excessive greed and irresponsibility and charged that companies owned by Guatemalans earned usurious profits, evaded taxes, and exported capital illegally with no regard for domestic consequences. The former Christian Democrat railed especially at political parties, which he tarred as a "wretched, sick, miserable lot" that had no relevance to the people for whom they claimed to speak. The only powerful sector that escaped this litany of ethical failings was the army, which Ríos Montt believed had thus far saved the nation from the morally bereft ethos of communism. By 1983, however, as criticism of the regime increased and his grasp on power weakened, even Ríos Montt assumed some blame for Guatemala's crisis in a public statement that struck a frankly confessional tone. "We as the government accept that we have sinned and abused our power," he said, "and we desire to reconcile ourselves to the Guatemalan people."[11]

The second element of Ríos Montt's plan for La Nueva Guatemala, order and discipline, was less readily achieved. Under Lucas, Guatemala had descended into a maelstrom of terror. In the countryside, political violence had become endemic and killing indiscriminate, while in the capital, murder and disappearances became so common that citizens refused to stop at traffic lights for fear of being shot. To Ríos Montt, this culture of fear had its root in moral weakness, specifically, in the lack of respect for authority, which he conceptualized in hierarchical, biblical terms that also mirrored patterns of military authority. This logic applied particularly to the guerrillas, whom Ríos Montt portrayed as dishonest, selfish, and utterly lacking in respect.[12] But to a lesser extent, it also applied to security forces in the capital, which Ríos Montt believed had exceeded the limits of their authority and abused the power given them.

On the night of 12 March 1982, Ríos Montt appeared on television and promised to restore proper authority and reinstate order. He commanded an end to the random and ubiquitous violence and decreed that there would be "no more cadavers on the roadsides." The next day, political murder in and around the capital dropped sharply, as rightist death squads felt the withdrawal of official sanction. Three days later, the city's *bomberos*, Guatemala's volunteer firefighters and morgue crews, reported that for the first time in months they had not picked up any dead bodies in the streets in the grisly morning ritual that had become their appointed task during the Lucas years.[13]

Shortly thereafter, Ríos Montt began a symbolic purge of the national security forces. In mid-December 1982, he forced the National Police, who had reportedly been among the most egregious offenders during the Lucas years, to take the anticorruption pledge. He had dozens of police officers arrested in a "depistolization" campaign designed to restore a sense of security to the capital and to distance the civil war from the city. Finally, he disbanded the secret police, replacing it with a new unit, the Special Operations Battalion, to combat subversion and common crime in the capital.[14] Cumulatively, these actions had the desired effect of restoring a sense of order and security in the capital. For the first time in two years, residents felt safe enough to go out at night or to travel to favorite tourist spots near the city; they laid this newfound security at the feet of Ríos Montt.

The matter of the violence in the countryside, however, could not be so easily dealt with, since during the Lucas years the confrontation between the armed resistance and the army had degenerated into outright civil war. In 1981, the guerrillas were at the peak of their power. They conducted daily operations in nine of the twenty-two departments and occupied territory in northern El Quiché; army forays into the area, however, prevented them from proclaiming an extended "liberated zone" (*territorio liberado*), as happened in neighboring El Salvador. At the time of the coup in March 1982, political conflagration had already claimed at least six thousand lives, the vast majority of whom were the victims of army reprisals against purported supporters of the guerrillas.[15]

To a much lesser extent, rural violence was the result of guerrilla *foquismo* techniques. Small cadres of armed combatants (who possibly numbered no more than three thousand or four thousand at their height) would surround themselves with civilians, who provide a measure of protection and, to some degree, strategic and logistical support.[16] As David Stoll has shown for the Ixil area, however, where the EGP occupied some strategically important towns beginning in 1979, *foquismo* had severe shortcomings. The most important was that, first, potential indigenous "*compañeros*" (comrades) tended to be suspicious of guerrilla cadres, which were generally ladino; as a result the guerrillas often won their support through hyperbolic promises and sometimes through coercion and force. Second, the *foquista* objective of making the armed resistance indistinguishable from the civilian population had disastrous consequences in Guatemala, where the combatants, always a relatively small and poorly armed force, failed to provide adequate protection for the civilian population, leaving them sitting ducks for army reprisals.

For Ríos Montt, the violence in the countryside represented the unraveling of moral society that would destroy the fabric of the nation if it continued unchecked. His interpretation of events was again cast in terms of moral reckoning: communism represented the ultimate rejection of morality and God-given authority; it had to be countermanded by his own divinely sanctioned "final battle against subversion," which he conceptualized in nearly apocalyptic terms. Of the legitimacy of his own authority in this matter, Ríos Montt had no doubt: "I have confidence in God, my master and king, that He will guide me. Only He can grant and take away power."[17]

Ríos Montt's first task in "ordering" the countryside was to legalize the civil war by declaring a state of siege on 1 July 1982. It was originally to run for thirty days, but he later extended it to last until the first anniversary of the March coup. The rationale for the state of siege was that it provided a legal framework for the apparatus that Ríos Montt set in motion to defeat the guerrillas. These included secret tribunals (*fueros especiales*), which could try suspected traitors without providing lawyers or revealing the charges, and mandated public executions of "subversives" convicted of certain types of murder, terrorism, sabotage, or treason. It also suspended certain civil rights, such as habeas corpus and the rights of freedom of assembly, mobility, and protest. The state of siege also mandated manipulation of information. The press was censored and news agencies infiltrated by paid informers known as *faferos*; moreover, the press was forbidden to publish any news of guerrilla activities, or for that matter, even print the word "guerrilla" without prior government approval.[18]

It was in the highlands, though, where Ríos Montt's crusade for order and authority was brought to bear. It is difficult to reconcile the brutal excesses of his "final battle against subversion" with his preachments on morality, but one must assume that the restoration of state authority from chaos and subversion formed for the general and his advisers a Kantian moral imperative that outweighed the enormous human cost. On 1 April 1982, Ríos Montt initiated the National Security and Development Plan, under which the army dramatically stepped up the systematic scorched-earth sweep of the highlands that had begun in February 1982, during the waning days of the Lucas administration.[19] The army concentrated its efforts most vigorously in the areas in which it believed the guerrillas enjoyed the widest support, across the Franja Transversal del Norte in particular, but elsewhere in the highlands as well. The army classified communities on a map by colored pin: green for those free of subversives; red for those in enemy hands; and pink or green for those "thought to be ambiguous."[20] For three months, the army assaulted the areas of conflict mercilessly in an attempt to "drain the sea in which the fishes swim."

Amnesty International estimated that at least two thousand campesinos were killed during Ríos Montt's first three months in office alone, a figure that seems low, given the number of bodies found in clandestine graves and the testimonies of survivors who surfaced in later years. The army swept through the highlands burning homes, churches, and crops and killing livestock; it forced perhaps a million residents, most of them Indians, to flee. Some went to distant havens like Mexico; others remained in Guatemala to suffer the terrible physical privations of "internal exile" in the remotest areas of the mountains or the rain forests, where some survivors eventually formed covert, autonomous, and completely self-sufficient communities known as Comunidades de Población en Resistencia (CPR).[21]

On 28 May 1982, Ríos Montt called a temporary halt to the army's siege of the highlands and offered a thirty-day general amnesty to the guerrillas and their supporters. His motive was as much ideological as it was pragmatic, for the amnesty cast the government as reconciler and benevolent authority. At the news conference during which he announced the amnesty, Ríos Montt urged insurgents to accept amnesty and to be part of a "conquest of love," in which they might "fight not with violence, but with understanding."[22]

Official sources claimed that during the monthlong amnesty, 2,000 people turned themselves in, although other estimates place the figure at fewer than 250, even allowing for those who surrendered under coercion. Despite this modest number of surrenders, the amnesty served its purpose, for it legitimated the resumption of what could now be classified as a "just war" against those who rebuffed the government's terms. But significantly, it is also the point at which survivors in the zones of conflict noticed a change in the nature of the violence; for many, as David Stoll suggests, "what count[ed was] a critical difference: . . . Ríos Montt replaced chaotic terror with a more predictable set of rewards and punishments, that is, what passe[d] for law and order under the country's normal level of repression." Even more telling is the solecism of one of Ṣtoll's informants, who misidentified the "ley de amnistía" (amnesty law) as the "ley de amistad" (friendship law).[23]

At the end of June 1982, with the authority of just war in his moral arsenal, Ríos Montt initiated a systematic and aggressive plan for the pacification of the highlands. The first component of Victoria '82 was the Plan for Assistance to the Areas of Conflict, more commonly known as "fusiles y frijoles"—rifles and beans. This operation was designed to eliminate the guerrillas by destroying their access to the general population as a base of support. In theory, soldiers who took part in the program took a pledge of good conduct and vowed, among other things, to respect women, children, and the elderly and to refrain from stealing or destroying crops or property.[24]

Despite this veneer of good intentions, the operative premise behind the program was simple, as inelegantly explained by one army officer: "If you are with us, we'll feed you; if you're against us, we'll kill you." In theory, nearly 80 percent of the program's resources went into "beans," that is, food, medical supplies, and other basic necessities. The army distributed these supplies throughout the zones of conflict and benefited, by the government's account, some 114,984 campesinos by the end of 1983.[25]

In tandem with this was the military program, through which the army renewed its earlier tactic of killing those who were suspected of being unrepentant guerrillas or their supporters. As a corollary, communities formed civil patrols (*patrullas de autodefensa civil*, PACs), manned by male villagers who served regularly, and, if only in theory, voluntarily on a rotational basis. Although the civil patrols system originated with the Lucas regime in 1981, it was greatly expanded under Ríos Montt. He recognized the value of inculcating in each community a sense of responsibility for its own security—and in allowing patrol members to take up arms (even if only the wooden rifles generally supplied to patrollers) *for* the government, instead of against it. By August 1982, the government had established PACs in thirteen hundred villages across the troubled zones, involving between twenty-five thousand and forty thousand men, a figure that had risen by 1984 to seven hundred thousand.[26]

These figures could not begin to compare with the number of people displaced and killed in the assault on the highlands. Surveys of the affected areas offered a distressing portrait of destruction: between 1981 and 1984, 440 villages disappeared from the map, and more than a million people fled into exile. In the Ixcán, the offensive either displaced or massacred nearly the entire population of 50,000. Nationwide, between 36,000 and 72,000 people were killed, leaving between 150,000 and 200,000 orphans or children who had lost one parent.[27]

The most vocal outrage at the high human cost of the campaign came from international human rights organizations, including church groups, which criticized Ríos Montt for his hypocrisy in authorizing mass killings in the name of God and peace. The government responded that the international press exaggerated the crisis to undermine the government, but Ríos Montt also claimed that the army's campaign was one not of scorched earth, but of "scorched communists."[28]

In a strictly strategic sense, Victoria '82 was an outstanding military triumph, so much so that it became known in Latin American military circles as "the Guatemalan solution." By mid-1983 the guerrillas were all but defeated. Ríos Montt conducted the campaign as a leader who, in the words of Vinicio Cerezo, himself later elected president, was "basically formed by the army," well schooled in the techniques of counterinsurgency and nurtured in an environment of military authoritarianism.[29]

Yet even for Ríos Montt as military man, the war in the countryside could not be completely divorced from its moral context. Poverty, insurrection, and violence, he believed, were not the product of inequality or class conflict, but the products of the "rottenness of mankind." This rottenness, he said in 1982 "has a name: communism, or the Antichrist, and all means must be used to exterminate it."[30] Thus it was that Ríos Montt revealed no irony when he admonished his people on national television during the bloody months of the *fusiles y frijoles* campaign, "We must give thanks to God, because through the army he has given us the opportunity to reorganize ourselves to get our affairs in order and to wipe away our differences."[31]

One of the most resounding criticisms of the counterinsurgency program was that *fusiles y frijoles* was too closely tied to the president's evangelical interests. The military campaign struck especially hard at politicized Catholics in the highlands active in Christian base communities and resulted in the deaths of literally hundreds of catechists involved in education, health promotion, agricultural extension projects, consciousness raising, political organization, and, occasionally, even with guerrillas. So brutal was the assault on Catholic activists that, in May 1982, the nation's bishops condemned the violence, labeling it as "genocide," and thus defined the conflict for the first time in ethnic rather than strictly political terms.[32]

The assault on Catholic activists had less to do with religious chauvinism than with politics, although sheer numbers meant that many more Catholics suffered for their "subversion" than Protestants suffered for theirs. Nevertheless, the war against "the Antichrist" knew no religious boundaries, as the number of Protestants who fled their villages or died at the hands of the army alongside their Catholic brethren attests. Protestant identity provided no security for those suspected of subversion, as graphically illustrated in April 1982, when thirteen members of a Quanjobal Pentecostal congregation in Xalbal, Ixcán, were burned alive by the army in their church. Other episodes, though spotty and anecdotal, provide further evidence, such as the kidnapping of a Nazarene pastor in Alta Verapaz by plainclothes security forces in the middle of a worship service or the discovery of the corpses of evangelicals and Catholic catechists killed by the army and left in kneeling positions or hanging from trees "as if crucified" in Kaibil Balam, Ixcán. Between 1982 and 1983, moreover, no fewer than forty-seven evangelical leaders and pastors were tried in the secret tribunals, the *fueros especiales,* and four of the men executed over the protest of Pope John Paul II during his visit to Guatemala in the summer of 1982 were evangelicals.[33]

Although press censorship was supposed to prevent widespread awareness in the capital, immigrants into the city spread the word of the breadth of destruction in the countryside. In late 1982, a small group of Protestants calling themselves the Confraternidad Evangélica (Evangelical Brotherhood) formed in Guatemala City to protest the government's gross violation of human rights and to beseech the president to stop identifying "Jesus' message with injustice and inhumanity."[34]

Despite this small voice in the wilderness, Protestant agencies were directly involved in the formation of La Nueva Guatemala, particularly after December 1982, when Ríos Montt pronounced *fusiles y frijoles* complete and unveiled the next stage of Victoria '82, *trabajos, tortillas y techo* (work, bread, and shelter), a civic action program to reconstruct the areas destroyed in the violence. At the head of the effort was a government agency, the Comité Nacional de Reconstrucción (National Reconstruction Committee, CRN), which was to oversee all public and private relief. But at its heart was a private agency, the Fundación de Ayuda al Pueblo Indígena (Assistance to the Indian People Foundation, FUNDAPI). This organization funded, staffed, and operated by several evangelical or church-affiliated groups, including Verbo's International Love Lift, Wycliffe Bible Translators/Summer Institute of Linguistics, and Partners in the Americas, an organization that had close ties to advisers in the Ríos Montt government and that operated primarily on money supplied by conservative Christian groups in the United States.[35] Technically, FUNDAPI reported to the CRN and worked autonomously from the Guatemalan government, but its workers traveled free on military transportation and received army escorts into controlled areas. While FUNDAPI staffers enjoyed these privileges, Catholic relief workers complained that military authorities would not even grant them assurance of free passage into army-controlled regions.[36]

Officially, however, the CRN did not demonstrate formal preference to any single church-based relief organization. In a gesture toward religious pluralism, Ríos Montt invited Catholic development organizations into the region and gave particular encouragement to the Catholic relief agency CARITAS to work in the zones of conflict.[37] Nonetheless, even evangelical groups that had no ties to FUNDAPI or the government informally enjoyed a greater freedom to travel and work in the army-controlled areas than did relief organizations that were not affiliated with churches. Several denominations, particularly the CAM, expanded their work significantly in the zones of conflict during Ríos Montt's tenure. The CAM became unofficially involved in the distribution of relief supplies for the government by issuing goods and food from its churches. In Chimaltenango and in the Ixil area, the CAM allowed the army to use its existing infrastructure to coordinate the distribution of supplies, to take censuses, and to communicate with the people of the area, and CAM pastors and lay activists sometimes acted as informal liaisons between the local populace and the military. The last earned them opprobrium and distrust that took years to dissipate.[38]

The Nazarene Church, too, which operated largely in the war-torn departments along the Mexican border, expanded its work considerably under the Ríos Montt administration. In April 1983, it launched a "Holiness Campaign" in northern El Quiché and Huehuetenango that within the month produced four new sizable Nazarene congregations.[39]

How much of this growth came from government encouragement of evangelical work and how much from the same factors that had attracted Guatemalans to Protestantism before Ríos Montt came into power is difficult to gauge. Nonetheless, it is apparent that at least some of the Protestant growth during this period in the war zones stemmed directly from implicit or explicit government support. One observer in a bipartisan task force for the British Parliament on a fact-finding mission to the area in 1983 was startled to note the number of new evangelical churches that had sprung up in army-controlled villages. "One cannot fail to notice the ubiquity of evangelical churches in most towns and villages," he wrote. "In one township in Quetzaltenango there were twenty-eight [Protestant] churches in a population of 20,000." The British observer conceded that this proliferation was not solely the result of the spontaneous growth of indigenous evangelical churches. He noted that in the model village of Acul, in El Quiché, there were four evangelical sects but not a single Catholic priest, despite the people's having repeatedly asked for one. He added that the popularity of the Protestant churches was at least partly due to expediency. "To be a member of a Protestant sect," he noted, "was said to give a certain amount of protection and security, even in some cases to gain preference in the receipt of food handed out by state organizations." [40]

In a similar vein, an American Nazarene pastor recorded that, during a government-sponsored visit he made to a military base in northern El Quiché in early 1983, the base commander openly acknowledged the political expediency of an association with a Protestant church. The pastor recalled that the commander called together one thousand civil patrol members from the area on a Saturday morning, and asked that the minister preach to them on Romans 13:1, the familiar admonition to "submit yourselves to the authority in power." The Nazarene pastor, however, demurred, preaching instead on humility and forbearance. [41]

Not all pastors were so demure, however. In July 1983, a team of Canadian observers at a military-sponsored rally in a newly subdued village in El Quiché noted an indigenous evangelical preacher admonishing his listeners: "He who lacks God in his heart is the one who is unable to love the authorities." [42]

It is clear that, during the Ríos Montt era, some *evangélicos,* particularly local pastors in the zones of conflict, cooperated willingly with the government's program, moving in quickly to fill local positions of authority left vacant by the death or flight of community leaders. Pastors sometimes acted as liaisons between their communities and the military; a survey conducted by the Alianza Evangélica, in fact, shows that in a disproportionate number of communities evangelicals held positions of leadership in the local civil patrols. [43]

The apparent collusion between the evangelicals and the military led to increased tensions between the Protestants and the rest of the community in the highland areas. Suspicion was nurtured by guerrillas, who distributed cartoons that portrayed FUNDAPI and evangelists as imperialist agents of the United States sent to divide and control the Guatemalan people. Yet where concrete evidence exists, it indicates that

Protestants, like their Catholic brethren, often cooperated with the army more for pragmatic than for ideological or theological reasons. David Stoll, in his documentation of the violence in the Ixil area, cites the case of Nicolás Toma, an Ixil pastor of the Pentecostal Complete Gospel Church of God, whom FUNDAPI workers credited with turning the tide of the war in the ravaged town of Cotzal. In 1982, Pastor Nicolás informed the army of the whereabouts of the EGP, thereby enabling the army to sweep the guerrillas out of the immediate area. Under his leadership, Toma's congregation provided the head of the first civil patrol and the first postwar mayor of Cotzal. Stoll notes, however, that in his extensive discussions with Nicolás, the pastor never mentioned religion or ideology as playing a part in his decision to cooperate with the army. Instead, his decision, made very deliberately, was a choice for survival; he believed the army better equipped to defend his people from the guerrillas than the guerrillas were to defend them from the army. "The guerrillas only provoke the army and they go," Nicolás told Stoll. "We are the ones who suffer the consequences." [44]

While there is some evidence that suggests that some of the army's excess actions during this period were beyond Ríos Montt's control, there can be little question that the destruction of the guerrillas' base of support through *fusiles y frijoles* accompanied the president's larger objective of restoring order and laid the groundwork for Ríos Montt's third major objective for La Nueva Guatemala—national unity. In specific terms, national unity required that citizens relinquish their selfish interests and serve one another and the nation. Echoing his own liberal heritage, Ríos Montt also recognized that Guatemala also lacked a clear sense of nationhood. His objective, then, was to create "a Guatemalan nationality" (una nacionalidad guatemalteca), a goal that had eluded the nation for 150 years. [45]

To this end, Ríos Montt paid lip service to the integrity of indigenous culture and identity. While the army was killing and displacing thousands of Indians in the countryside, Ríos Montt was going out of his way to attend festivities surrounding Día de la Raza (October 12) and other celebrations of the country's mythic Indian past. In his Sunday sermons, he offered a stunning reversal of old-time indigenist thinking by pointing to Indians as models of hard work, service, and nonacquisitiveness. [46] To great public fanfare, he also appointed ten Mayan representatives to the Council of State.

Despite these gestures, Ríos Montt made it abundantly clear that a national identity based on unity was one in which state authority superseded all other provincial, ethnic, political, or even religious loyalties. The bywords of national unity, "Debemos integrarnos" (We must become one), demanded the price of indigenous identity and autonomy.[47]

It was in this respect that the national unity program intersected with the restoration of order and authority. One of the cornerstones of the reclamation of the highlands was the establishment of "model villages" (resettlement villages) and "development poles" (*polos de desarrollo y servicios*) in which citizens from the zones of conflict, the vast majority of whom were Indians, could live under government protection and control. The model villages—part strategic hamlet, part kibbutz—were used to resettle civilians from war zones or in internal exile into new communities, where they were provided with housing, food, and work in a rigidly controlled, closely monitored environment. The development poles were only slightly different in that each "pole" consisted of one or, usually, more villages built on or near the site of a destroyed settlement; these, too, were maintained under the vigilant eyes of the army. In late 1982, the army began construction of the first model villages, located in the Departments of Huehuetenango and El Quiché, around the Ixil Triangle of the villages of Nebaj, Chajul, and San Juan Cotzal and somewhat later established development poles in the Ixil Triangle, the Ixcán, and the Petén.[48]

While the official purpose of the model villages and development poles was to house campesinos who had lost their homes and crops and to provide an additional measure of security and control in conflict regions, they also served as a mechanism for indigenous integration. Presumably by intent, refugees from different villages and linguistic groups were thrown together in the model villages, where they were settled in configurations that discouraged the reestablishment of old community patterns. From the moment of their arrival, residents of the model villages received courses in Spanish language, and Spanish became the lingua franca. Army overseers discouraged the revival of any type of traditional community ritual or organization and instead encouraged new types of activities, such as beauty pageants in which young women were crowned "queen." One exception was churches, which formed freely in the model villages, a factor that in itself may account in part for the enormous increase in Protestant church growth not only in the zones of conflict, but also all over rural Guatemala during this period.[49]

Because so many Protestants in the highlands were recent converts, it is difficult to discern a clear pattern of political action among them. Without doubt, Protestants, heeding the famous exhortation about respect for authority, tended to be supportive of the government; with important exceptions, they also tended to believe that the guerrillas, as Marxists, were inherently hostile to their religion. After Ríos Montt took office, Protestant "apoliticalism" often translated into a more active support of the government, because the president's evangelical profile lent their faith a new legitimacy and practical expediency that it had not enjoyed before. Yet this begs the question: Did people support the government because they were Protestants, or did they become Protestants to gain the protection of the government? Or, as in the case of Pastor Nicolás, did the intensified counterinsurgency war under Ríos Montt spark pragmatic support for the government on the part of both Catholics and Protestants?

The equation of Protestant conversion with simple political or economic expediency is an extension of the old *ánima por lámina* argument of the immediate postearthquake period, although during the Ríos Montt era, craven opportunism surely accounted in part for the pace of "conversion." It is more likely, however, that conversion in the Ríos Montt years had less to do with the president's own religion or the influence of North American evangelicals than with his pacification program. The all-out military assault on the highlands destroyed families, villages, and, where it had still been strong, the *costumbre* that had lent Indian communities their distinctive identities for hundreds of years. In the face of such loss, people may have found a new sense of control, a place for the individual, and a sense of order in Protestant churches.

Why did the Protestant churches provide this haven when the Catholic Church did not? For one thing, Protestant churches, unlike the Catholic Church, had no articulated theology that linked them to the political struggle. To those who, for ideological reasons or simply for their own safety, sought to remove themselves as much as possible from the strife, Protestant churches offered a fresh alternative. Sheldon Annis has noted that Guatemala's war was "always a psychological as well as a military struggle. Beyond merely wiping out the guerrillas' bases of popular support, the larger challenge faced by the army was to create a psychological identification and new social organization that would allow campesinos to be non-guerrillas." He argues that, until Ríos Montt, the guerrillas held the "moral high ground."[50] When Ríos Montt seized the standard of moral legitimacy, he offered an alternative to those who were weary of the war or wary of guerrilla promises.

Conversion to Protestantism may also have been a response to rampant violence. Although the spiritual impact of violence would be difficult to assess, the theological messages of Guatemalan Protestant churches can provide some insight. By far, the most popular Protestant denominations in the highlands were Pentecostal and evangelical (in the North American sense of the word), the sorts of churches that focused on concrete biblical certainties instead of on teleological abstractions. The fastest-growing churches in the zones of conflict were also premillenarianist; that is, they emphasized that the Second Coming of Christ was imminent, and that a time of great tribulation must precede the coming of the New Day. In Ríos Montt's time, premillenarianism offered an explanation and rationale for the appalling destruction and promised the believer a better life in the next world—which, in Guatemala in the early 1980s, seemed very close at hand.

The common denominator in this period was Pentecostalism. One had only to observe the war's victims in a Pentecostal church, their eyes focused on the beyond and their faces streaming with tears, to grasp what a psychological outlet such churches provided. Moreover, Pentecostal practices such as miraculous healing, ecstatic trances, and glossolalia also bore at least a superficial resemblance to some of the syncretic rituals and shamanism once practiced widely, but now scorned by most—but not all—Catholics. It is significant that Catholic church attendance increased in the zones of conflict during this period as well, but only in a heretofore small movement called Renovación (Renewal).[51] Renovación emphasized baptism in the Holy Spirit, repentance, reconciliation, and "signs and wonders." It permitted extensive lay participation in worship and distinctly distanced itself from the social activism of Catholic Action. It was, in short, a type of Catholicism that was functionally little different from Protestant Pentecostalism.

Indigenous congregations were tiny, local sects, usually with only the loosest affiliation, if any, to a larger denomination. By the mid-1980s, there were approximately ten thousand Protestant churches in Guatemala divided among nearly three hundred distinct denominations, some two hundred of which were classified as "independent."[52] The tiny sects, often numbering no more than a dozen people, met in houses or storefronts. Most were led by pastors whose only training was divine revelation but whose power was often absolute. Like the earlier independent churches, these were highly schismatic by nature; virtually all splintered periodically into new congregations. Each of these congregations provided members with kinship, identity, authority, and the satisfaction of believing they were uniquely part of God's unfolding plan.

In the context of violence and upheaval, one might expect to find many Protestant churches in the model villages or, for that matter, in any part of the highlands where communities were destroyed outright by war. Even if a convert might have initially joined to receive preferential treatment—such as better housing or better food—from the army or FUNDAPI, she would likely remain in the church because she found herself better able to cope as a Protestant than as a Catholic in this new world.[53] Since the "community" in which the converts lived was completely artificial anyway, comprising by design Indians from different villages and language groups who shared no *costumbre*, a convert might consider herself better off facing life as a Protestant, as part of a small, self-sufficient group, than as part of the larger Catholic "community," which, for all intents and purposes, had ceased to exist. If, in the process, she happened to become more affluent, to travel the route that Annis's informants in San Antonio Aguascalientes called "del suelo a cielo"— from a dirt floor to heaven—then the incentive to be a Protestant was all the greater.[54]

In fact, the evidence indicates that, whereas Protestant growth was indeed significant in the heart of the zones of conflict, the greatest growth in Protestant churches occurred in areas affected by violence but outside the actual war zone. For example, Protestant conversion was greater in such places as Totonicapán, around Quetzaltenango, and communities in Chimaltenango than it was in, say, the Ixil area. Communities in this "second tier" of affected areas did not actually collapse in the midst of the violence, but their traditional economic and social structures were pushed beyond their limits. As Carol A. Smith has demonstrated in her study of one *municipio* affected by secondary violence, Totonicapán, the formation of PACs and limitations on travel imposed by the Guatemalan army in the highlands disrupted Indian control of trade and marketing so severely that they threatened the very autonomy of the community. "Totonicapán's indigenous economy—the material basis for its ethnic strength—" Smith wrote in the mid-1980s, "is . . . near death." If Totonicapán can be used as a paradigm, and if Protestant churches did indeed provide a haven in the midst of community collapse, it is not surprising that by the mid-1980s, there were 270 Protestant churches, three times the number in 1980.[55]

Although this analysis helps explain the attraction of Protestantism on one level, it fails to take into account the fact that Protestant growth was expanding dramatically in the highlands even before Ríos Montt took power and continued unabated after he left office. In terms of aggregate church growth, the Ríos Montt era brackets little; conversion rates rose at a steady pace from 1976 to late 1984 and only then slowed somewhat, when backsliding and some "reconversion" began to come into play. Conversion, moreover, was as much a part of the spiritual landscape in territory occupied by the guerrillas as it was in army-controlled regions in the late 1970s. Some Protestants actively supported the popular resistance, albeit less readily than did their Catholic brethren, and a few churches adopted an overtly leftist stance. Thus, while Ríos Montt's "moral mandate" may well have turned the tide of the war, it was not in itself a determining factor in Protestant growth.[56]

To be sure, the evangelical development groups such as FUNDAPI and some churches did enjoy the support of conservative religious organizations in the United States, for Ríos Montt's religious affiliation had had a strong impact among North American conservative fundamentalist groups. The vision of this Christian soldier waging war on a communist insurgency proved irresistible to the emerging right-wing, fundamentalist Moral Majority in the United States, a powerful political coalition that had formed to support the presidential campaign of Ronald Reagan in 1980. When Ríos Montt took power, conservative Protestant groups in the United States began to channel money for "reconstruction and relief" into Guatemala through organizations like World Vision and FUNDAPI and to specific denominations and congregations to aid in church growth. Donations of funds, equipment, and services from U.S. evangelical groups during the Ríos Montt era totaled only around twenty million dollars, a substantial amount, but far less than the billion dollars the general had been promised by Pat Robertson. Nevertheless, public fanfare surrounding the aid exaggerated the role that foreign evangelicals played in the Ríos Montt administration and left them open to charges that, in the words of one observer (speaking from the safety of Mexico), they were "the Franciscans and Dominicans of our time . . . plainly a part of American penetration."[57]

The gap between perception and reality was even greater in the matter of domestic support (which reached its height in the last months of 1982) for the Ríos Montt regime. By coincidence or something more, it happened that the year marked the first one hundred years of Protestantism in the republic, calculated from the arrival of John Clark Hill in 1882. In honor of the centennial, newspaper editorials revived the reputation of Protestantism's local mentor, Justo Rufino Barrios, and marveled at Protestantism's growth in recent years. The publicity on the centennial lasted for most of 1982, although national interest in the Protestant churches shifted away temporarily during the visit of Pope John Paul II to the republic in June of that year. A massive revival in October 1982 capped off the centennial celebrations with a reported five hundred thousand Guatemalans crowded into the Campo de Marte in Guatemala City to hear the famous Argentine evangelist Luis Palau, widely known as "the Latin Billy Graham," commend the centennial and lavish praise on Ríos Montt's "miracle."[58]

The Protestant centennial proved to be the single biggest show of public support for Ríos Montt during his seventeen months in power, but this display of evangelical strength alone, taken on top of the cataclysm in the countryside, worried the Catholic hierarchy deeply. The president's own brother, Mario Enrique Ríos Montt, then auxiliary bishop of the Diocese of Escuintla, articulated Catholic fears succinctly. "What is going on in Guatemala may have grave consequences," he warned. "It could well turn into a religious war more serious than our own political war." Indeed, even some evangelical leaders felt that the enormous show of public support at the centennial suggested that the evangelical community could, if mobilized, become a lasting base of political support. Some talk even circulated about the possible formation of a political party built around an "evangelical agenda."[59]

Yet the display at the centennial celebration had been deceptive, for below the surface the evangelicals were bitterly divided. Factions split along the traditional fault lines that divided the mainline sects from the Pentecostals. At an institutional level, this tended to translate into active support for Ríos Montt, and only passive support or even outright criticism of the regime from the non-Pentecostals, particularly from the more liberal denominations, where human rights were an issue. As one prominent Protestant leader later complained, "The government of General Ríos Montt suffered from the same kinds of sectarianism that has always divided the evangelical community. One sect surrounded the President and another encircled the president of the Council of State, and all the rest lamented that no one else could have access to the two and were only allowed to observe."[60]

But even Pentecostals were divided in their support of Ríos Montt. Many were outraged that the president, who was so widely associated with evangelicalism, rarely called for the advice of Protestant leaders outside of his own church. Church leaders were privately resentful that after so many years of minority status they were excluded from influence in the unprecedented experiment of evangelical government. Thus, when opposition from right-wing political forces and disgruntled senior army officers forced Ríos Montt out of the presidency, the divided evangelical community did not rally to his defense. Evangelical mobilization failed because of the very qualities that made evangelicals such good citizens of the military governments—sectarianism, passivity, apoliticism, and a lack of articulated politics. Such qualities made them poor allies in an actual political showdown.

Ríos Montt was ousted in a coup on 8 August 1983, which put in power Gen. Oscar Humberto Mejía Víctores, Ríos Montt's own minister of defense, and Guatemala's last military president before the return of civilian government in 1986. The public rhetoric of the coup addressed the religious issue head on and clearly implied that Ríos Montt was a deluded religious zealot. The Mejía government issued a statement to the press on the day of the coup that called Ríos Montt and his advisers from the Church of the Word part of "a fanatical and aggressive religious group that took advantage of their position of power as the highest members of government for their benefit, ignoring the fundamental principle of the separation of church and state."[61]

The charge of evangelical political railroading rang hollow even at the time, for despite the evangelical tone of the Ríos Montt administration, no one from the Church of the Word outside of the president and his two advisers had held any pivotal position in government, nor had any high-ranking military officer been an evangelical Christian.[62] At the heart of the matter was the fact that, with the insurgency in the countryside beat into submission, few others in positions of power shared Ríos Montt's idiosyncratic vision of La Nueva Guatemala. He still enjoyed considerable support among the urban poor and even in the rural areas affected by the violence, where people paradoxically credited him with restoring order and authority. But in the higher circles, once the urgency of national crisis had passed, Ríos Montt wore thin. His cavalier dismissal of demands for new presidential elections—"¿Elecciones, para qué?" (Elections, what for?)—and his insistence that he governed as a servant of the people anointed to restore order and authority did little to endear him to senior officers and influential right-wing political parties, which came to regard him as capricious and unpredictable. But most unforgivable of all was his inability to rebuild the economy, where two key commodities, coffee and tourism, were so damaged by the war that by the end of 1982, the GDP had dropped to an unprecedented 3.3 percent. As one analyst noted, "Businessmen might be willing to sit still while moralizing Ríos Montt admonished them to give up their mistresses, but when the GDP fell . . . there was cause for grave concern."[63]

In terms of the religious rationalization for the coup, the only quantifiable complaint coup participants had with Ríos Montt's religion seems to have been their profound opposition to his moralistic, church-inspired anticorruption campaign, which had severely stanched the flow of graft to military officers and government officials. By one account, one of the soldiers muttered to Ríos Montt as he escorted him out of the National Palace during the coup, "A government that doesn't abuse its power doesn't govern."[64]

The ouster of Ríos Montt, however, had little immediate effect on the growth of Protestantism in the country, although in the weeks following the coup there was a brief surge of public reprisals against the Protestant community. In late August 1983, pastors complained of being intimidated by the National Police, of anonymous death threats, and of general public harassment. Finally, at the urging of the leaders of the Alianza Evangélica, General Mejía Víctores ended the harassment by reaffirming the Freedom of Worship decree of 1873 and by offering protection to evangelical activities. The following day, on August 29, the National Police sent out a bulletin that asserted that there were no restrictions on religious activities and assured Protestants, with no apparent irony, that they would continue to have the same protection under the law that they had enjoyed before.[65]

With the assurance that there would be no public or government backlash, the evangelicals resumed their efforts, only slightly subdued by the ouster of the Protestant president. When the dust had settled, it became apparent that Ríos Montt's presidency had had little effect on the growth of the Protestant Church in Guatemala, at least not in the short run. The Servicio Evangelizador para América Latina (SEPAL), a newly formed data bank for national Protestant work, estimated that the rate of church growth increased and decreased only negligibly with Ríos Montt's fortunes, although the rapid increase in congregational expansion did begin to plateau toward the latter part of the 1980s. At the time, however, only the Church of the Word suffered a noticeable and precipitous decline in membership, when five hundred people left the church in the wake of the coup.[66]

In some respects, Ríos Montt's seventeen-month administration in the early 1980s brings the story of Protestantism in Guatemala full cycle. By invoking the rhetoric of nineteenth-century missionaries and their Liberal mentors—the calls to moral rectitude and national unity and the full-bore effort to deal with the "Indian problem" through as-similation or, if need be, elimination—Guatemala's first Protestant president advanced farther than any of his predecessors in asserting the will of the state over the governed. This was the very objective that had so seduced Justo Rufino Barrios and had compelled him to invite mis-sionaries into the country in the first place. While the likes of Hay-maker, Bishop, Smith, and Burgess would undoubtedly have found Ríos Montt's methods reprehensible and perhaps even tyrannical, they nonetheless would have concurred utterly with his definition of Guate-mala's problems in strictly moral terms and would have agreed that the solutions lay in the ethical and moral framework provided by Protestant belief.

Yet the explanation for the expansion of Protestantism in Guatemala in general lies somewhere outside this construct. Under Ríos Montt, the howling forces of modernization, violence, and community disintegra-tion that drove people into Protestant churches in the 1960s and the 1970s accelerated dramatically. Where political change and economic shifts had weakened the power of local sources of community authority gradually as the century progressed, Ríos Montt sometimes eliminated them entirely. Where the Catholic Church's spiritual hegemony ebbed through the twentieth century and fractured into competing bits, Ríos Montt's very public membership in a Protestant church served notice that new types of religious institutions were there to fill the void. But above all, Protestant congregations offered a new community, a new "way of being" for those who chose to convert and provided a new iden-tity to take the place of an identity that was once tied to a lifestyle, to family, or even to a physical location that might no longer even exist. Whether this new identity is the product or the source of the disinte-gration of traditional community integrity remains a central point of controversy, especially within the communities themselves. What is im-portant to bear in mind is that these new identities, which we ambigu-ously label "Protestant," are locally constructed, understood, and, in-deed, valued by those who subscribe to them. The new community of *hermanos* may be both larger and smaller than the *municipio*—but it has an internally logical corpus of rules, authority, belonging, and cohesion that makes members integrally a part of something that is larger than they. This has profound implications in a place where traditional sources of authority, order, and truth may be dramatically altered or even fully collapsed by new patterns of power and labor, migration, economic transition, factionalism, or massacre and exile.

EPILOGUE

AFTER Ríos Montt's ouster in 1983, Protestantism continued to expand dramatically until around 1985. In that year, the rate of growth, measured by conversions, began to level out at around 10 percent per year, a rate markedly lower than the halcyon days of the early 1980s, but significant nonetheless. In his study of this pattern, Timothy Evans demonstrates that this slowdown in Protestant conversion stemmed from a variety of fairly predictable factors: backsliding, "conversion," reconversion from one Protestant denomination to another or even back to the Catholic Church, and recidivism into old habits proscribed by the churches, such as the consumption of alcohol or adultery. As a result, by 1990, church growth experts felt it necessary to scale back their earlier projections, which had estimated that Guatemala would be more than half Protestant by the year 2000. "Our growth rate has slowed in part because we are working from a larger aggregate statistical base," one Protestant statistician working for SEPAL explains, "but the simple fact is that some people will always remain Catholic no matter what."[1]

Nevertheless, by the mid-1980s, even by conservative estimates, Protestants accounted for approximately one third of Guatemala's total population, the highest percentage in all of Spanish America. This figure seemed destined to increase, even if at a slower rate than church partisans had once thought, for the same issues of community fragmentation and political and economic crisis continued to feed the Protestant movement, though in a slightly different guise.[2] After Ríos Montt's ouster, the military retained power for three years, but finally relinquished the presidency to civilian control when international and economic pressures became too great. Even more significantly, in December 1996, the Guatemalan government and the URNG signed a peace accord that finally ended the civil war that had defined Guatemala's reality since the early 1960s.

The return to democracy at the end of the twentieth century—if "return" is indeed an accurate word, since Guatemala has rarely enjoyed this political luxury—raises hopes that Guatemala may indeed, in Paul Burgess's phrase, be able to "untangle the yarn and reestablish the pattern of weaving," at least in the fabric of political life. Yet the reconstruction of civil society within the framework of democracy remains a challenging goal indeed. Hyperurbanization, crime, and economic stagnation have all increased under civilian rule. The constant threat of social unrest and praetorian intervention has created an uncertainty about the future that is unprecedented, even under the false *pax* of the generals. Compounding these political problems, in 1986, the national economy began a free fall from which it has never fully recovered. The quetzal, the value of which was once tied to the dollar, was devalued to a fifth of its official rate in 1985, and the national debt increased as foreign investment remained static. Common crime, poverty's stepchild, which the military government had been able to keep in check, became endemic in the capital. Those who had remained aloof from the political violence of the early 1980s, particularly members of the urban middle class, now found themselves vulnerable.

What resulted was a Guatemala nearly immobilized by malaise. The civilian regimes have brought some relief from human rights violations, but have not been as successful in controlling crime; kidnappings, robberies, and nonpolitical murders have become so common that some have compared Guatemala City to Bogotá.

In such a context, it is perhaps not all that surprising that Efraín Ríos Montt remains a key political figure in the 1990s. Although prohibited by the 1985 Constitution from placing his name on the presidential ballot, he heads a political party, the Frente Republicano de Guatemala (Republican Front of Guatemala, FRG), that holds an influential number of seats in the National Assembly.

In the midst of this political restructuring, Protestant churches have been among the few institutions that continue to thrive, particularly as violence in the countryside and the illusion of economic opportunity lure Guatemalans into the capital. Beginning in the mid-1980s, Protestant growth increased significantly for the first time among members of the middle and upper classes in the capital. The attraction of Protestant churches for the urban poor was similar to its attraction for the rural poor, for a great many of the former were recent migrants from the countryside. Urban migrants, having been pushed into the city's slums by the exigencies of war or by false perceptions of economic opportunity, joined the same kinds of Pentecostal churches as their brethren in rural areas. The uncertainty of the mid-1980s, it seems, produced a fertile environment for Protestantism—with its emphasis on eternal truths and verities—to flourish among the poor, whether they resided in the damaged communities of the countryside or the miserable *barrancas* (slums) of the city.

Alongside these churches a parallel movement that shared little more than name with either the rural autochthonous churches or the old missionary denominations took its place among the sophisticated middle and upper classes. Unlike Protestant growth among the poor, conversion among the middle and upper classes was basically a phenomenon of the 1980s and the 1990s. In these sectors, the most successful churches were also Pentecostal, but with a difference. Although they were usually indigenous in that they had a local pastor and no formal affiliation with a missionary agency, they nonetheless exhibited a strong kinship to the values and ethics of conservative (and often affluent) Christians in the United States.

Besides embracing traditional Pentecostal beliefs, these neo-Pentecostal churches in Guatemala place great emphasis on "healing in the atonement," which roughly translates into empowerment on earth through proper faith in God. Closely related is the belief that material prosperity is the entitlement of the faithful; money, good health, and security are all tangible evidence of God's benediction. The believer is thus right to demand such things from God, for personal prosperity is witness to His power and grace. This message is underscored by the preaching of televangelists broadcast from within Guatemala and by satellite from the United States. This strong emphasis on prosperity in Guatemalan neo-Pentecostal churches has been dubbed "theonomy" by some, "health-and-wealth theology" by others.[3]

It is not surprising that the health-and-wealth churches enjoy a tremendous popularity among Guatemala's ambitious middle class and affluent elite, who aggressively cultivate ties to U.S. consumerism. Although this emulation of things American has been evident among the Guatemalan elite for many years, it became even more apparent in the early 1980s, when wealthy Guatemalans perceived Reagan's America to be on "their side" in the civil war. Moreover, as materialism became the guiding ethos of the United States in the 1980s, it also did so, albeit on a less blatant level, in Guatemala. To the wealthy or near-wealthy, then, neo-Pentecostal churches not only affirmed the impulses to emulate and accumulate, they sanctified them.[4]

A second reason for the neo-Pentecostal churches' newfound popularity in the early 1980s was economics, for, as we have seen, Protestantism of all stripes is clearly associated with prosperity in Guatemala. This association was obvious in rural areas, where converts spoke of the urban poor's ascension from "a dirt floor to heaven," and now it appeared among the wealthy as well. As civil strife, political turmoil, and capital flight destroyed the national economy, even members of the elite felt the squeeze. To them, and to aspirants to the middle class, neo-Pentecostal churches offered both the means and the rationale for upward mobility in a society in which it was otherwise unattainable.[5]

At a less deterministic level, neo-Pentecostalism offered the same kinds of spiritual answers as traditional Pentecostalism, but without the latter's lower-class associations. Although the middle and upper classes in Guatemala had not suffered the genocide and cultural calamity that afflicted the Indian population, even for them, the past few decades had not been easy. Many elite Guatemalans were Catholic only in the most nominal sense to begin with, and in times of crisis, their marginal faith did not see them through. Others were alienated by real and perceived associations between Catholic activism and the armed rebellion, and this drove them from the Church. By the mid-1980s, neo-Pentecostal churches had emerged to fill this spiritual void.[6]

In practical terms, the health-and-wealth churches offer a message that is quite similar to the theology of the so-called Gospel of Wealth that was popular in the United States in the late 1890s, likewise a period of great social tumult and uncertainty. Numbering among its apostles the likes of David Rockefeller and J. P. Morgan, the Gospel of Wealth promised that "godliness [was] in league with riches." Material acquisition and financial success were thought to be evidence of right living and God's blessing, while poverty and penury were fair punishment for idleness and vice. In the United States during the Gilded Age, the Gospel of Wealth explained a social order that permitted the very rich to live without guilt or fear of the large, poor, immigrant working class. A century later, this theology had an apt application in Guatemala.[7]

The characteristics associated with right living in the modern health-and-wealth churches—punctuality, thrift, efficiency, a concern with law and order—were never a part of the traditional Guatemalan ethos, and are in many ways contrary to the traditional worldview of the national elite. It is perhaps for this very reason that members of the middle and upper classes began to look to the health-and-wealth churches for fresh formulas for personal, social, and spiritual advancement. If Protestant churches in rural areas help render the outside world comprehensible to indigenous members and provide a locus of identity and belonging, neo-Pentecostal churches function in a similar way for wealthy urban dwellers. On the one hand, they insulate members from the violence and social decay that surround them; on the other, health-and-wealth theology offers a moral justification for members who seek personal aggrandizement instead of social reform. Neo-Pentecostal churches offer a spiritual rationale for the gaping social inequities of Guatemala and bring order to what is otherwise a capricious world. Where the fatalism and paternalism of old-time Catholicism once quieted these jarring dissonances, so now, for some, does this variety of Protestantism.

When such a movement collides with power and money, it is not surprising that politics increasingly defines itself along religious lines. Although this is not to imply a simple dichotomy between liberal (leftist) Catholics and conservative (rightist) Protestants, it is true in part because Guatemala's Protestants remain a notoriously divided lot, who have well earned the moniker "protest-ant." The large Protestant population in Guatemala is divided internally by class, ethnicity, geography, theology, and political opinion; it also includes a large faction who believe that political participation of any kind is profane. In recent years, wealthy urban Pentecostals, a small but influential minority, have made a concerted effort to create a confessional-based political bloc, but the fissures inherent within Guatemalan Protestantism, coupled with a lack of a single, overarching "Protestant" ideology, have thus far rendered these efforts ineffective. In politics as in theology, Protestants are so differentiated that Jean-Pierre Bastian suggests that they be referred to as "non–Roman Catholics" rather than as "Protestants," as the latter implies consistent orthodoxy of belief and practice.[8]

Despite this lack of coherence, however, "Protestant" when used as an adjective instead of a noun has important social and political cachet in Guatemala in the post–Ríos Montt era. The lingering aura of Ríos

Montt's regime, now given a softer edge in popular memory, has caused Guatemalans, Catholic and Protestant alike, to associate Protestantism with desirable and "modern" (and distinctly Weberian) traits like honesty, integrity, discipline, and personal initiative. Stories abound of job applicants lying about their church affiliation in the belief that they are more likely to be perceived as "honest and trustworthy" if employers think they are Protestant. In a variation on this theme, people are said to carry Bibles with them on visits to local prisons in the belief that capricious guards are more likely to trust Protestants than Catholics when admitting visitors into prison compounds.[9]

The presidential election of 1990 offers the clearest example of how religion and, specifically, a minority faith, has become a defining element in national politics. This election is particularly important in that it marks Guatemala's first peaceful transition from one civilian president to another in the twentieth century.[10] It also marks the first time that candidates from parties from the Left and Center-Left freely competed against parties of the Center-Right and far Right. Although a few of these competing factions, such as the Christian Democratic Party, carried some religious association, none were explicitly affiliated with a specific church or denomination.

Midway through the presidential campaign, Efraín Ríos Montt threw his hat into the political arena. He did not attempt to run as a "Protestant candidate" per se, but he made it clear, particularly in his calls for "Protestant values" such as discipline and law and order, that his second term as president would strongly reiterate the themes of the first. Ríos Montt quickly dominated the field, gaining strong support across all social sectors. Most surprising of all, he was the leading contender even in areas where voters were survivors of his scorched-earth campaigns.

The possibility that Ríos Montt might actually win the presidency was so great that the Supreme Court ruled his candidacy illegal. Yet the battle lines of confessional politics had already been drawn. In early 1991, Guatemalans elected Jorge Serrano Elías, a Center-Right businessman whose lackluster campaign for president had floundered until Ríos Montt left the race. Until Ríos Montt was forced to withdraw, Serrano had been politically indistinguishable from most of the other candidates, but he was the only Protestant on the ballot.[11] Serrano's election is eloquent proof of the enduring resonance of religious identity in Guatemalan society.

This equating of Protestantism with honesty and rectitude was undercut only slightly by Serrano's ouster from office in 1992 amid charges of autocracy and corruption; the collateral damage most affected Serrano's church, Elim, which had a greater association with wealth and power than did most evangelical churches. Despite the stain of the Serrano era, in 1994, General Ríos Montt returned to the political arena to run for the presidency again, in defiance of an explicit constitutional prohibition against the candidacy of anyone who had ever seized power by force. Although he was prohibited by the 1985 Constitution from appearing on the official presidential ballot, Ríos Montt's platform of "efficiency and order" and his record put him ahead in the popular polls and made him the object of a national movement to return to the law-and-order rule of the man who believed he governed with the "authority of God."

But what of the Roman Catholic Church? No candidate in an authentic election in Guatemala could possibly win without the solid support of Catholic voters, who still compose two thirds of the national population. In the 1990s, however, a single clear-cut Catholic political identity was still inchoate. Guatemalan Catholicism, as we have seen, has never been monolithic, and within the institutional Church a variety of different, and sometimes conflicting, political and religious ideologies have long coexisted. Yet the repression of sectors of the Church since the 1970s, coupled with the recasting of the political idiom, is forcing the Church to redefine its place in a society that is moving away from the ideal of secularism, that elusive goal that nineteenth-century liberals believed to be the sine qua non of nation building. But the irony is that it is Protestantism, and not Catholicism, that has already set the stakes. Thus the "Mother Church" finds its new political identity in opposition—a role normally reserved for minority faiths.

The Roman Catholic Church is moving cautiously but decisively out of this marginalized position. In a break with precedent, the archbishop who succeeded Casariego in 1983, Próspero Penados del Barrio, issued a series of bold pastoral letters that unabashedly sought to win back the moral high ground from the Protestants and reassert the Catholic Church's ethical hegemony over the hearts and minds of Guatemalans. Three of these letters articulated the new political vision of the Church. Two, "Clamor por tierra" (Cry for Land) (1988) and "Pastoral indígena" (Pastoral Letter on Indigenous Peoples) (1992), stand in strident opposition to long-standing government policies on land tenure and ethnic rights, two issues on which the institutional Church has historically been noticeably silent. A third, "Signo de verdad y esperanza" (Symbol of Truth and Hope) (1989), asserts that the Catholic Church is "moving toward a moment of special vitality" as it reestablishes its position of authority in Guatemalan society. This assertion is not as premature as it may appear, even given the Protestant onslaught.[12] For the first time in the more than one hundred years since the liberal reform, Guatemala's Catholic seminaries are filled to overflowing; in 1987, 483 young men were studying for the priesthood, a figure equal to the total number of ordained priests and other religious in the country in 1964 and an astonishing 637 percent increase in seminary enrollment over 1972.[13] The masses, to borrow Christian Lalive d'Epinay's phrase, seem to be finding their refuge in Protestant and Catholic churches alike.

It merits noting at the end of the twentieth century that Protestantism is no longer Guatemala's newest religious movement; to the contrary, the "newest" movements go back much farther than the Protestant Reformation. The first of these is the emergence of a "Maya" Catholic Church. This radical innovation in formal Catholicism embraces a "contextualized theology" that intentionally fuses Catholic beliefs with Maya cosmology; it is under the leadership of a Maya priesthood and operates with the tacit blessing of the official Church. And even beyond this, traditional non-Christian Mayan religion is claiming its place in the formal religious sphere. As part of the cultural renaissance of the pan-Mayan movement, traditional Maya religion is enjoying an efflorescence that gives a public face to the many ancient beliefs and practices that have long been, in the words of Enrique Sam Colop, "hidden beneath a discourse of concealment."[14] Both movements are clearly responses to the cultural devastation of the early 1980s and to the rising tide of Mayan political activism at century's close. Yet both may owe a debt, like it or not, to the Protestant move to provide a usable template for pluralism, theological fluidity, and contextualized growth.

This book began with a gloss of the canon of social science's conventional treatment of religious change, with particular attention to Max Weber's articulation of the relationship between modernization, economic rationality, and Protestantism. At first glance, the Guatemalan case seems to largely refute this equation, since the type of Protestantism—Pentecostalism—that has taken hold in the country would not seem to inculcate the "Protestant virtues" like Puritanism and rationality that Weber associates with the "spirit of capitalism." To the contrary, many Guatemalan converts value Pentecostalism for its very "irrationality" and otherworldliness, two traits that seem eminently at odds with a "modern" Weltanschauung. And yet, non-Pentecostals perceive their brethren to be very Puritan-like: trustworthy, frugal, honest, and no-

nonsense. Do these qualities, either real or perceived, point to what Irving Zeitlin calls the "elective affinity" between Protestantism and capitalism, or, more broadly, to late-twentieth century "Western" consumer culture in general?[15]

There can be no doubt that in many large health-and-wealth-oriented neo-Pentecostal churches, the affinity is both elective and eagerly sought out. In these churches, matters of personal economy and lifestyle are firmly embedded in theology. It is ironic that these churches are not directly tied to the old mission denominations, for they offer a message of salvation that is every bit as culturally encoded as that of the early missionaries in the late nineteenth century—a message for which the missionaries were reviled. It perhaps attests to the anomie of the current era that the health-and-wealth churches are valued precisely because they provide an identity, albeit one that is imported from abroad.

Is this also true for the much more numerous Indian churches in the countryside, where many Pentecostal congregations have become new foci of small-group and even ethnic identity? If the answer is no, as I believe it is, then we must accept the possibility that the dynamic and function of Pentecostalism or even of Protestantism in general is quite different in this context, that they both mold and are molded by a distinctly non-Western cultural milieu, and that it is only in that context that it can be understood and valued. Many Mayan Protestants reject the notion that Protestantism inevitably leads to assimilation and cultural degradation; they note that for them it is no more contradictory to be an indigenous Protestant than to be an indigenous Catholic. Catholicism, of course, is a foreign religion imposed by conquest but that quickly assumed a Mayan vernacular. Mayan Protestants presume that Protestantism, to which they subscribe voluntarily and of their own agency, will do no less. This is perhaps expressed best in the words of Vitalino Simalox, a Mayan activist and Presbyterian minister (1988): "Cristianizar no se puede ser equivalente de occidentalizar," he writes. "El cristianismo ha de respetar a todos los pueblos. . . . Ha de tratar de ser griego con los griegos, guatemalteco con los guatemaltecos y Maya con los Mayas. Y esto en todos planos de la creación cultural. (1 Cor. 9.) [De decir menos] . . . se menosprecia y se marginan los valores objectivos y subjectivos de las culturas Mayas en nuestro medio" (To Christianize cannot be the same as to Westernize. Christianity must respect all peoples. . . . It must try to be Greek with the Greeks, Guatemalan with the Guatemalans, and Maya with the Maya. And this on all planes of cultural creation. [1 Cor. 9.] To say anything less diminishes and marginalizes the objective and subjective values of the Maya cultures in our environment).

Simalox's words offer testimony to the fact that, since colonial times, religion in Guatemala has exhibited a marvelous elasticity in the hands of the faithful, if not always by Church institutions. It has shown an enduring ability to expand, contract, and take new shapes and contours while retaining its fundamental density. In recent decades, violence, repression, and "development" have radically redefined the contours of society and politics in Guatemala, but they have also created new opportunities for socioreligious innovation. As Guatemala teeters on the edge of the millennium, religion may become, in Daniel Levine's words, a "convenient place from which to begin . . . cultural reconstruction," not so much a "refuge for the masses" as a moral base from which to reconstruct identity, belonging, and meaning.[16]

Notes

INTRODUCTION

1. Except where specifically noted, I use the term "evangelical" as synonymous with "Protestant," as is common in Spanish usage.
2. The best-known books by these prolific authors include Emile Durkheim (1915) and Max Weber (1930).
3. David Martin (1990), p. 285.
4. David Stoll (1990), p. xvi.
5. Daniel Levine (1991).
6. See Virginia Garrard-Burnett, "Conclusion: Is This Latin America's Reformation?" in Virginia Garrard-Burnett and David Stoll, eds. (1993); see also Duncan Earle (1992).

1. "ORDER, PROGRESS, AND PROTESTANTS"
The Beginning of Mission

1. Mary P. Holleran (1949), pp. 15–44; J. Lloyd Mecham (1966), pp. 5–37.
2. Ernesto Chinchilla Aguilar (1953), p. 7; Gonzalo Báez-Camargo (1960), p. 39.
3. Wilton M. Nelson (1982), p. 21.
4. Chinchilla Aguilar (1953) pp. 67, 69.
5. Ralph Lee Woodward, Jr. (1965).

6. For a classic account of liberalism in Guatemala during this period, see Mariam Williford (1963).

7. Guatemala (1830), p. 27; *Boletín Oficial* (10 October 1837).

8. W. George Lovell and Christopher Lutz (1992).

9. I am indebted here to Rachel Ballard (1993), who explores the documents generated as a result of the cholera epidemic.

10. *Boletín de Noticias de Cólera Morbus* (12 May 1837). Unless otherwise noted, all translations are mine.

11. Ibid. (21 April 1837); Ballard (1993), p. 14.

12. Ballard (1993), p. 14.

13. Lorenzo Montúfar (1879), pp. 349–352.

14. *Boletín de Noticias de Cólera Morbus* (12 May 1837).

15. The term "ladino" is problematic, and in this context is particular to Guatemala. The best working definition comes from Richard N. Adams and Charles Hale (1991, p. 9): "'Ladino' is an ethnic designation that is used only in the region of the surviving Mesoamerican Indian peoples, i.e., from Chiapas to El Salvador, western Honduras and occasionally in Nicaragua. It is not used in [southeastern Central America]. While its original colonial usage referred to Indians who took on 'Latin' traits—specifically language and religion—gradually it came to denote a separate segment of the population, more or less the equivalent of 'mestizo.' It was specifically an issue of culture, however, not race. A racially pure Maya could become a *ladino*. Sometimes these cultural go-betweens were scorned by both Indians and whites, and legally excluded the rights of the other. Even today the term is confusing ethnically; those who are called ladinos find it difficult to define a single identity for them collectively."

16. Hazel Ingersoll (1972), p. 274.

17. For a more comprehensive analysis of the church's role in this period, see Douglass Sullivan-González (1994).

18. For a thorough assessment of Carrera's policies and reforms, see R. L. Woodward., Jr. (1993). For a much more condensed account of some of these issues, see idem (1990), pp. 52–71.

19. Sullivan-González (1989). See also Hubert J. Miller (1991).

20. See Ingersoll (1972), chap. 3.

21. Woodward (1990), p. 80.

22. Henry Dunn (1828), p. 139.

23. These included two businessmen who tried to establish an Anglican mission in Guatemala City in 1824; a Baptist pastor named Bourne, who went to Izabal in 1824; a Scots representative of the British and Foreign Bible Society, James Thomson, who went to Guatemala City in 1926; Bp. Dunn, who visited Guatemala under the auspices of the British and Foreign Bible Society in 1827; and Alexander Henderson of the British and Foreign Bible Society, who came to Guatemala from Belize City in 1834. See Kenneth Grubb (1937), American Bible Society (1916); Dunn (1828); British and Foreign Bible Society to Rev. D.

Morgan, 20 October 1970, archives of the Iglesia Episcopal de Guatemala, Guatemala City.

24. Although it is concerned primarily with British penetration farther south along the Atlantic coast, a good study of British expansion in Central America is Robert A. Naylor (1960).

25. Frederick Crowe (1850), p. 561.

26. Ora-Westley Schwemmer (1966), p. 80. See also David Escobar (1984), p. 27; British and Foreign Bible Society to Rev. D. Morgan, 20 October 1970, archives of the Iglesia Episcopal de Guatemala, Guatemala City; Juan C. Varetto (1940), p. 43; Holleran (1949), pp. 128–146; Crowe (1850), p. 561.

27. Woodward (1990), p. 83.

28. David McCreery (1976).

29. Benedict Anderson (1983), pp. 19, 145.

30. Lovell and Lutz (1982, p. 7) calculate the overall population of Guatemala in 1870 at 1,080,000; they estimate that 756,000 were Indians.

31. McCreery (1983), pp. 17, 42–43.

32. Jim Handy (1984), p. 67.

33. Hubert Miller (1991), p. 121

34. Joel S. Migdal (1988) in Steigenga (1989), pp. 5–6.

35. Steigenga (1989), p. 6

36. Miller, "Concordat," p. 119.

37. Ramón A. Salazar (1892), p. 29. It is worth noting that, although Germans migrated to Guatemala in large numbers during this period, there is no evidence that they took advantage of this legal right. The German Deutsch-Evangelisches Pfarramt Kirchlich sent a missionary to serve the German population in Alta Verapaz in 1907, but did not establish a permanent church until 1929, when it built the Evangelisches-Lutheranische Landeskirche La Epifania in Guatemala City. "Gründungsffestgottesdienst," *Evangelisches Gemeindeblatt für Guatemala ünd das ubrige Mittelamerika Deutsche-Evangelischen Esiphanisagemeinde Guatemala* 6(2): 3–4, "Amtsreise," Evangelisches Gemeindeblatt 5(5):4.

38. *Guatemala* (1830), vol. 1, p. 174.

39. See Hubert Miller (1991), p. 119.

40. See Thomas E. Bogenschield (1992), p. 41.

41. Deborah Baldwin (1990), p. 17.

42. Bogenschield (1992), p. 42.

43. Ibid.

44. Ibid., p. 49.

45. Thomas E. Bogenschield (1991), pp. 6–7.

46. McCreery (1983), p. 70.

47. Edward Haymaker (1947), p. 15; Presbyterian Church of the U.S.A., Board of Foreign Missions (hereafter P B F M) to John Hill, 3 January 1883, P B F M, Latin American Letters (hereafter P B F M letters), 1882–1902, archives of the Iglesia Nacional Presbiteriana de Guatemala, Guatemala City.

48. Helen J. Sanborn (1886), p. 85.
49. Ibid., p. 118.
50. PBFM to Hill, 30 December 1882; Hill to PBFM, 3 January 1885; United States Ministry to PBFM, 2 February 1886; PBFM to Hill, 2 February 1886; PBFM to Hill, 24 November 1886; Hill to PBFM, 26 January 1887; all in PBFM letters, 1882–1902.
51. See Baldwin (1990), pp. 11–29.
52. Nelson Manfred Blake (1972), p. 466.
53. Despite this, the relationship between Protestantism and Freemasonry was close in many regions of Latin America during the nineteenth century, in that both movements found themselves marginalized as "dissenters." See Jean-Pierre Bastian, ed. (1990).
54. Haymaker to PBFM, 22 April 1902, PBFM letters, 1903–1911.
55. Haymaker (1947), p. 36.
56. Bogenschield (1991), p. 75.
57. PBFM to Haymaker, 19 January 1899, PBFM letters, 1882–1902.
58. PBFM to Haymaker, 28 March 1888, PBFM letters, 1882–1902.
59. Haymaker to PBFM, 16 September 1898, PBFM letters, 1882–1902.
60. Lidia Solís de Mansilla, "El Reverendo Eduardo Haymaker," *Ecos Feminiles* 28(3): 4. Iglesia Evangélica Presbiteriana de Guatemala, *Apuntes para la Historia* (1980), p. 82. The spelling of Maya words here corresponds to the new orthography authorized by the Academia de las Lenguas Mayas de Guatemala in 1987. See Edward F. Fischer and R. McKenna Brown, eds. (1996), p. 16.
61. PBFM letters, 1901–1902; letter dated 13 July 1901, no names; letter dated 3 January 1906, no names.

2. "BETTER THAN GUNSHIPS"
The Institutional Expansion of Missions

1. James S. Dennis (1897), vol. 3, pp. 358–359.
2. Blake (1972), pp. 462–463.
3. For a more amplified articulation of these ideas, see Dennis (1897).
4. Josiah Strong (1891), p. 225.
5. Louis A. Pérez, Jr. (1992).
6. Oliver Otis Howard (1898), p. 20, in ibid., p. 107.
7. Haymaker (1917), no page.
8. American Bible Society (1916), p. 31; Mario Ríos Paredes (1982), p. 4; Guatemala Mission to PBFM, Mission Report 1901, PBFM letters 1901–1902.
9. See George Marsden (1980).
10. *Central American Bulletin* (hereafter *CAB*) 1(3): 2. This newsletter was privately published in small runs, with erratic notations of dates and issue and volume numbers, especially in the early decades of publication. Years and issues are cited whenever possible in these notes. See also Adolph Blakeney (1956), p. 59.

11. *CAB* 3 (1897): 8; Wilkins Bowdre Winn (1963), p. 240; Paul Enyart (1970), p. 19.
12. Haymaker to PBFM, 29 October 1902, PBFM letters, 1901–1902.
13. *CAB* 6(1): 6.
14. Haymaker to PBFM, 29 October 1902, PBFM letters, 1901–1902.
15. Ibid.
16. William McBath to PBFM, 6 January 1900, PBFM letters, 1901–1902; Guatemalan Mission to PBFM, Mission Report 1900, PBFM letters, 1882–1902.
17. Haymaker to PBFM, 29 October 1902, PBFM letters, 1901–1902.
18. Ibid.
19. Hugh Milton Coke, Jr. (1978), p. 316.
20. Gates to PBFM, 23 October 1902, PBFM letters, 1882–1902; Gates to PBFM 30 May 1902, PBFM letters, 1903–1911.
21. Blake (1972), p. 656.
22. Bogenschield (1991), pp. 114–121.
23. Ibid., pp. 124–125.
24. Arnoldo Izaguirre (1977), p. 1; Harold Ray (n.d.), p. 1; Margaret Birchard to Virginia Garrard, 23 January 1985.
25. Ray (n.d.), p. 1; Birchard to Garrard, 23 January 1985.
26. Carlos Marroquín Vélez, ed. (1983), p. 1. It is telling that the only regularly scheduled ecumenical meeting attended by all missionaries was always held at Thanksgiving, a holiday not celebrated in Guatemala. This provides a window into the small ways in which the missionaries, even those who lived in Guatemala for their entire adult lives, still consciously, if fitfully, reaffirmed their North American identity.
27. Bogenschield argues that the initial partition was made in 1903, since neither the Quakers nor the Nazarenes were fully established in Guatemala in 1902. I agree that my date is early, but both CAM and Presbyterian documents seem clear on this point, and it is worth noting that a year later, neither of the smaller missions had really gained a foothold. I would surmise that the 1902 agreement was actually an accommodation between the Presbyterian and the CAM missions, and that the other participating denominations were incorporated at a somewhat later date. In any event, the agreement was not formally codified until 1936, when the work of all of the principals was firmly established.
28. Luis Corral Prieto (1984), p. 17; James Hudson interview; Pauline Burgess Sywulka interview. The Comity Agreement gave the Departments of Guatemala, El Progreso, Quetzaltenango, Suchitepéquez, and Retalhuleu to the Presbyterian mission.
29. To the CAM went the Departments of Chimaltenango, Sacatepéquez, Sololá, San Marcos, Huehuetenango, Escuintla, Santa Rosa, Jalapa, and Jutiapa. The Nazarene Mission took the Departments of Alta and Baja Verapaz and laid claim to the Department of the Petén, although that remote and underpopulated region was not specifically included in the agreement. The Friends claimed the Departments of Chiquimula, Zacapa, and Izabal. With Solomonic wisdom, the agreement divided Guatemala City in half, designating half to the

Presbyterian Church and the other half to the Central American Mission. In 1914, when the Primitive Methodist Church, a tiny offshoot of the United Methodist Church in the United States, came into Guatemala, the original four denominations agreed to include them in the territorial division. They gave to the new church the Department of Totonicapán and part of El Quiché, which the Methodists were to share with the Presbyterians: Coke (1978), p. 190; James Hudson interview; Pauline Burgess Sywulka interview; Lovell and Christopher Lutz (1990), pp. 32–51.

30. Lovell and Christopher Lutz (1990), p. 37.

31. Bogenschield (1992), p. 151.

32. Handy (1984), p. 79.

33. Haymaker (1947), p. 30.

34. Ibid.; *CAB* 18 (1912): 6.

35. Haymaker (1947), p. 30; Archivo General de Centro América, Ministerio de Relaciones Exteriores, "Religiosos y asuntos religiosos," signatura B104-17, legajo 8319.

36. Haymaker (1947), p. 30.

37. Canfield interview.

38. Presbyterian missionaries began publishing *El Mensajero* from Guatemala City in 1889, and *El Noticiero Evangélico* from Quetzaltenango prior to 1915. *El Mensajero* was also published in English as *The Messenger*.

39. *CAB*, no. 140 (1925): 2; *CAB*, no. 178 (1931): 20; *CAB*, no. 194 (1934): 5; *El Cristiano* 34(380): 8; *El Cristiano* 35(384): 8.

40. Archivo General de Centro América, Ministerio de Relaciones Exteriores, "Religiosos y asuntos religiosos," signatura B104-17, legajo 8317.

41. Amilcar Madrid (1975), p. 84; *Harvester* 30(12): 1–6.

42. Virgilio Zapata Arceyuz (1982), p. 93; Izaguirre (1977), p. 6; *El Cristiano* 34(371): 4–5.

43. Bogenschield (1992), p. 105.

44. See, for example, "Qué es el Adventismo de Séptima Día? De dónde proviene? ¿Hacia dónde conduce?"; "Los Adventistas explicados," all in *CAB* 22 (14): 4.

45. The Plymouth Brethren came to Guatemala in 1917; see Albert Julian Lloret (1976), p. 185.

46. Dennis Teague (1975), pp. 59–60.

47. Bogenschield (1992), pp. 232, 233.

48. For insight into shifting religious affiliations in a contemporary context, see Lesley Gill (1993), pp. 180–198.

49. Teague (1975), pp. 16, 62–63; Samuel Cadwallader (n.d.), p. 27; Samuel Berberian (1980), pp. 12–13. In English, the name of this denomination is conventionally rendered in the singular when referring to a single church and in the plural when referring to the denomination at large. In Spanish, both individual congregations and the denomination are normally referred to in the plural.

50. For a careful and specific analysis of the Pentecostal movement, see Everett

Wilson (1997). For an example of independent effort, see Mattie Crawford (1922) about her eighteen-month hegira through Central America.

51. Teague (1975), p. 37; Anna Marie Dahlquist (1985), p. 121.

52. Teague (1975), pp. 59–61; Lloret (1976), p. 116; Cadwallader (n.d.), p. 27.

53. Teague (1975), pp. 62–63; Lloret (1976), p. 191.

54. *Harvester* 32(1–2): 3; Ríos Paredes (1982), p. 9.

55. *Harvester* 32(1–2): 3.

56. *CAB*, no. 115 (1921): 2.

57. *CAB*, no. 115 (1921): 8.

58. Haymaker (1947), p. 36.

59. "Comulgantes," *Libros de Actas* 1924, archives of the Iglesia Evangélica Nacional Presbiteriana Central, Guatemala City.

60. Tord Wallstrom (1955), p. 259.

61. Dana Munro (1918), p. 13.

62. *Harvester* 32(1–2): 3; *CAB* (1914), all issues; PBFM letters, 1903–1911, 1904.

63. McBath to PBFM, 14 July 1905, 7 January 1905, PBFM letters, 1903–1911.

64. PBFM to Guatemalan Mission, 8 December 1910, PBFM letters, 1903–1911.

65. *CAB* 17(1): 5–6.

66. McBath to PBFM, 6 January 1906, PBFM letters, 1903–1911.

67. "Roster of Pentecostal Mission, Southern Pentecostal Union and Nazarene Missionaries, 1901–1980," Iglesia del Nazareno National offices, typewritten, pp. 1–4, n.d.; Ray (n.d.).

68. McBath to PBFM, 14 July 1905, PBFM letters, 1903–1911.

69. *CAB* 17(1): 5–6; Canfield interview.

70. *CAB*, no. 117 (1921): 13.

71. Iglesia Evangélica Presbiteriana de Guatemala, *Apuntes para la Historia*, pp. 493–504; "Roster of Pentecostal Mission, Southern Pentecostal Union and Nazarene Missionaries, 1901–1980"; *CAB* (1891–1940), all issues.

72. Marroquín Vélez (1983), pp. 215–216.

3. ETHNICITY AND MISSION WORK

1. See Alan Knight (1989).

2. Some of the most influential Guatemalan indigenist writers include Batres Jáuregui (1894), J. García Granados (1927), and J. Fernando Juárez Muñoz (1931). For a more in-depth analysis of Guatemalan indigenism, see E. Barillas (1988) and Antonio Goubaud Carrera, ed. (1964).

3. I am indebted here to Richard N. Adams, who shared with me two as yet unpublished papers that greatly enhanced my understanding of this topic. See Adams and Hale (1991), and Adams (n.d.).

4. For a thorough discussion of the neo-Liberals' "Indian policy" in Guatemala, see McCreery (1983); McCreery in Carol A. Smith, ed. (1990), pp. 96–115.

5. McCreery (1990), pp. 107–108.

6. Alastair White (1973), p. 93.

7. McCreery (1990), p. 108; see also David Browning (1971), p. 208.

8. Jim Handy (1994), pp. 9–10. The impact of the new system should not be understated. Robert Carmack (1983) has estimated that the municipality of Momostenango provided approximately 336,000 man days of labor to plantations and public works projects annually (in Murdo MacLeod and Robert Wasserstrom, eds. [1983], pp. 242–243).

9. See Handy (1984), p. 79. For contemporary, partisan accounts of the development of agrarian capitalism during the Estrada Cabrera period, see Felipe Estrada Paniagua (1904) and Raul Agüero (1914).

10. Haymaker (1917), pp. 39–40.

11. Ibid., no page.

12. *CAB* 18(20): 19.

13. *CAB* 2(3): 1.

14. Iglesia Evangélica Presbiteriana de Guatemala, *Apuntes para la Historia*, p. 82.

15. McBath to PBFM, 23 May 1913, PBFM letters, 1903–1911.

16. *CAB* 14(4): 5–6.

17. George Lovell and Christopher Lutz estimate that the Maya constituted 67 percent of the national population between 1893 and 1921. These figures are taken from official census records recorded in Francis Gall, ed. (1976–1983). See also George Lovell and Christopher Lutz (1994).

18. *CAB*, no. 103 (1919): 11. Cameron Townsend and his wife, a Swede, were very much hindered by a lack of training in linguistic field methods, as might be expected. The obstacles they encountered in this project anticipated those faced by missionaries of other denominations who attempted to elicit grammars and dictionaries for the complex Maya languages. In 1920, Mrs. Townsend plaintively wrote in the *CAB* (no. 110: 14–15): "Do pray that we may quickly learn this awful language. With no grammar or books of any kind from which to study, it is indeed hard. We have a little book of our own in which we mark down different words and phrases they, the Indians, tell us when we visit them. However, some of the words have such awful sounds that it is impossible to write them down. But surely the day of the Cakchiquels is the Lord's just as much as English, Spanish, or Swedish, and we know that he will give us this Indian language that we may soon be able to explain the Gospel to them in their own tongue."

19. David Scotchmer (1991), pp. 98–99.

20. Ibid., pp. 99–100.

21. Birchard to Garrard, 23 January 1985.

22. *CAB* 3(1): 6.

23. David Stoll (1982), p. 40.

24. Amilcar Madrid (1975), p. 83.

25. *CAB* 18(1): 20–21; Ruth Bunzel (1952), p. x; Oliver La Farge (1947), p. 101.

26. *CAB* 1 (1904): 6; *CAB* 13 (1907): 11.

27. *El Protestante* (August 1910, November 1910, March 1911).

28. *El Cristiano* (1907, all issues); see also Ríos Paredes (1982), p. 5; Lloret (1976), p. 77; *CAB* (1900–1920), all issues; PBFM to Guatemala Mission, 10 June 1910, PBFM letters, 1903–1911.
29. McBath to PBFM, 25 February 1905, PBFM letters, 1903–1911.
30. Mecham (1966), p. 370; see also pp. 318–319. Edward L. Cleary and Hannah Stewart-Gambino, eds. (1992), p. 170.
31. Cleary and Stewart-Gambino (1992), p. 170; Oliver La Farge (1927): 476–495, cited in La Farge (1947), p. xii.
32. Louis Luzbetak (1966).
33. Sandra Orellana (1975).
34. See Robert M. Hill II (1989).
35. First quotation from David McCreery (1992). For elucidation on the evolution of the *guachibales* as distinct entities, see Robert Hill II and John Monaghan (1987). Second quotation from McCreery (1992), p. 15.
36. Adams and Hale (1991), p. 44; and Carmack, "State and Community in Nineteenth-Century Guatemala," in Carol A. Smith, ed. (1990), pp. 116–140.
37. See Adams (n.d.), p. 36.
38. Sol Tax (1953). A classic case study of the redistributive function of the *cofradía* is Frank Cancian (1965). Handy (1994, p. 141) writes: "The survey of fifty-six municipalities conducted by the Instituto Indigenista Nacional in the 1940s and 1950s revealed the varying strengths of the traditional village structures. Few municipalities had elected an Indian as first *alcalde* for decades before the revolution. In many the cofradías no longer performed important functions and the *principales* no longer met, nor were they consulted when major decisions needed to be made." This suggests a precipitous decline in the external political influence of the *cofradía,* but it does not provide much evidence about the cultural and spiritual hegemony that the brotherhoods may or may not have continued to maintain. Manning Nash, in his study of Cantel in the mid-1950s (1958, pp. 88–89), suggests that the *cofradía* was going through what he believes to be a "cycle" of distress, as evidenced by the increasing difficulty in filling the posts in the civil-religious hierarchy. He notes, however, that, despite this decline, the community at large—excluding the village's 161 Protestant families— "still subscribe[s] to the value system of cofradía support, to cofradía importance, and to the necessity for religious brotherhoods, and because of the important role such a system plays in structuring the entire society. . . . It is the one mechanism . . . which relates family to family in an orderly manner and enables members of the community to relate to one another in the customary formal manner . . . [Cantel residents] believe that the community must be in harmony with the saints and the special provinces they control, and that this harmony can be achieved through the care of the saints by the cofradías in the public name."
39. Rojas Lima (1988), p. 83; quotation from James C. Scott (1986).
40. The percentage Protestant comes from a partisan and polemical source, the Roman Catholic paper *Acción Social Cristiana* (30 December 1948). It seems ac-

curate, however, when held up alongside the statistics that appear in Grubb (1937), a work that was published by a British mission society and is thus equally biased in its own way. See also *CAB* 18(20): 19.

41. Bogenschield (1992), pp. 201, 202–204.
42. Bogenschield notes (ibid., pp. 201–202) that the first recorded Ki'che Protestant in Cantel was Pedro Poz Raimundo, a policeman who converted while serving in the local militia in 1909. Poz was baptized by Paul Burgess at the Presbyterian mission in Quetzaltenango. The seminal study of Cantel is Manning Nash (1958), which is based on fieldwork conducted over a fourteen-month period in the mid-1950s. Nash was primarily interested in observing the impact of industrialization on a "traditional" community.
43. Adams (n.d.), p. 12.
44. M. Nash (1958), pp. 18–19.
45. Ibid., p. 85; Bogenschield (1992), p. 201.
46. Bogenschield (1992), p. 205.
47. Cited in ibid., p. 172.
48. Asturias (1923), p. 32; La Farge (1947), p. 100.
49. Adams (n.d.), pp. 14–17; J. J. Fernando (1931); Juárez Muñoz (1931), pp. 81–85, 159–166.
50. Cited in Robert Abzug (1994), p. 86.
51. By the late 1800s, the equation of Christian (Protestant) identity and temperance in the United States was further enhanced by subtle nativist sentiments, a reaction against the foreigners—mostly Mediterranean Catholics and Eastern European Jews, who clung to conventional Old World attitudes about alcohol, among other alien practices—who immigrated in vast numbers to the United States during the final decades of the century. By the early twentieth century, temperance was so encoded with Protestant, American identity that it was universally promoted by American missionaries abroad, even by those from denominations that took a more moderate view of alcohol use in general. For a classic study of the growth of the North American temperance movement, see J. A. Krout (1925).
52. Dahlquist (1985), p. 168.
53. Quotation from Blake (1972), p. 447. While at McCormick, Burgess imbibed the ideas of progressive activists like William Jennings Bryan and Jane Adams. Around the time of his graduation, Burgess became enamored of socialism and even published several articles in *Christian Socialist* (Dahlquist, 1985, pp. 30–50).
54. Bogenschield (1992), p. 174–179.
55. John M. Watanabe (1992), chaps. 3–5.

4. PROTESTANTS AND POLITICS

1. *CAB* (1920): 1; Ríos Paredes (1982), p. 6.
2. "Revisión de valores políticos," *El Unionista*.

3. This is not to put too fine a point on the situation. Handy estimates that under José María Orellana, president from 1921 to 1926, some 290 political dissidents were killed by order of his minister of war, Jorge Ubico. The peaceful conveyance of the presidential sash to Lázaro Chacón in 1926 may be better attributed to Orellana's sudden death from a heart attack than to democratic impulses. See Handy (1984), pp. 88–89, and Kenneth Grieb (1979), p. 3.

4. See Marc Christian McLeod (1993), pp. 59, 69, 71; Woodward (1985), p. 209.

5. Handy (1994), p. 49.

6. Asturias (1923), cited in ibid. For a thorough discussion of indigenism during the 1920–1940 period, see Dennis R. Casey (1979).

7. Stoll (1982), p. 31.

8. "Acontecimientos recientes," *El Noticiero* 11(12): 1; *El Unionista* article cited in Blakeney (1956), p. 62.

9. See Stoll (1982).

10. *CAB,* no. 103 (1919): 11; *CAB,* no. 140 (1925): 2; *CAB,* no. 178 (1931): 20; *CAB,* no. 194 (1934): 5; *El Cristiano* 34(380): 8; *El Cristiano* 35(384): 8.

11. Lloret (1976), p. 82; Pauline Burgess Sywulka interview.

12. In 1944, the school was attached jointly to the Primitive Methodist Mission and moved to Santa Cruz del Quiché. See Paul Burgess (1957), pp. 49–50.

13. *CAB,* no. 140 (1925): 2; *CAB,* no. 178 (1931): 20; *CAB,* no. 194 (1934): 5; Scotchmer, "Symbols," pp. 102–104.

14. Georgina R. Allcott (1970), p. 57; Archivo General de Centro América, Ministerio de Relaciones Exteriores, "Inscripciones de extranjeros," signatura B104-17, legajo 8315–8320.

15. Piero Gleijeses (1991), p. 11; Handy (1984), pp. 89–90; see also Grieb (1979), p. 12.

16. Ubico quoted by Carlos Samayoa Chinchilla (1950), pp. 62, 107, in Gleijeses (1991), p. 18. See also Gleijeses (1991), pp. 8–29. An excellent study of Ubico's background prior to his presidency is Joseph Pitti (1975).

17. Archivo General de Centro América, Ministerio de Gobernación, carta no. 100, Jorge Ubico to Ministerio de Gobernación, 18 November 1931; Archivo General de Centro América, Ministerio de Relaciones Exteriores 542, "Inscripciones de extranjeros"; Zapata (1982), p. 62; Haymaker (1947), p. 45.

18. Handy (1984), p. 94.

19. Archivo General de Centro América, Ministerio de Relaciones Exteriores 542, "Inscripciones de extranjeros."

20. See Thomas P. Anderson (1971).

21. Rodolfo Barón Castro (1942) in Adams and Hale (1991), p. 20.

22. Gleijeses (1991), p. 12. Demitrio Coxtí Cuxil has noted that the falsification of ethnicity census data is not unusual in Guatemala, as the censuses "do not provide trustworthy data because their goal is not to reflect the reality of the Indian nationalities but rather to produce results that conform to Ladino expectations: hide and minimize the existence of the Indian population" ("Los censos nacionales de población: ¿medios de opresión de pueblo indio?" *A Saber* 1 [1990] 36, cited in Fischer and Brown [1996], p. 18).

23. Adams and Hale (1991), p. 29. For a description of this process in one community, see Ricardo Falla (1978), pp. 288–289.
24. Handy (1984), pp. 97–98.
25. Adams and Hale (1991), p. 27; George Lovell (1988): 25–27.
26. Gleijeses (1991), p. 17.
27. Dahlquist (1977); idem (1985), pp. 125–130; Pauline Burgess Sywulka interview; Grieb (1979), pp. 79–80.
28. See Grieb (1979), pp. 67–81.
29. "Los católicos diocesanos del pueblo de Guatemala"; Anita Frankel (1969), p. 193.
30. "Undertow" (1983). In 1941, to demonstrate his dedication to the Allied cause, the president took action against the Evangelisch-Lutheranische Landeskirche, the German Lutheran Church in Guatemala City. He deported the pastor to Germany and dissolved the congregation. See Clarence T. Kuehn (1950).
31. Gleijeses (1991), pp. 17–18.
32. Archivo General de Centro América, Ministerio de Relaciones Exteriores, signatura B99-34-13, legajo 6901, "Colonización," affidavit, 21 July 1933; *Harvester* 31(7): 7; Pauline Burgess Sywulka interview; Birchard to Garrard, 23 January 1985; Guerra interview; *Anunciador Evangélico* 2(13): 10; *Boletín de la Iglesia Evangélica Nacional Presbiteriana Central* 11(45): 4; Grieb (1979), p. 48. For their part, the Protestant missionaries responded to their new status with a certain nervous obsequiousness. The Presbyterian journals began to run large photographs of the caudillo on their front pages, while the Quakers' *Harvester* published effusive felicitations on Ubico's birthday each November 4. Eventually, it became a tradition for the Evangelical Synod to send the president a birthday telegram each year, which he always acknowledged with exaggerated courtesy.
33. See Grieb (1979), p. 48.
34. "Comunistas convertadas," *El Cristiano* 32(355): 1–2; "Convertido del comunismo," *El Noticiero Evangélico* 35(355): 1; "La religión, el ópio del pueblo," *Harvester* 22(154): 3; "Asesinado por los comunistas," *Harvester* 30 (1936): 3–4; "El comunismo," *El Mensajero* 30(4): 1–2; "Dos mundos en conflicto," *El Cristiano* 34(369): 1–2. A number of articles heralded Chiang Kai-Shek, who was a Methodist, as a shining example of appropriate democratic leadership for a Third World nation. See, for example, "Chiang-Kai Chek," *El Noticiero Evangélico* 23(158): 1.
35. *Boletín de la Iglesia Evangélica Nacional Presbiteriana Central* (3 March 1929, 18 September 1938).
36. "Dios en la formación de una nación," *Rayitos de Luz* (4 July 1937): 733; "Dios provee un caudillo," *Rayitos de Luz* (11 July 1937): 735; "Dios anima a un caudillo," *Rayitos de Luz* (18 July 1937): 738; see also "Dios requiere justicia social," *Rayitos de Luz* (5 September 1935); "El lugar de la religión en la vida de una nación," *Rayitos de Luz* (22 August 1937).

37. Archivo General de Centro América, Ministerio de Relaciones Exteriores 542, "Inscripciones de extranjeros"; "Ingresos de religiosos."
38. Handy (1984), p. 105.

5. THE REVOLUTIONARY YEARS

1. Thomas M. Leonard (1984), p. 84; Stephen Schlesinger and Stephen Kinzer (1983), p. 37; Thomas Melville and Marjorie Melville (1971), pp. 27–32; Richard Immerman (1982), pp. 43–57; Leo A. Suslow (1949).
2. Juan José Arévalo Bermejo (1946), pp. 147–149, cited in Handy (1984), p. 25.
3. Handy (1994), pp. 24, 50.
4. Ibid., p. 25.
5. Gleijeses (1991), p. 33; Antonio Guerra interview.
6. The Catholic weekly *Acción Social Cristiana* (30 December 1948) estimated that the Protestant population in 1945 was somewhere around 2 percent. The 2 percent figure actually seems excessive when compared with the statistics that appear in Kenneth Grubb (1937). Grubb placed the number of Protestants in Guatemala in 1937 at 40,657, out of a total population of 2.2 million (p. 67).
7. Fischer in Fischer and Brown (1996), p. 73.
8. See Goubaud Carrera (1964), introduction.
9. Fischer in Fischer and Brown (1996), p. 73. Adrián Inés Chávez, an indigenous scholar and autodidact in indigenous language pedagogy, presented his alphabet to the Primera Convención de Maestros Indígenas de Guatemala in Cobán in June 1945. He believed that orthographic revision was necessary to "reveal the beauty of the language." Chávez constructed the alphabet so that it could be used to write not only Ki'ché, but all Mayan languages, thus stressing linguistic and Mayan unity. The government declined use of the alphabet, perhaps because of these very implications, or because of the orthographic complexity of the alphabet. Chávez is now considered to be one of the intellectual progenitors of the contemporary pan-Maya movement (ibid., p. 57).
10. Handy (1994), p. 71.
11. *Boletín de la Iglesia Evangélica Nacional Presbiteriana Central* (23 March 1947); *Harvester* 56(1): 4; *Harvester* 27(3): 6–1; *CAB*, no. 266 (1946): 3; *Mensajero Evangélico* 41(5): 23.
12. Minutes of Meeting of the Guatemala Station, 3 January 1945, Iglesia Evangélica Nacional Presbiteriana (hereafter IENP); Doyle Brewington to Paul Burgess, 24 March 1945, IENP; PBFM to Guatemala Mission no. 302, 3 January 1946, p. 3, IENP; *CAB*, no. 266 (1946): 3; *Harvester* 26(12–1): 10; "Resultados de la campaña de alfabetización por el comité del sínodo," *El Cristiano* 42(472): 5–6.
13. Minutes of the Annual Meeting, October 1945, p. 1, IENP; *El Mensajero* 41(2): 18; *PAN* 3(2): 3.

14. *PAN* 3(2): 3.
15. *Noticiero Evangélico* 30(276): 9-10; "A Mission's Contribution to the Indian Problems of Guatemala," *Guatemala News* 39(3-4): 3; *CAB*, no. 266 (1946): 3.
16. *PAN* 2(8): 1, 4; *Mensajero Evangélico* 41(7): 23-25; *El Mensajero* 39(10): 5; *El Mensajero* 39(9): 4; Paul Winn to Virginia Garrard, 12 February 1985.
17. See Archer C. Bush (1950); R. L. Woodward (1962); Schlesinger and Kinzer (1983), pp. 38-39; Melville and Melville (1971), p. 31.
18. T. N. Harer to PBFM, 27 August 1944, IENP.
19. Kuehn (1950), p. 42. In this case, the gesture may have been less an embrace of Protestant missions than a demonstration of the regime's new political openness and a signal of the readmission of German Guatemalans back into the body politic.
20. Minutes of the Annual Meeting of the Guatemala Mission: Report to the General Assembly of the Presbyterian Church, May 1944, IENP; Kuehn (1950), p. 42; Schlesinger and Kinzer (1983), pp. 38-39; Melville and Melville (1971), p. 31.
21. *Noticiero Evangélico* 29(263): 110-111.
22. Enyart (1970), p. 65.
23. Paul Burgess to PBFM, 3 November 1950, IENP.
24. Narrative Report of the Guatemala Station, 1949, IENP.
25. The Rev. Robert F. Gussick of the Lutheran Missouri Synod came to Guatemala at the suggestion of a German Lutheran chaplain he had met at an internment camp in North Dakota during World War II. Lutheranism first came to Guatemala in 1907, when the Deutsch-Evangelisches Pfarramt Kirchlich sent a pastor to minister to Germans living in Guatemala City and Alta and Baja Verapaz. In 1929, the German Lutherans established a permanent church, the Evangelisches-Lutheranische La Epifania, in Guatemala City. The Deutsch-Evangelisches Pfarramt Kirchlich continued to supply pastors until World War II prevented them from doing so. See "Gründungs-ffestgottesdienst," *Evangelisches Gemeindeblatt für Guatemala ünd das ubrige Mittelamerika deutsch-Evangelischen Epifania-gemeinde Guatemala* 6(20): 3-4; "Amtsreise," *Evangelisches Gemeindeblatt* 5(5): 4; Clifton Holland (1981), p. 75.
26. Kuehn (1950), pp. 21-23, 43-45, 82-83. The Anglican Church, also known as the Church of England or, in the United States, the Episcopal Church, had maintained a presence in Guatemala since the mid-nineteenth century, although no Anglican clergy were registered as resident in the republic until 1918. Anglican congregations, which were made up almost exclusively of British citizens and banana workers who had come to Guatemala from Jamaica, were under the jurisdiction of the Diocese of British Honduras and were served by priests who resided in what is now Belize. Anglican services were conducted in English; the denomination made few attempts to proselytize among Spanish speakers because they were already Christians, albeit Catholics. This policy was codified at the Edinburgh Conference in 1916, when the Church of England officially removed Roman Catholic Latin America from its missionary agenda.

See "Calendar of Selected Documents on Rafael Carrera 1838–1865," British Foreign Office 15/19, Wyke to Claredon, 30 April 1856; *Christian Work in Latin America: Report of Commission I, II, III to Congress of Christian Work in Latin America, Panama, February 1916* (1916), p. 6; "The Diocese of British Honduras," *The Honduras Evangel* (March 1918), from archives of the British and Foreign Bible Society, London.

27. Enyart (1970), pp. 15–16.
28. Cadwallader (n.d.), p. 29; Kuehn (1950), p. 13; "Aclaración," *El Anunciador Evangélico* 5(49–51): 5.
29. "Aniversario de la obra bautista en Guatemala," *Nueva Era Bautista* 42(1): 3–4; Cadwallader (n.d.), pp. 37–42.
30. Jorge Enrique Díaz (1975), pp. 108–110.
31. Frankel (1969), p. 194. Quotation from Allcott, p. 29.
32. *CAB*, no. 279 (1948): 16.
33. Opus Dei was founded in Spain in 1928 by Josemaría Escrivá de Balaguer, a priest from Madrid, as a religious sodality designed to combat liberal theological and social trends through codified pious discipline and devotion. In 1934, Escrivá published a book of spiritual maxims entitled *Consideraciones espirituales: el camino*, which, among many other things, embodied the central precepts of national Catholicism. See Michael Walsh (1989). Catholic Action was established by Pius XI as a lay organization to be run under the direct control of diocesan bishops. Catholic Action was chartered to "work . . . where religion or morals are directly or indirectly related to the good of the individual or the community, or the universal good of the Church." Although expressly defined by the church to be a nonpolitical movement, Catholic Action organized along class lines and particularly focused its efforts among labor and students, two groups thought to be susceptible to the lures of socialist or secular ideologies; see Robert C. Broderick, ed. (1987), pp. 98, 99. See also Edward Cleary (1986), p. 108.
34. The central premise of National Catholicism was the indivisible dual identity of Spanish and Catholic. In the words of one historian, "Love of country was to be associated with the rejection of all heterodoxy, Protestant or Jewish, liberal or socialist. Religious faith and political identity were one" (Walsh 1989, pp. 42–43). See also Frances Lannon (1982), pp. 467–590.
35. "Aclaraciones del Exmo. y Revmo. Sr. Arzobispo Metropolitano, sobre la recta y firme postura de la iglesia de Guatemala con relación al presente momento político y protesta por las insidiosas calúmnias de partidos políticos contra el clero de nuestro país," in Hubert J. Miller (1988).
36. "Los católicos diocesanos del pueblo de Guatemala"; Frankel (1969), pp. 169–170, 192, 193.
37. María Cobos Batres (1945); "Los católicos diocesanos del pueblo de Guatemala."
38. Narrative Report of the Guatemala Station, 1949, IENP; Leonard (1984), pp. 75–80, 96.

39. Dahlquist, p. 159; Leonard (1984), pp. 75–106.
40. Arbenz himself always denied any association with the Communist Party. His wife, however, was openly affiliated with the Salvadoran Party, and several of his prominent advisers were Communists. These associations are what provoked the U.S. secretary of state, John Foster Dulles, to make his famous remark regarding Arbenz's communist sympathies: "If it walks like a duck and quacks like a duck, it's a duck."
41. Burgess to PBFM, 20 September 1950, IENP.
42. Archivo General de Centro América, Ministerio de Relaciones Exteriores 565, "Ingresos de religiosos," March 1953.
43. "Informe anual del Instituto Lingüístico de Verano en Guatemala, 1983 (1984), p. 7; Fischer and Brown (1996), p. 57.
44. Burgess to Ruth Wardel, 18 November 1950, IENP; Archivo General de Centro América, Ministerio de Relaciones Exteriores 565, "Ingresos de religiosos."
45. Burgess to Ruth Wardel, 18 November 1950, IENP; Archivo General de Centro América, Ministerio de Relaciones Exteriores 565, "Ingresos de religiosos."
46. Archivo General de Centro América, Ministerio de Relaciones Exteriores 565, "Ingresos de religiosos."
47. Handy (1994), p. 90.
48. The historiography of the showdown between the U.S. government and the Arbenz administration over the UFCO expropriations is extensive. Two good studies that examine the international dimensions are Immerman (1982) and Schlesinger and Kinzer (1983). Two excellent and more recent works that offer fresh perspectives on the "ten years of spring" are Gleijeses (1991) and Handy (1994).
    Perhaps nothing captures the polemics of this issue as vividly as the studies of the Arbenz overthrow written in its immediate aftermath. Few contemporary topics have attracted so much debate or scholarly attention and acrimony. Some of the most noteworthy of these include Juan José Arévalo Bermejo (1961); Luis Cardoza y Aragón (1954); Manuel Galich (1956); Daniel James (1954); Ronald M. Schneider (1958); Stacy May and Galo Plaza (1958).
49. Annual Report, La Patria School, 1953, IENP.
50. Northern Presbytery Annual Report, 1954, IENP.
51. "Aclaraciones," in Miller (1988), pp. 6–7.
52. CAB, no. 318 (1953): 10; Presbyterian Board to Guatemala, 21 February 1950; Minutes of the Executive Committee, 12 September 1951, IENP; Boletín de la Iglesia Evangélica Nacional Presbiteriana Central (1 June 1952, 8 June 1952, 5 July 1953, 6 December 1953).
53. Verbum (25 September 1949): 1–2, in Miller (1988), pp. 101–11.
54. Jim Handy (1994, p. 150) notes that the "Arbenz administration did not advocate the expropriation of all community land, nor was it interred in promoting a wholesale transform of municipal land to comunidades or the state. Nevertheless, substantial municipal land was denounced and 297,460 manzanas were taken."

55. *CAB*, no. 276 (1948): 13; Handy (1994), pp. 54–55. For a more thorough account of this incident, see idem (1989).
56. Falla (1978), pp. 27–47; see also Rubén E. Reina (1960); Stoll (1982), p. 48; Roland Ebel (1970); idem (1988), pp. 174–194.
57. "Carta Abierta, Cantel Enero 1954, A los politicastros evangélicos: David Ordóñez Colop, Gabriel Sam Chuc, Obispo Salanic Salanic, Felipe Santiago Colop García, Juan Itcep y otros, con motivo de la manifestación de los 'revolsos' no REVOLUCIONARIA del 13 de diciembre próximo pasado," IENP (original emphasis).
58. M. Nash, pp. 130–131. The configuration of political parties here comes from Nash's study, which was based on fieldwork done in 1952. It is confusing, because some of the parties described in this section seem to show up in Cantel before they appear on the scene nationally. (Most notable among these is the PAR, which did not become a national party until 1952.) Jim Handy has suggested that Nash may have projected back and labeled the existing political parties and entities with contemporary names (Handy to Garrard-Burnett, July 1996).
59. M. Nash (), pp. 135–136. A detailed account of the electoral alliances and results is found in idem (1958), pp. 130–136.
60. M. Nash (), p. 78. Nash estimates that there were between 450 and 500 Protestants in Cantel when he did his fieldwork, but he admits that his figures are imprecise: "No one is sure exactly how many Protestants there are in the municipio, due to only partial commitment by some of those who attend Protestant churches. The best count I could get, [is] based on reported membership by the Protestants themselves and on the Catholic priest's counteroffensive . . . The largest group is the Presbyterian, next the Cramerista, then the Adventists, and finally the Pentecostals."
61. M. Nash (1958), p. 78; "Presbyterian Agrarians," *Guatemala News* 44(6) (1953): 3–5.
62. "Presbyterian Agrarians," *Guatemala News* 44(6) (1953): 3–5; *Guatemala News* 45(1) (1954): 3; W. Stanley Rycroft (1954), p. 354.
63. "Confidential Crisis Strategy," from PBFM, IENP; PBFM to Stanley Wick, 2 March 1953, IENP.
64. Unnamed writer to PBFM, 25 June 1954, IENP; PBFM to Robert Thorpe, 24 June 1954, IENP.
65. Schlesinger and Kinzer (1983), p. 42; *Guatemala News* 43(1) (1954): 3.
66. Archivo General de Centro América, Ministerio de Relaciones Exteriores 565, "Ingresos de religiosos," 16 August 1952, 16 July 1951, 22 July 1950, 4 September 1953, 24 July 1952, 16 July 1951, 24 July 1952, 16 August 1952.
67. Archivo General de Centro América, Ministerio de Relaciones Exteriores 565, "Ingresos de religiosos," 22 July 1950, 16 July 1951, 24 July 1952, 16 August 1952, 4 September 1953.
68. Archivo General de Centro América, Ministerio de Relaciones Exteriores 565, "Ingresos de religiosos," 16 July 1951, 16 August 1952.
69. Christmas letter from the Paul Burgess family, 1954, IENP.

6. THE POSTREVOLUTIONARY YEARS

1. Canfield interview.
2. See Immerman (1982), pp. 173–186; Schlesinger and Kinzer (1983), pp. 203–255; Melville and Melville (1971), pp. 83–119.
3. "New Government," *Guatemala News* 45(4): 2; "Religious Freedom in Guatemala," *Guatemala News* 46(5): 6–7.
4. "Manifesto al Pueblo de Guatemala," *El Imparcial* (2 June 1955).
5. Stanley Wick to Stanley Rycroft, 7 July 1954, IENP.
6. Mecham (1966), pp. 320–321; Adams (1970), p. 310.
7. Mecham (1966), p. 320; *Guatemala News* 49(4) (1955): 1; Kay B. Warren (1978), p. 90.
8. Robert Thorpe to PBFM, 15 May 1955, IENP; Archivo General de Centro América, Ministerio de Relaciones Exteriores 565, "Ingresos de religiosos," 30 September 1954.
9. "Mínimo de libertades perdidas por las Iglesias Evangélicas de Guatemala," *El Imparcial* (12 November 1954).
10. Falla (1978), p. 39.
11. For the Mam incident, see *El Noticiero Evangélico* 34(5): 4. Concerning the incident in El Quiché, see *Guatemala News* 45(4): 6. Regarding the Santiago Atitlán incident, see Falla (1978), pp. 34–35.
12. Alianza Evangélica, "Protesta contra hostilidades a los evangélicos," *El Imparcial* (2 September 1956).
13. Agustín Estrada Monroy (1979), p. 504; Falla (1978), p. 427. The tally of clergy was given by Bishop García Caballeros in his 1944 address to a national congress on priestly vocations, as cited by Hubert J. Miller (1997). On Rossell's deployment of Catholic Action, see Warren (1978), p. 88.
14. Adams (1970), p. 295.
15. See Bruce J. Calder (1970).
16. Calder in Watanabe (1978), p. 195.
17. Watanabe (1978), p. 203, quoted in Warren (1978), chap. 4. Warren's analysis of Catholic Action in San Andrés offers invaluable insight into the impact of Catholic Action on one indigenous community, and I am indebted to her for much of the material set forth in this section. See also Falla (1978), pp. 288–290.
18. Douglas E. Britnall (1979b), p. 147; Peter Berger (1967).
19. Warren (1978), p. 87.
20. Iglesia Evangélica Presbiteriana de Guatemala, *Apuntes para la Historia*, p. 259; "La obra con los Kek'chis," Iglesia Evangélica Nacional Presbiteriana, pamphlet.
21. Allcott (1970), p. 64; Rubem César Fernandes (1981); Enrique Domínguez and Deborah Huntington (1984), p. 13.
22. Jean-Pierre Bastian (1981); Allcott (1970), pp. 80–88.
23. Mecham (1966), p. 427.

24. See Ralph Winter (n.d.); "La cruz o la hora," *El Estudiante Bíblico* 10(3–6); "Comunismo en la Iglesia," *El Noticiero Evangélico* (1962): 13; *CAB*, no. 319 (1955): 15; "Dios y gobierno," *El Noticiero Evangélico* (June 1963): 9. See also "Nuestra responsabilidad cristiana hacia el gobierno," *El Noticiero Evangélico* (May 1963): 5–6; "Será un lindo paraíso mi nación," *El Noticiero Evangélico* (March 1963): 18.

25. Bastian (1981), pp. 7–12.

26. Domínguez and Huntington (1984), pp. 13–14; Bastian (1981), pp. 7–12; Fernandes (1981), pp. 29–39; *Guatemala News* 53(3): 4–5; Robert Lawrence (1983), pp. 34–40.

27. *CAB*, no. 266 (1946): 22; *CAB*, no. 377 (1948): 2; *El Noticiero Evangélico* 29(259): 6; Archivo General de Centro América, Ministerio de Relaciones Exteriores 565, "Ingresos de religiosos," 11 September 1953; *Harvester* 5(4): 45.

28 Domínguez and Huntington (1984), p. 15; Ríos Paredes (1982), pp. 13–14; "La manipulación de la religión en Guatemala: testimonio del sector 'Libertad de Conciencia y Religión' de la Comisión de Derechos Humanos de Guatemala" (no year).

29. Even so, the CAM's growth during this period was fairly modest. Church records report an annual growth rate of 7.3 percent in 1965, compared to 3 percent in 1960 (*CAB*, no. 403 [1967]: 10–11). On sociopolitical factors, see Rafael Baltodano interview.

30. Handy (1984), p. 154; Domínguez and Huntington (1984), p. 16; see also Miguel Ydígoras Fuentes (1963); G. E. Aguilar Peralta (1971); George Black, Milton Jamail, and Norma Stoltz Chinchilla (1984). The best overall study of Guatemala in the 1960s remains Adams (1970). On the evangelicals' response to the counterinsurgency campaign, see Fernandes (1981).

31. Handy (1984), p. 150.

32. Ibid., p. 160.

33. Sheldon Annis (1987), p. 140.

34. James Painter (1987), p. 13; Guatemala, Dirección General de Estadística (1985), p. 45.

35. The first government-sponsored project to colonize the Petén was under Arévalo, who initiated a project in Poptún in 1945 that failed because of bad communications and malaria. The project was revived in 1963 by General Peralta Azurdia, and then codified into the National Development Plan for 1965–1969 (Peter Calvert, 1985, p. 150). See also Artimius Millet (1971). I have used as sources for this section Guy M. Lawson (1995) and Juanita Sundberg (1993). For the Ixcán, see James A. Morrissey (1978).

36. "Una nueva campaña de cooperativas," *El Noticiero Evangélico* 50(11): 11–12; "El nuevo programa de extensión agrícola," *El Noticiero Evangélico*, nos. 5–6 (November–December); *Official Minutes: California Yearly Meeting of Friends Church 1970–1973*, pp. 38–41.

37. Ruben Lores (1976): 4–6.

38. Minutes to the Annual Meeting of the Presbyterian Mission, 1945, IENP. On the native Presbyterian church, see Ríos Paredes (1982), p. 11; Lidia Solís de Mansilla interview. Quotation from Linn P. Sullenburger to PBFM, 20 February 1952, IENP.
39. William R. Read et al. (1969), p. 159; Allcott (1970), p. 41. On the closing of the American Hospital, see Guerra interview.
40. Ariel Curet-Cuevas (1954).
41. Hudson interview; Handy (1984), p. 152.
42. Chema de Muñoz interview; member of Asambleas de Dios, anonymous by request, interview held 6 March 1985 at Iglesia Asambleas de Dios Central in Guatemala City.
43. Chema de Muñoz interview.
44. Chema de Muñoz interview.
45. These denominations were Iglesia Getsemaní, Iglesia Jesús Viene, the Asociación Evangélica Interdenominacional, the Misión Evangélica Independiente, and a group that eventually joined the Southern Baptist Conference; see CAB, no. 403 (1967): 89; Cadwallader (n.d.), pp. 37–42; Corral Prieto (1984), pp. 33–40.
46. Corral Prieto (1984), p. 45; Ríos Paredes (1982), p. 18.
47. Berberian (1980), pp. 13–14.
48. Ríos Paredes (1982), pp. 17–18.
49. Samuel Berberian interview (18 March 1985).
50. Solís de Mansilla interview.
51. Harvey Cox (1995), p. 15.
52. Ríos Paredes (1982), pp. 18–19.

7. THE EARTHQUAKE AND THE CULTURE OF VIOLENCE

1. See Black, Jamail, and Stoltz Chinchilla (1984), p. 152.
2. Edgardo García interview.
3. Julian Lloret interview; Harold Ray interview.
4. García interview.
5. García interview.
6. The most notable of these relief agencies, some of which still operate in Guatemala, include the following: World Vision, a U.S.-based nondenominational and nonpolitical organization sponsored in part by the ministries of evangelists Jimmy Swaggart and Jerry Falwell, which focuses its efforts on community development and child care; Partners in the Americas, a nonsectarian group that unofficially helped channel aid from the U.S. embassy into the altiplano in and around Chimaltenango; Christian Children's Fund; the World Relief Committee of the Association of Evangelicals; Episcopal Presiding Bishop's Fund for World Relief; Norwegian Church Aid; Baptist World Relief; and Wycliffe Bible Translators/Summer Institute of Linguistics. Major local organizations

that emerged to cope with the disaster include the Coordinadora Cakchiquel Desarrollo Integral (CODAPI), a nondenominational agency that provided technical and health aid around Chimaltenango, and the Fundación Cristiana para la Educación y Desarrollo (FUNDACED), which originally provided housing to victims of the earthquake and later shifted its focus to reforestation and community development in highland areas affected by the civil war. See Proyecto Centroamericano de Estudios Socio-Religiosos (PROCADES) (1981), pp. 385–390; Lloret interview; Harris Whitbeck interview; "Consejos cristianos de agencias de desarrollo," *Esfuerzo* 84(2) (1983): 14.

7. Concerning church membership, see Domínguez and Huntington (1984), p. 26; "lámina por ánima" from Marlise Simons (1982), p. 112; "rice Christians" came out of the missionary experience in Asia in the interwar period, where church attendance and "conversions" ran high only as long as missions gave out food aid. The church membership statistics that appear in this and the following chapter, unless otherwise noted, are those compiled by PROCADES (Proyecto Centroamericano de Estudios Socio-Religiosos) and its sister organization, SEPAL (Servicio Evangelizador para América Latina), both of which are church-growth agencies that utilize the methodologies of the social sciences to analyze the efficacy of evangelism. In 1980, PROCADES's sponsoring organization, the Pasadena, California–based Institute for In-Depth Evangelization (IINDEF), conducted a study of Protestant work in Guatemala, the results of which were published in a directory in 1981. The directory listed 210 evangelical denominations (as opposed to individual congregations) and estimated the overall Protestant population of the country at 1,337,812, based on a formal report of 334,453 adult members multiplied by a factor of four. Although PROCADES justified the use of this mulitiplier to account for congregations in formation, children and other household members, and nonmembers who attended worship, the methodology has been faulted for inflating the actual numbers of Protestants in Guatemala. In *Is Latin America Turning Protestant?* (1970, pp. 337–338), David Stoll offers a more conservative estimate of 18.92 percent Protestant population in Guatemala in 1985, with a growth factor of 6.7 between 1960 and 1985. Stoll's estimates are based on figures derived by the Worldwide Evangelization Crusade, a British organization, and the World Christian Encyclopedia (1982), which multiplied church membership figures by a factor of 2.5. For further discussion of this issue, see Phillip Berryman (1994), pp. 146–147.

8. Holland (1981), p. 79.

9. See Bryan Roberts (1968) and Ruth A. Wallace (1975).

10. Estrada Monroy (1979), p. 672.

11. Adams (1970, pp. 137, 283–284) mentions that it is difficult to get a precise figure for the number of clergy in the country. For example, his source, the Conferencia Nacional de Religiosos y Religiosas de Guatemala's *Boletín Informativo y Tercer Informe General,* placed the number of clergy in February 1965 at 472 priests and brothers and 739 nuns; for summer 1965, however, it listed 470 priests and 775 nuns. This leads Adams to conclude that "precision may not be

necessary since the number is constantly changing." The total population of Guatemala in 1964 was 4,284,473, with an annual national growth rate of 3.1. See Domínguez and Huntington (1984), p. 119, for the priest-to-congregant ratio.

12. Carlos Martínez interview; Roberts (1968), pp. 761–762. A good analysis of the conjuncture of alcohol, conversion, and gender relations is found in Elizabeth E. Brusco (1995).

13. David Scotchmer (1989).

14. Although women often play important roles in these congregations, particularly in the offering of *testimonios,* and often make up the majority of the congregation, they almost never serve as pastors in Guatemala.

15. David Stoll (1993), p. 65. See also Gabriel Aguilera Peralta (1980); Berryman (1994), p. 108. For discussion of the organization and repression of trade unions during this period, see James A. Goldston (1989). For information on the founding and activities of the CUC, see Rigoberta Menchú (1984).

16. Sheldon H. Davis (1988), p. 27; Handy (1984), p. 176.

17. Beatriz Manz (1988), p. 15.

18. There is an extensive literature that outlines and critiques the changes wrought by Vatican II and the Medellín conference. A good study of Liberation Theology that deals in particular with the Guatemalan case is Phillip Berryman (1984). For a regionally based account of the aftermath of religious activism during the early 1980s, see Stoll (1993).

19. Berryman (1984), p. 15. Although he does not address his expulsion or relations with the guerrillas, one of the priests involved in this episode has written a useful political account of this period; see Melville and Melville (1971).

20. See Rachel Garst (1993).

21. Berryman (1984), pp. 107–108.

22. See Ricardo Falla (1994) for a vivid account of the war in this afflicted region. Falla wrote the first study in Spanish to document the violence of this period to be published in Guatemala itself (1992), and its revelations prompted considerable controversy in the country. See also Black, Jamail, and Stoltz Chinchilla (1984), p. 46.

23. Berryman (1984), pp. 101–111; *Iglesia Guatemalteca en el Exilio* (hereafter IGE), 1980–1985.

24. Richard Foulkes interview; Itzmar Rivera interview.

25. Hudson interview.

26. Guerra interview; Presbyterian layworker interview held 6 June in San José, Costa Rica, location withheld by request.

27. This is the verse from the New Testament on which some evangelicals base their aversion to political involvement. The biblical context of the verse is the Apostle Paul's warning to the early Christians suffering persecution around A.D. 57 not to resist Roman rule. A fuller rendering of the verse reads (Romans 13:1–5, Jerusalem Bible): "You must obey the governing authorities. Since all government comes from God, the civil authorities were appointed by God, and so anyone who resists authority is rebelling against God's decision, and such an

act is bound to be punished. Good behavior is not afraid of magistrates; only criminals have anything to fear. If you want to live without being afraid of authority, you must live honestly and authority may even honor you. The state is there to serve God for your benefit. If you break the law, however, you may well have fear; the bearing of the sword has its significance."

28. Anonymous Presbyterian layworker interview.

29. June Nash (1960).

30. Guerra interview.

31. United Presbyterian layworker interview held 4 June 1985 in San José, Costa Rica, location withheld by request; Samuel Berberian interview (18 March 1985). See also David Stoll (1985).

32. Arnoldo Dubón interview; *The Primitive Methodist Journal* (September 1982): 7.

33. Rivera interview; Dubón interview.

34. Dubón interview; interview with indigenous Presbyterian layworker; interview with pastor's wife, Iglesia Nacional.

35. Interview with North American Presbyterian layworker.

36. IGE bulletin (September 1982); publication of Direction, International Mission Board of the Primitive Methodist Church, 13–15 April 1982.

37. EGP communiqués, July 1980. Evangelicals did respond to the EGP's call to arms, but they were never sufficiently numerous to make up a separate cell of the organization and usually organized into ecumenical groups with radical Catholics. One of the most active ecumenical branches of the EGP was the Frente Vicente Menchú, named after one of the victims of the Spanish embassy fire (and father of 1992 Nobel Peace Prize winner Rigoberta Menchú), which operated around Quetzaltenango. Evangelicals also participated in the smaller revolutionary organizations. Radical evangelicals were particularly active in the guerrilla group that operated in the far western part of the country, the Organización del Pueblo en Armas (Organization of the People in Arms, ORPA). By 1981, enough evangelicals were involved in the guerrilla fronts that they formed an autonomous auxiliary organization called the Confraternidad Evangélica de Guatemala (Evangelical Brotherhood of Guatemala). See *En Comunión*, official publication of the Confraternidad Evangélica de Guatemala.

38. Stoll (1993), p. 102.

39. Falla (1994), p. 188.

8. THE PROTESTANT PRESIDENT

1. Ángel Aníbal Guevara, a general, member of the Democratic Institutional Party (Partido Institucional Democrático, PID), and Lucas's hand-picked successor, won the presidency in patently rigged elections in 1982. In a show of strained partnership, young officers in the army who did not like the way the Lucas regime was conducting the counterinsurgency war joined forces with the Christian Democrats and the MLN to prevent Guevara from taking office. See

Calvert (1985), p. III. See also Joseph Anfuso and David Sczepanski (1984), p. 20.

2. Woodward (1985), p. 245; *Directorio de la Provincia Eclesiástica de Guatemala, 1992–1994* (1994), p. 45. Early polls showed Ríos Montt to be ahead, but after television screens reporting the vote went blank, the final results were Kjell Laugerud (MLN), 41.2 percent, Ríos Montt (Democracia Cristiana), 35.7 percent; and Ernesto Paiz Novales (Partido Revolucionario), 23.1 percent. See Calvert (1985), p. 85; Gyl Catherine Wadge (1987), p. 43.

3. *Time* (5 May 1982): 30.

4. Jorge Serrano Elías interview; Whitbeck interview; Wadge (1987), p. 36.

5. Statement to the press from Iglesia Cristiana Verbo, 10 August 1983; Deborah Huntington (1983).

6. Jean-Marie Simon (1987), p. 121. See also Stoll (1990), pp. 191–192.

7. Serrano Elías interview; Víctor Gálvez Borrell (1991), p. 29. I am deeply indebted to the work of Alejandra Batres Grenados, whose work I have relied on heavily in this chapter. In an unpublished paper entitled, "Morality, Order, and Unity: The Experience of Ríos Montt in Guatemala" (1994), she has done a systematic study of the 1982–1983 Ríos Montt administration based largely on synopses of his Sunday night "sermons" published regularly in *El Imparcial* in 1982 and 1983.

8. "Ríos Montt señala causas que mantienen el empobrecimiento en que está el país," "Ríos Montt se califica como mismo, mayordomo del pueblo," *El Imparcial* (9 August 1982), p. 1; "Ahora o nunca, para un cambio en Guatemala, dijo Ríos Montt," *El Imparcial* (10 May 1982), p. 1; "5 militares cambaten los focos de subversión, dijo Ríos Montt," *El Imparcial* (19 July 1982), p. 1; Anfuso and Sczepanski (1984), p. 153.

9. "Juran 'no robar, no mentir, no abusar,'" *El Gráfico* (8 November 1982); "Funcionarios empleados honestos serán mejorados," *El Imparcial* (22 November 1982), p. 1; "Este gobierno tiene el compromiso de cambiar; no robo, no miento, no abuso," Guatemalan government press release, December 1982.

10. "Calmar sed de justicia preve Ríos Montt," *El Imparcial* (12 April 1982), p. 1; "Juicio a Lucas habrá caso de aumentarlo," *El Imparcial* (15 July 1982), p. 1; "Ahora o nunca, para un cambio en Guatemala, dijo Ríos Montt," *El Imparcial* (10 May 1982), p. 1.

11. Bernard Debusmann, "Guatemala City, July 15, 1982, Reuters North European Services; "Nosotros como gobierno aceptamos que hemos pecado y abusado del poder y por ello queremos reconciliarnos con el pueblo," *El Imparcial* (July 1982); "No habrá elecciones en el 84," *El Imparcial* (9 May 1983), p. 1.

12. "Ríos Montt defiende a los generales," *El Imparcial* (13 June 1983), p. 1.

13. Anfuso and Sczepanski (1984), p. 122; Serrano Elías interview; "Ningún asesinado a tiros hoy," *El Imparcial* (27 March 1982), p. 1.

14. "Policía juran no robar, no mentir, no abusar," *Prensa Libre* (18 December 1982).

15. Manz (1988), p. 15; Black, Jamail, and Stoltz Chinchilla (1984), p. 46.

16. Black, Jamail, and Stoltz Chinchilla (1984), pp. 166–167.
17. "President Efraín Ríos Montt of Guatemala has said that the state of siege which came into force on July 1st marks the start of the final battle against subversion," *Latin American Weekly Report* (10 July 1982); "General Efraín Ríos Montt believes he rules on mandate from God," Reuters North European Service, 8 August 1983.
18. Wadge (1987), p. 51; "Presidente se refiere al estado de sitio," *El Imparcial* (5 July 1983), p. 1; Beverly Treumann (1982), p. 281.
19. Although the Ríos Montt administration is justifiably associated with some of the most brutal slaughters of the scorched-earth campaign, some of the worst massacres committed by the army occurred in the last months of the Lucas administration. Some of the most notorious massacres in the Ixcán region occurred immediately prior to Ríos Montt's taking office. Although this list is by no means inclusive, these include the massacres in eastern Ixcán from February 13 to 28, in which around 100 people from 6 *aldeas* and cooperative settlements died; at Cuarto Pueblo, March 14–17, 1982, one week before Ríos Montt took power, in which at least 366 villagers died. The prototype for the systematic elimination of villages took place somewhat earlier, at San Francisco Nentón, where more than 300 villagers were executed by the military in July 1982. See Falla (1994), chaps. 4–11; idem (1983); Washington Office on Latin America (WOLA) (1984), p. 7.
20. Carmack (1988).
21. Amnesty International (1982), p. 1; Americas Watch (1982); "Death and Disorder in Guatemala," *Cultural Survival Quarterly* 7(1) (1983). See also AVANSCO (1992).
22. "Guatemalan Amnesty," BBC Summary of World Broadcasts, 25 May 1982.
23. *Central America Report* (25 June 1982: 191) recorded that 237 guerrilla sympathizers and only 3 combatants surrendered under the amnesty. See also "1857 subversivos se acogieron a la Amnistía," *El Imparcial* (1 July 1982); Stoll (1993), pp. 94, 111.
24. Tom Barry (1986), pp. 19–20; José Efraín Ríos Montt (1982), pp. 11–14.
25. Lawrence (1983), p. 40; Ríos Montt (1982), no page; Simon (1987), p. 119.
26. In theory, each *municipio* in the republic was responsible for organizing a civil patrol, and membership in patrols was voluntary, at least according to law. In practice, participation in civil patrols was mandatory during this period in the zones of conflict, "*flojo*" (lax) in areas, such as in the Petén or the Oriente, where the establishment of "order" was not so important. Beatriz Manz (1988) reports that in the mid-1980s "the usual twenty-four-hour shift falls anywhere from every five days to every three months, depending on local circumstances. . . . The system . . . serves primarily to control the men who have to participate and monitor the activities of the rest of the population, allowing the army to concentrate on other military activities." See also Wadge (1987), p. 67.
27. WOLA (1984), p. v; sources in this report include the Programa de Ayuda para

los Vecinos del Altiplano (Aid Program for Altiplano Neighbors, PAVA) and the Juvenile Division of the Guatemalan Supreme Court. The figure for destroyed villages comes from the Guatemalan army.

28. "Guatemalan President's News Conference in Honduras," BBC Summary of World Broadcasts, 7 December 1982.

29. Linda Drucker (1983), p. 6; Batres Grenados (1994), p. 14.

30. Black, Jamail, and Stoltz Chinchilla (1984), p. 131.

31. Anfuso and Sczepanski (1984), p. 153.

32. See Amnesty International (1982); "Guatemala: A Commentary on Human Rights," *Plenty International* (1982); Comisión de Derechos Humanos de Guatemala (July–October 1983); Berryman (1994), p. 121.

33. See Stoll (1993), chaps. 3 and 4; Falla (1994), chap. 10, pp. 131, 135; "Testimonio de Carmelita Santos," *Polémica* 7(8) (1983): 77–78; "La iglesia evangélica en Guatemala," *Polémica* 9: 4–5; "An Urgent Communiqué to the LAM Family, San José, Costa Rica," photocopy; "Represión de los gobiernos militares de Guatemala al sector protestante," communiqué from the Iglesia Guatemalteca en el Exilio, no date.

34. Berryman (1994), p. 121.

35. Some of the participants in FUNDAPI included Wycliffe Bible Translators/ Summer Institute of Linguistics, the Church of the Word, Partners in the Americas, and World Vision.

36. See Simons (1982), p. 110; William Hamman interview; Raymond and Helen Elliott interview; Whitbeck interview.

37. Whitbeck interview.

38. Lloret interview.

39. "Campaña de Sanctidad," circular no. 4, 19 April 1983, archives of the national Iglesia del Nazareno in Guatemala City.

40. "Bitter and Cruel: An Interim Report of the Parliamentary Human Rights Groups," British Parliamentary Human Rights Group (November 1984), pp. 26–27.

41. Letter from Harold Ray to unspecified recipient, 15 April 1983, archives of the Iglesia del Nazareno in Guatemala City.

42. "Guatemala," *Plenty International* (1982): 28–29.

43. Virgilio Zapata Arceyuz interview; Stephen Sywulka interview; see also "Guatemalan Pastors: Between a Rock and a Hard Place," *Christianity Today* 25(9) (1982): 13; "Guatemala," *Christianity Today* 22(23) (1982): 44–45.

44. "Los que matan en nombre de Dios," Organización del Pueblo en Armas, June 1983, mimeographed communiqué; Stoll (1993), p. 103.

45. Ríos Montt's particular definition of unity is summed up in part by a conclusion to one of his Sunday sermons. "Padre: te suplico, Señor," he said, "que me traigas al corazón de los guatemaltecos; que traigas confianza a un pueblo, Señor, y que consolide a su familia" ("Calma sed de justicia preve Ríos Montt," *El Imparcial* [12 April 1982], p. 1); "Ríos Montt anuncia cambios de ministros," *El Imparcial* (21 May 1982), p. 1.

46. "Triple cimera centroamericana aquí," *El Imparcial* (6 December 1982), p. 1; Raúl Villatoro (1982), p. 1.
47. Simon (1987), p. 121.
48. WOLA (1984), p. 27
49. Ibid., p. 39.
50. Annis (1987), pp. 5–6.
51. See Stoll (1993), pp. 104–105; Falla (1994), chap. 2.
52. Servicio Evangelizador para América Latina (SEPAL), "Retrato de Guatemala," report for Amanecer project, 15 December 1988. SEPAL is a Protestant data bank based in Guatemala City.
53. I have elected to use the female pronoun here because of the inordinately high numbers of widows left by the violence; by 1984, they accounted for nearly the entire adult population of some communities. See WOLA (1984), pp. 6–10.
54. Annis (1987), pp. 89–90.
55. See Carol A. Smith (1988), p. 230; PROCADES (1981), pp. 178–184; SEPAL (1988), p. 4.
56. See Timothy Evans (1990); Luis Arturo Isaacs Rodríguez interview; Dubón interview; interview with pastor of Iglesia Evangélica Príncipe de Paz; Flavio Gaspar Zapeta Vásquez interview.
57. Some of the most prominent U.S. Christian groups that sent funds, supplies, and personnel to Guatemala during this period included Jimmy Swaggart's Crusade, Jerry Falwell's Old Time Gospel Hour, the Billy Graham Crusade, the 700 Club, and Youth with a Mission. See "Reagan y sectas con armas y dinero a Ríos Montt," *Barricada* (10 September 1982); "Juventud con una misión," *El Imparcial* (13 April 1983). Quotation from Simons (1982), p. 150.
58. This was the number reported in the press, although even participants in this rally believe the report was grossly inflated; the event was, however, very well attended. See "Gran concentración de los evangélicos" (*Prensa Libre* [29 November 1982]). One panoramic (and doctored) photo of the event shows the same section of audience in two different places.
59. Simons (1982), p. 116; José María Ruiz Furlán interview; see also "¿Evangelización? ¿Colonización?"; Domínguez and Huntington (1984), p. 27.
60. Zapata, Berberian (18 March 1985), Hudson, and Guillermo Galindo interviews.
61. Calvert (1985), p. 113; "Motivos del golpe: abusos de un grupo de religiosos, fanático y agresivo," *La Razón* (9 August 1983); "Golpe contra la secta 'El Verbo' y la corrupción," *La Razón* (9 August 1983).
62. The president of the Council of State, Jorge Serrano Elías, was a fellow evangelical who by most accounts won the 1991 presidential election on Rios Montt's coattails; at the time, Serrano belonged to Elim Church, which had notoriously hostile relations with the Church of the Word. Ríos Montt's "personal representative" (*personal del presidente*) also was a member of a Protestant church, but belonged to the Union Church, a denomination that fell on the

other side of the mainline-Pentecostal fault line and that mainly catered to the English-speaking foreign community. See James Janowiak (1983).

63. "No habrá elecciones en el '84," *El Imparcial* (9 May 1982), p. 1; quotation from Stan Persky (1984), p. 326.

64. Whitbeck interview.

65. "Evangélicos denuncian persecución," *El Gráfico* (21 August 1983); "Virgilio Zapata Arceyuz defiende a los evangélicos," *Prensa Libre* (22 August 1983); "Policía Nacional ajena a molestias a evangélicos," *El Gráfico* (22 August 1983); "Denuncian a Mejía persecución de evangélicos," *El Gráfico* (29 August 1983).

66. "La gente se aleja de la Iglesia del Verbo," *La Razón* (22 September 1983).

EPILOGUE

1. SEPAL (1987, 1988); Congreso Amanecer '84 (1983); Roy A. Wingard, Jr. (1987), p. 12; Timothy E. Evans (1990, 1991); SEPAL staff member interview.

2. These are estimates that appear in David Stoll (1990, pp. 333–334) and that are compiled from three independent sources: Johnson, Holland, and Barrett.

3. A study of Guatemalan electronic ministry that touches on this slightly is Aníbal F. Duarte Alonso (1988). In Guatemala City, the growth of neo-Pentecostal churches since 1982 has been meteoric. Fraternidad Cristiana de Guatemala, a church that used an old movie theater as its sanctuary as late as the 1980s, by the late 1990s had 11,000 members. Cristo Centro, a church that split off from the traditional Pentecostal El Calvario Church in the mid-1980s now "shepherds" 125 related neo-Pentecostal congregations. Elim, the largest neo-Pentecostal denomination, has over 7,000 parishioners in its church in Zone 7, one of the most exclusive neighborhoods of the city. The Zone 7 Elim Church is only one of several congregations of comparable size scattered throughout the capital.

4. Berberian interview (5 May 1989). See also Dennis A. Smith (1988), pp. 12–14.

5. Berberian interview (5 May 1989); Lloret interview.

6. See Samuel Berberian (1983).

7. For more on the Gospel of Wealth, see Henry S. Commager (1950); Richard Hofstadter (1945); Paul F. Boller, Jr. (1981).

8. Jean-Pierre Bastian (1993).

9. Edmundo Madrid interview.

10. In 1985, the army permitted free elections and a return to civilian rule. Marco Vinicio Cerezo, the Christian Democratic candidate, was elected president and took office in spring 1985. Despite numerous coup attempts, Cerezo successfully completed his term.

11. Serrano Elías served as president of the Council of State during Ríos Montt's administration and was a member of a large and affluent Pentecostal denomination based in Guatemala City until he left the country following his unsuccessful *auto-golpe*. There is less collusion of interests between Serrano and Ríos

Montt, however, than these facts might indicate. First, Serrano's position under Ríos Montt lay outside the executive branch of government. Second, the church that Serrano attended at that time, Elim, has a long history of hostility toward Ríos Montt's church, Verbo, over doctrinal and liturgical differences.

12. This new orientation is summarized in Conferencia Episcopal de Guatemala (15 August 1992).

13. *Statistical Yearbook of the Church 1987; Catholic Almanac 1975,* cited in Cleary (1986), p. 186.

14. See Edward Cleary (1997); Bruce Calder (1995); Enrique Sam Colop (1996).

15. Irving Zeitlin in Carlos Alberto Torres (1992).

16. Daniel Levine (1991), pp. 21–22.

Bibliography

ARCHIVES AND LIBRARIES CONSULTED

Archivo General de Centro América. Ministerio de Gobernación. Guatemala City. Correspondencia. 1932.

Archivo General de Centro América. Ministerio de Relaciones Exteriores. Guatemala City.

Signatura B99-34-13, legajo 6901, "Colonización."

Signatura B99-34-7, legajos 6847–6852, "Asuntos religiosos."

Signatura B99-34-1, legajo 6802, "Asuntos religiosos."

Signatura B99-3-11-1, legajos 5022–5023, "Asuntos religiosos."

Signatura B99-34-2, legajos 6803–6804, "Asuntos religiosos."

Signatura B104-9, legajos 8466, 8215, "Asuntos religiosos."

Signatura B104-17, legajo 8315–8323, "Asuntos religiosos."

542, "Inscripciones de extranjeros."

565, "Ingresos de religiosos, 1937–1954."

566, "Colonización, 1937."

Biblioteca Nacional de Guatemala. Hemeroteca. Guatemala City.

British Foreign and Bible Society. Archives. London.

Central American Mission. International headquarters. Dallas, Texas.

Central American Mission. Seminario Teológico de Centroamérica. Guatemala City.

Coordinador Pastoral de la Comunicación. International offices. San José, Costa Rica.

Iglesia del Nazareno. National offices. Guatemala City.

Iglesia Episcopal de Guatemala. Archives. Guatemala City.

Iglesia Evangélica Nacional Metodista Primitiva. Instituto Bíblico Metodista. Santa Cruz del Quiché, Guatemala.

Iglesia Evangélica Nacional Presbiteriana Central. Archives. Guatemala City.

Iglesia Evangélica Nacional Presbiteriana de Guatemala. Archives. Guatemala City.

El Imparcial, Diario Independiente. Archives. Guatemala City.

Junta Anual de Iglesias Evangélicas de Centroamérica "Amigos." National offices. Chiquimula, Guatemala.

Seminario Bíblico Latinoamericano. Archives. San José, Costa Rica.

Tulane University. Latin American library. New Orleans, Louisiana.

University of Texas. Nettie Lee Benson Latin American Collection. Austin, Texas.

INTERVIEWS AND CORRESPONDENCE

Ainsely, Vera. Presbyterian missionary. Correspondence, 10 February 1985.

Baltodano, Rafael. Instituto Internacional de Evangelización a Fondo. Interview, San Francisco de Dos Ríos, Costa Rica, 7 June 1985.

Behrhorst, Carroll. Fundación Guatemalteca para el Desarrollo Carroll Behrhorst, Chimaltenango. Interview, New Orleans, Louisiana, 21 November 1983.

Berberian, Samuel. Universidad Mariano Gálvez. Interviews, Guatemala City, 18 March 1985, 14 September 1987, 5 May 1989.

Birchard, Margaret. Nazarene missionary. Correspondence, 23 January 1985.

Brown, Nola. Presbyterian missionary. Correspondence, 25 January 1985.

Canfield, Paul. Misión Amigos. Interview, Chiquimula, Guatemala, 12 April 1985.

Dahlquist, Anna Marie. Daughter of Central American Mission and Presbyterian missionaries. Correspondence, 2 February 1985.

Dubón, Arnoldo. Iglesia Jerusalén Metodista Primitiva. Interview, Santa Cruz del Quiché, Guatemala, 23 May 1985.

Elliott, Raymond, and Helen Elliott. Wycliffe Bible Translators, Summer Institute of Linguistics (SIL), Nebaj. Interview, SIL headquarters, Guatemala City, 18 March 1985.

Foulkes, Richard. Seminario Bíblico Latinoamericano. Interview, San José, Costa Rica, 5 June 1985.

Frey, William. Anglican missionary. Correspondence, 25 April 1985.

Galindo, Guillermo. Alianza Evangélica. Interview, Guatemala City, 18 March 1984.

García, Edgardo. Consejo Cristiano de Agencias de Desarrollo. Interview, Guatemala City, 6 February 1985.

Gilmore, Ronald. Global Missionary Evangelicism. Interview, Antigua, Guatemala, 1 September 1983.

Guerra, Antonio. Colegio La Patria. Interview, Guatemala City, 21 January 1985.

Hamman, William. Iglesia Cristiana Verbo. Interview, Guatemala City, 11 March 1984.

Haydus, Marian. Asambleas de Dios. Interview, Guatemala City, 5 March 1985.

Heap, Gwladys. Nazarene missionary. Correspondence, 12 April 1985.

Hudson, James. Iglesia del Nazareno. Interview, Guatemala City, 4 February 1985.

Kaqchikel lay pastors. Seminario Teológico Centroamericano. Interview, Guatemala City, 28 February 1985. Names withheld by request.

Layworker, United Presbyterian Church. Interview, San José, Costa Rica, 6 June 1985. Name withheld by request.

Lloret, Julian. Central American Mission. Interview, Guatemala City, 5 March 1985, 3 May 1989.

McAnlis, Mrs. J. Albert. Presbyterian missionary. Correspondence, 27 March 1985.

Madrid, Edmundo. Alianza Evangélica. Interview, Guatemala City, July 1990.

Mansilla, Lidia de Solís. Iglesia Presbiteriana "El Divino Salvador." Interview, Guatemala City, 21 January 1985.

Martínez, Carlos. Iglesia de Dios de la Séptima Día. Interview, Guatemala City, 4 March 1985.

Martínez, Juan C. Asambleas de Dios Central. Interview, Guatemala City, 7 March 1985.

Muñoz, Chema de. Iglesia Príncipe de Paz Central. Interview, Guatemala City, 6 March 1985.

Muñoz, Marduqueo. Iglesia Presbiteriana Central. Interview, Guatemala City, 9 March 1984.

Pastor. Asambleas de Dios Central. Interview, Guatemala City, 7 March 1985. Name withheld by request.

Pastor. Iglesia Evangélica Nacional Presbiteriana. Interview, San José, Costa Rica, 7 June 1985. Name withheld by request.

Pastor. Iglesia Evangélica Príncipe de Paz. Interview, Chichicastenango, Guatemala, 24 May 1985. Name withheld by request.

Pastor's wife. Iglesia Nacional. Interview, Santa Cruz del Quiché, Guatemala, 23 May 1985. Name withheld by request.

Piedra Solano, Arturo. Seminario Bíblico Latinoamericano. Interview, San José, Costa Rica, 3 June 1985.

Ray, Harold. Iglesia del Nazareno. Interview, Guatemala City, 18 April 1985.

Rivera, Itzmar. Iglesia Metodista Primitiva. Interview, Santa Cruz del Quiché, Guatemala, 23 May 1985.

Rodríguez, Luis Arturo Isaacs. Guatemalan Army Public Relations Office. Interview, Guatemala City, 27 June 1989.

Ruiz Furlán, José María. Iglesia Católica Santa Cura de Ars. Interview, Guatemala City, 6 March 1985.

Scotchmer, David. Presbyterian missionary. Correspondence, 28 April 1984, 31 January 1995; interview, Austin, Texas, April 12, 1994.

Serrano Elías, Jorge. President, Council of State, 1982–1983, President of the Republic, 1991–1993. Interview, Guatemala City, 11 February 1985.

Staff member. SEPAL. Interview, SEPAL office, Guatemala City, 4 May 1989. Name withheld by request.

Sywulka, Pauline Burgess. Misión Centroamericana, La Democracia, Huehuetenango, Guatemala. Interview, Seminario Teológico Centroamericano, Guatemala City, 22 February 1985.

Sywulka, Stephen. Radio TGNA, Seminario Teológico Centroamericano. Interview, Guatemala City, 28 February 1985.

Wallis, Calvin. Presbyterian missionary. Correspondence, 12 April 1985.

Wallis, Matilda. Presbyterian missionary. Correspondence, 12 April 1985.

Whitbeck, Harris. Interview, Guatemala City, 18 February 1985.

Whitesides, Robert. Wycliffe Bible Translators and Summer Institute of Linguistics. Interview, Guatemala City, 6 February 1985.

Wick, Stanley. Presbyterian missionary. Correspondence, 16 March 1985.

Wingard, Roy. Encargado de estadística, Servicio Evangelizador para América Latina. Interview, Guatemala City, 14 September 1987.

Winn, Paul. Presbyterian missionary. Correspondence, 12 February 1985.

Zapata Arceyuz, Virgilio. Alianza Evangélica. Interview, Guatemala City, 25 January 1985.

Zapeta Vásquez, Flavio Gaspar. Asambleas de Dios. Interview, Chichicastenango, Guatemala, 24 May 1985.

JOURNALS, PERIODICALS, AND NEWSPAPERS

Acción Social Cristiana, October 1945–December 1948.

El Anunciador Evangélico (Zacapa, Guatemala), 1940–1944.

Austin American-Statesman, 16 March 1987.

Barricada, 10 September 1982.

Boletín de la Iglesia Evangélica Central Presbiteriana (Guatemala City), 1920–1950.

Boletín de Noticias de Cólera Morbus, 12 May 1837.

Boletín Oficial, 10 October 1837.

British Broadcast System Summary of World Broadcasts, 7 December 1982.

Central American Bulletin, 1891–1984.

Central America Report, 25 June 1982.

Chispas (Guatemala City), 1967.

Corazón y Vida (Chiquimula, Guatemala), 1936–1947.

El Crepúsculo, January–December 1872.

El Cristiano (Cobán, Guatemala), 1907–1908.

Diario de Centro América, September 1910–May 1921.

Ecos Feminiles (Guatemala City), 1961–1985.

En Comunión (Panama), May–June 1983.

Enfoque Evangelismo Juvenil (Guatemala City), April 1967.

El Estudiante Bíblico (Huehuetenango, Guatemala), 1946–1957.
Evangelisches Gemeindeblatt (Guatemala City), 1938–1940.
El Gráfico, March 1982–October 1984.
Guatemalan Challenge (Guatemala City), 1958–1962.
Guatemala News (Guatemala City), 1943–1964.
El Guatemalteco, September 1879–June 1883.
Harvester (Chiquimula, Guatemala), 1936–1952.
La Hora, May 1944–July 1945; March 1982–September 1983.
Iglesia Guatemalteca en el Exilio, 1980–1985.
Impacto, June 1982–April 1983.
El Imparcial, 1932–1983.
Latin American Weekly Report, 10 July 1982.
El Malacate, January–December 1871.
Manantial de Aguas Vivas (Guatemala City), 1946–1950.
El Mensajero (Guatemala City), 1909–1947.
Mensajero Evangélico (Quetzaltenango, Guatemala), 1947–1967.
Messenger (Guatemala City), 1909–1947.
La Nación (Costa Rica), 5 April 1979.
El Nazareno (Guatemala City), 1933.
Newsweek, 13 December 1982.
New York Times, 1982–1983.
El Noticiero Evangélico (Quetzaltenango, Guatemala), 1926–1965.
Nueva Era Bautista (Guatemala), 1970–1978.
La Palabra, March 1982–June 1985.
Pescadores (Guatemala City), July 1943.
Prensa Libre, November 1982–September 1983.
The Primitive Methodist Journal, 1982.
Pro-Alfabetización Nacional (Guatemala City), November 1945–November 1947.
El Protestante (Chichicastenango, Guatemala), August 1910–March 1911.
Rayitos de Luz (Cobán, Guatemala), 1936–1944.
La Razón, August–September 1983.
Reuters North European Service, 8 August 1983
El Unionista, 1920–1929.
Vocero Evangélico (Guatemala City), 1946–1955.
Wall Street Journal, 14 April 1982.

SECONDARY SOURCES

Abzug, Robert. *Cosmos Crumbling: American Reform and the Religious Imagination.* New York: Oxford University Press, 1994.

Adams, Richard N. *Crucifixion by Power: Essays on Guatemalan National Social Structure, 1944–1966.* Austin: University of Texas Press, 1970.

———. "La población indígena en el estado liberal: 1900–1944." Manuscript, n.d.

Adams, Richard N., and Charles Hale. "Sociedad y etnia, 1930–1979." Manuscript, 1991.

Adolfo, Felipe. "Evangélicos y compromiso con el pueblo." *Cristianismo y Sociedad* 68(2) (1981): 13–22.

Agüero, Raúl. *Guatemala: la revolución liberal de 1871 y las administraciones del benemérito Estrada Cabrera.* San José, Costa Rica: Imprenta Alsina, 1914.

Aguilar, Alfonso. *Pan-Americanism from Monroe to the Present: A View from the Other Side.* New York: Monthly Review Press, 1968.

Aguilar Peralta, G. E. *La violencia en Guatemala cómo fenómeno político.* Cuernavaca, Mexico: N.p., 1971.

———. "Terror and Violence as Weapons of Counterinsurgency in Guatemala." *Latin American Perspectives* 25 (1980): 91–113.

Allcott, Georgina R. "An Historical Survey of Evangelical North American Mission Boards in Guatemala." Master's thesis, Columbia Bible College, 1970.

American Bible Society. *Hundredth Annual Report of the American Bible Society.* New York: American Bible Society, 1916.

Americas Watch. "Human Rights in Guatemala: No Neutrals Allowed." New York: Americas Watch Committee, 1982.

Amilcar Madrid, Edgar. *Breve historia de los Amigos.* Chiquimula, Guatemala: Junta Anual "Amigos" de Centroamérica, 1975.

Amir, Raymond Gene. "Religious and Political Changes in a Guatemalan Village." Master's thesis, University of California, 1954.

Amnesty International. *Guatemala: Massive Extrajudicial Executions in Rural Areas under the Government of Ríos Montt.* London: Amnesty International, 1982.

Anderson, Benedict. *Imagined Communities: Reflections on the Origin and Spread of Nationalism.* New York: Verso, 1983.

Anderson, Thomas P. *Matanza: El Salvador's Communist Revolt of 1932.* Lincoln: University of Nebraska Press, 1971.

Anfuso, Joseph, and David Sczepanski. *He Gives—He Takes Away: The True Story of Guatemala's Controversial Former President Efraín Ríos Montt.* Eureka, Calif.: Radiance Press, 1984.

Annis, Sheldon. *God and Production in a Guatemalan Town.* Austin: University of Texas Press, 1987.

Arévalo Bermejo, Juan José. "Conservadores, liberales y socialistas." In *Escritos políticos,* 2nd ed. Guatemala City: Tipografía Nacional, 1946.

———. *The Shark and the Sardines.* New York: Lyle and Stuart, 1961.

Argueta, Rodrigo. "Responsabilidad misionera de la Iglesia Evangélica de Guatemala." Licenciatura thesis, Seminario Teológico Centroamericano, 1984.

Assman, Hugo. *La iglesia electrónica y su impacto en América Latina.* San José, Costa Rica: Editorial Departamento Ecuménico de Investigaciones, 1987.

Asturias, Miguel Ángel. *Sociología guatemalteca: el problema socio del indio.* Guatemala City: Tipografía Sánchez y de Guise, 1923.

AVANSCO. *¿Dónde está el futuro? Procesos de reintegración en comunidades de retornados.* Cuaderno de Investigación, no. 8. Guatemala City: AVANSCO, 1992.

Aybar, José. *Dependency and Intervention: The Case of Guatemala in 1954.* Boulder, Colo.: Westview Press, 1979.

Báez-Camargo, Gonzalo. *Protestantes enjudiciados por la Inquisición en Iberoamérica.* Mexico City: Casa Unida Publicaciones, 1960.

Baldwin, Deborah. *Protestants and the Mexican Revolution: Missionaries, Ministers, and Social Change.* Urbana: University of Illinois Press, 1990.

Ballard, Rachel. "Differences, Disease and Nation: Liberals and Public Health in Guatemala in 1837 and the 1930s." Unpublished, 1993.

Barillas, E. *El "problema del indio" durante la época liberal.* Apontes de la Investigación, 1–88. Instituto de Investigaciones Históricas, Antropológicas y Arqueológicas, Escuela de Historia. Guatemala City: Universidad de San Carlos, 1988.

Barrientos, Alberto. "Profile of an Expanding Church." *Latin American Evangelist* 57(2): 1–3.

Barry, Tom. *Guatemala: The Politics of Counterinsurgency.* Albuquerque, N.M.: Inter-Hemispheric Educational Resource Center, 1986.

Bastian, Jean-Pierre. "Guerra fría, crisis del proyecto liberal y atomización de los protestantes latinoamericanos, 1949–1959." *Cristianismo y Sociedad* 68(2) (1981): 7–12.

———. *Protestantismo y sociedad en México.* Mexico City: CUPSA, 1983.

———. "Protestantismos latinoamericanos entre la resistencia y la sumisión, 1961–1983." *Cristianismo y Sociedad* 82 (1984): 49–68.

———. *Breve historia del protestantismo en América Latina.* Mexico City: Casa Unida Publicaciones, 1986.

———. *Los disidentes: sociedades protestantes y revolución en México, 1872–1911.* Mexico City: El Colegio de México, Fondo de Cultura Económica, 1989.

———. "The Metamorphosis of Latin American Protestant Groups: A Sociohistorical Perspective." *Latin American Research Review* 28(2) (1993): 33–61.

———. *Le protestantisme en Amérique Latine: une approche socio-historique.* Geneva: Éditions Labor et Fides, 1994.

———. *Sociedades de ideas, heterodoxia religiosa y cambio social en México, siglos XIX y XX.* Mexico City: CIPSA, forthcoming.

———, ed. *Protestantes, liberales y francmasones: sociedades de ideas y modernidad en América Latina, siglo XIX.* Mexico City: Fondo de Cultura Económica–Cehila, 1990.

Batres Grenados, Alejandra. "Morality, Order, and Unity: The Experience of Ríos Montt in Guatemala." Unpublished, 1994.

Batres Jaureguí, Antonio. *Los indios: su historia y su civilización.* Guatemala City: Tipografía La Unión, 1894.

Batz, Luis. *Las cofradías de San Pedro la Laguna, Sololá.* Guatemala City: CENALTEX, Ministerio de Educación, 1991.

Bayle, Constantino. *La cruz y el dólar: propaganda protestante en la América Latina.* Madrid: Editorial Razón y Fe, 1930.

Berberian, Martha Saint de. "Análisis de la educación cristiana en Guatemala." Licenciatura thesis, Universidad Mariano Gálvez, 1983.

Berberian, Samuel. "Movimiento carismático en Latinoamérica, 1960 – 1980." Licenciatura thesis, Universidad Mariano Gálvez, 1980.

———. *Movimiento carismático en Latinoamérica, 1960 – 1980.* Guatemala City: Ediciones Sa-Ber, 1983.

Berger, Peter. *The Sacred Canopy.* Garden City, N.Y.: Doubleday, 1967.

Berryman, Phillip. *The Religious Roots of Rebellion: Christians in Central America's Revolutions.* Maryknoll, N.Y.: Orbis, 1984.

———. *Stubborn Hope: Religion, Politics and Revolution in Central America.* Maryknoll, N.Y.: Orbis, 1994.

Bishop, Edwin. "The Guatemalan Labor Movement, 1944 – 1959." Ph.D. dissertation, University of Wisconsin, 1959.

Black, George, Milton Jamail, and Norma Stoltz Chinchilla. *Garrison Guatemala.* New York: Monthly Review Press, 1984.

Blake, Nelson Manfred. *A History of American Life and Thought.* 2nd ed. New York: McGraw-Hill, 1972.

Blakeney, Adolph. "The Origin and Growth of Protestantism in Guatemala, 1824 – 1950." Master's thesis, University of Alabama, 1956.

Bogenschield, Thomas E. "The Roots of Fundamentalism in Western Guatemala, 1900 – 1944." Paper presented to Latin American Studies Association Conference, April 1991.

———. "The Roots of Fundamentalism in Liberal Guatemala: Missionary Ideologies and Local Responses, 1882 – 1944." Ph.D. dissertation, University of California, Berkeley, 1992.

Boller, Paul F., Jr. *American Thought in Transition: The Impact of Evolutionary Naturalism, 1865 – 1900.* Washington, D.C.: University Press of America, 1981.

British Parliamentary Human Rights Group. "Bitter and Cruel: An Interim Report of the Parliamentary Human Rights Group." London: British Parliamentary Human Rights Group, November 1984.

Britnall, Douglas E. "A Model of Changing Group Relations in the Maya Highlands of Guatemala." *Journal of Anthropological Research* 36(3) (1979a): 294 – 315.

———. *Revolt against the Dead: The Modernization of a Mayan Community in the Highlands of Guatemala.* New York: Gordon and Breach, 1979b.

Broderick, Robert C., ed. *The Catholic Encyclopedia.* Nashville, Tenn.: Thomas Nelson, 1987.

Browning, David. *El Salvador: Landscape and Society.* Oxford: Clarendon Press, 1971.

Brusco, Elizabeth E. *The Reformation of Machismo: Evangelical Conversion and Gender in Colombia.* Austin: University of Texas Press, 1995.

Bunzel, Ruth. *Chichicastenango: A Guatemalan Village.* Publication 22. Locust Valley, N.Y.: American Ethnological Society, 1952.

Burgess, Paul. *Justo Rufino Barrios.* New York: Dorranca and Co., 1926.

———. *Historia de la obra evangélica presbiteriana en Guatemala: bodas de diamante.* Guatemala City: Privately published, 1957.

————. *Historia de la obra evangélica presbiteriana en Guatemala: bodas de diamante.* Quetzaltenango: Tipografía "El Noticiero," 1957.

Burns, E. Bradford. *The Poverty of Progress: Latin America in the Nineteenth Century.* Berkeley & Los Angeles: University of California Press, 1980.

Bush, Archer C. *Organized Labor in Guatemala 1944–1949.* Latin American Seminar Report 2. Hamilton N.Y.: Colgate University Area Studies, 1950.

Cabrera Gonzales, Daniel. "Religión indígena y cristianismo en Guatemala." Licenciatura thesis, Seminario Bíblico Latinoamericano, 1980.

Cadwallader, Samuel. "Historical Background for an Understanding of Guatemala Baptist Missions." Seminario Teológico Centroamericano, Guatemala City. Mimeographed, n.d.

Calder, Bruce. "Growth and Change in the Guatemalan Catholic Church, 1944–1964." Master's thesis, University of Texas at Austin, 1968.

————. *Crecimiento y cambio de la iglesia guatemalteca, 1944–1966.* Estudios Centroamericanos del Seminario de Integración Social Guatemalteca, no. 6. Guatemala City: Editorial José Pineda Ibarra, 1970.

————. "The Catholic Church and the Guatemalan Maya, 1940–1969: Building a Base for the 1990s." Paper presented at Latin American Studies Association Conference, April 1995.

Calvert, Peter. *Guatemala: A Nation in Turmoil.* Boulder, Colo.: Westview Press 1985.

Cancian, Frank. *Economics and Prestige in a Maya Community: The Religious Cargo System in Zinacantán.* Stanford: Stanford University Press, 1965.

————. *The Decline of Community in Zinacantán: Economy, Public Life, and Social Stratification, 1960–1987.* Stanford: Stanford University Press, 1992.

Cardoza y Aragón, Luis. "Guatemala y el imperio bananero." *Cuadernos Americanos* 64 (March 1954): 19–45.

Carmack, Robert M. "Spanish-Indian Relations in Highland Guatemala, 1800–1944." In Murdo MacLeod and Robert Wasserstrom, eds., *Spaniards and Indians in Southeastern Mesoamerica.* Lincoln: University of Nebraska Press, 1983.

Carmack, Robert M., ed. *Harvest of Violence: The Maya Indians and the Guatemala Crisis.* Norman: University of Oklahoma Press, 1988.

Carrasco, David. *Religions of Mesoamerica.* San Francisco: Harper & Row, 1990.

Carrera, José C. "Lecciones de historia de la Iglesia Presbiteriana de Guatemala." Archives of the Iglesia Evangélica Nacional Presbiteriana. Mimeographed, n.d.

Casey, Dennis R. "Indigenismo: The Guatemalan Experience." Ph.D. dissertation, University of Kansas, 1979.

Chinchilla Aguilar, Ernesto. *La Inquisición en Guatemala.* Guatemala City: Ministerio de Educación Pública, 1953.

Christian Work in Latin America: Report of Commission I, II, III to Congress of Christian Work in Latin America, Panama, February 1916. New York: New York Missionary Education Movement, 1916.

Cleary, Edward L. *Crisis and Change: The Church in Latin America Today.* Maryknoll, N.Y.: Orbis, 1986.

―――. "Birth of Maya Catholic Theology." Paper presented at Latin American Studies Association, Guadalajara, Mexico, April 1997.

Cleary, Edward L., and Hannah Stewart-Gambino, eds. *Conflict and Competition: The Latin American Church in a Changing Environment.* Boulder, Colo.: Lynne Rienner, 1992.

―――. *Power, Politics and Pentecostals in Latin America.* Boulder, Colo.: Westview Press, 1997.

Coke, Hugh Milton, Jr. "An Ethnohistory of Bible Translation among the Maya." Ph.D. dissertation, Fuller Theological Seminary, 1978.

Colby, Benjamin N., and Lore M. Colby. *The Daykeeper: The Life and Discourse of an Ixil Diviner.* Cambridge, Mass.: Harvard University Press, 1981.

Colby, Benjamin N., and Pierre L. van den Berghe. *Ixil Country: A Plural Society in Highland Guatemala.* Berkeley & Los Angeles: University of California Press, 1969.

Colop, Enrique Sam. "The Discourse of Concealment." In Edward F. Fischer and R. McKenna Brown, eds., *Maya Cultural Activism in Guatemala*, pp. 107–113. Austin: University of Texas Press, 1996.

Comisión de Derechos Humanos de Guatemala. "The Repression of Christians in Guatemala: Preliminary Report Submitted to the United Nations on the Situation of Human Rights and Basic Liberties in Guatemala." July–October 1983.

―――. "La manipulación de la religión en Guatemala." Presented at Conferencia Latinoamericana de Personalidades Cristianas por la Dignidad y Soberanía, Mexico City, 26–29 May 1984.

Comité Central Pro-Centenario de la Revolución de 1871. *Índice general de las leyes emitidas por los gobiernos de la Revolución de 1871, La Reforma: época de los presidentes Miguel Granados y Justo Rufino Barrios.* Guatemala City: Gobierno de Guatemala, 1871.

Commager, Henry S. *The American Mind: An Interpretation of American Thought and Character since the 1880s.* New Haven: Yale University Press, 1950.

Conferencia Episcopal de Guatemala. *Directorio de la Provincia Eclesiástica de Guatemala, 1992–1994.* Guatemala City: Secretariado de la Conferencia Episcopal de Guatemala, 1994.

―――. "500 años sembrando el Evangelio." Bishops of Guatemala pastoral letter, 15 August 1992.

Congreso Amanecer '84 (Emilio Antonio Núñez, Jim Montgomery, and Galo E. Vásquez). *La hora de Dios para Guatemala.* Guatemala City: Editoriales SEPAL, 1983.

Congreso Evangélico Centroamericano. *Memoria del II Congreso Evangélico Centroamericano.* Comayaguela, Honduras: Central American Mission, 1953.

Congress on Christian Work in Latin America. *Christian Work in Latin America: Reports of Commissions I, II, III.* New York: Missionary Education Movement, 1916.

Corral Prieto, Luis. "Las iglesias evangélicas de Guatemala." Licenciatura thesis, Universidad Francisco Marroquín, 1984.

Costas, Orlando E. *Theology of the Crossroads in Contemporary Latin America: Missiology in Mainline Protestantism, 1969–1974.* Amsterdam: Rodopi, 1976.

Cox, Harvey. *Fire from Heaven: The Rise of Pentecostal Spirituality and the Reshaping of Religion in the Twenty-first Century.* Reading, Mass.: Addison-Wesley, 1995.

Crawford, Mattie. *On Mule-Back thru Central America with the Gospel: A Thrilling Missionary Story.* Los Angeles: Privately printed, 1922.

Crowe, Frederick. *The Gospel in Central America.* London: Charles Gilpin, 1850.

Curet-Cuevas, Ariel. "Guatemala." *The Christian Century* (14 July 1954): n.p.

Dahlquist, Anna Marie. "La pluma de Pablo Burgess." *Ecos Feminiles* 27(4) (1977): 3–4.

———. *Burgess of Guatemala.* Langley, B.C.: Cedar Books, 1985.

Damboriena, Prudencio. *El protestantismo en América Latina.* Fribourg, Switzerland: Oficina Internacional de Investigaciones Sociales de FERES, 1962.

Davis, Sheldon H. "Introduction: Sowing the Seeds of Violence." In Robert M. Carmack, ed., *Harvest of Violence: The Maya Indians and the Guatemalan Crisis.* Norman: University of Oklahoma Press, 1988.

De León Barbero, Julio César. "Para una reflexión teológica en la sociedad guatemalteca." Paper presented at conference held at Universidad Mariano Gálvez, 14 January 1984.

———. "La realidad guatemalteca del pueblo evangélico." Paper presented at conference held at Universidad Mariano Gálvez, 12 January 1985.

Dennis, James S. *Christian Missions and Social Progress: A Sociological Study of Foreign Missions.* 3 vols. New York: Fleming H. Revell, 1897.

Denton, Charles. "Protestantism and the Latin American Middle Class." *Practical Anthropology* 18 (1971): 24–28.

Díaz, Jorge Enrique. "Los Bautistas de ayer: un estudio sencillo sobre la historia de los Bautistas." Licenciatura thesis, Instituto Superior Teológico Bautista de Guatemala, 1975.

Domínguez, Enrique, and Deborah Huntington. "The Salvation Brokers: Conservative Evangelicals in Central America." *NACLA* 17(1) (1984): 2–36.

Drucker, Linda. "One Year of Ríos Montt: A Talk with Guatemala's Vinicio Cerezo Arévalo." *New Leader* 21 (March 1983).

Duarte Alonso, Aníbal F. "Radiofonia religiosa en Guatemala: un análisis cuantitativo de la programación." Thesis, Universidad de San Carlos, 1988.

Dunn, Henry. *Guatimala.* New York: G & G Carvill, 1828.

Durkheim, Emile. *The Elementary Forms of the Religious Life.* New York: Free Press, 1915.

Earle, Duncan. "Authority, Social Conflict, and the Rise of Protestant Religious Conversion in a Mayan Village." *Social Compass* 39(3) (1992): 379–389.

Ebel, Ronald H. "Political Modernization and Community Decision-Making Process in Guatemala." *Annals of the Southeastern Conference on Latin American Studies* 1(1) (1970): 123–140.

———. "When Indians Take Power: Consensus and Conflict in San Juan Ostuncalco." In Robert M. Carmack, ed., *Harvest of Violence: The Maya Indians and the Guatemalan Crisis*. Norman: University of Oklahoma Press, 1988.

Ejército Guerrillero de los Pobres. Communiqué. June 1980.

Enyart, Paul. *Friends in Central America*. Pasadena, Calif.: William Carey Library, 1970.

Escobar, David. "La expulsión de Frederico Crowe." *Ecos Feminiles* 25(6): 13–16.

———. *Frederico Crowe: expedientes oficiales de su residencia en, y expulsión del territorio de Guatemala*. Aberdeen, Md.: Privately published, 1984.

Estrada Monroy, Agustín. *Datos para la historia de la Iglesia en Guatemala*. Vol. 3. Guatemala City: Sociedad de Geografía e Historia de Guatemala, 1979.

Estrada Paniagua, Felipe. *Administración Estrada Cabrera*. Guatemala City: Tipografía Nacional, 1904.

"¿Evangelización? ¿Colonización?" Pamphlet, Confederación de Sacerdotes, Diocesanos de Guatemala, circa 1984.

Evans, Timothy. "Percentage of Non-Catholics in a Representative Sample of the Guatemalan Population." Paper presented to the Latin American Studies Association Conference, Crystal City, Virginia, 4–6 April 1991.

———. "Religious Conversion in Quetzaltenango, Guatemala." Ph.D. dissertation, University of Pittsburgh, 1990.

Falla, Ricardo. "Evolución político-religiosa del indígena rural en Guatemala (1945–1965)." *Estudios Sociales Centroamericanos* 1(1) (1972): 27–47.

———. *Quiché rebelde: estudios de un movimiento de conversión religiosa, rebelde a las creencias tradicionales en San Antonio Ilotenango, Quiché 1948–1970*. Guatemala City: Editorial Universitaria de Guatemala, 1978.

———. "Masacres de la finca San Francisco, Huehuetenango, Guatemala." Document 1. Copenhagen: International Work Group for Indigenous Affairs, 1983.

———. *Masacres de la selva: Ixcán, Guatemala, 1975–1982*. Guatemala City: Editorial Universitaria, 1992.

———. *Massacres in the Jungle: Ixcán, Guatemala, 1975–1982*. Boulder, Colo.: Westview Press, 1994.

Fernandes, Rubem César. "Fundamentalismo a la derecha y a la izquierda: misiones evangélicas y tensiones ideológicas." *Cristianismo y Sociedad* 69 & 70(3 & 4) (1981): 21–50.

Fernando, J. J. *El indio guatemalteco: ensayo de sociología nacionalista*. Guatemala City, 1931.

Fischer, Edward F. "Induced Culture Change as a Strategy for Socio-Economic Development: The Pan Maya Movement in Guatemala." In Fischer and Brown, eds., *Maya Cultural Activism in Guatemala*, pp. 51–73. Austin: University of Texas Press, 1996.

Fischer, Edward F., and R. McKenna Brown, eds. *Maya Cultural Activism in Guatemala*. Austin: University of Texas Press, 1996.

Fiske, John. *Outlines of a Cosmic Philosophy, Based on the Doctrine and Evolution, with Criticisms on the Positive Philosophy*. Boston: Houghton Mifflin, 1874.

————. *The Unseen World and Other Essays*. Boston: Houghton Mifflin, 1876.

————. *Darwinism and Other Essays*. Boston: Houghton Mifflin, 1879.

Frank, Luisa, and Philip Wheaton. *Indian Guatemala: Path to Liberation*. Washington, D.C.: EPICA Task Force, 1984.

Frankel, Anita. "Political Development in Guatemala, 1944–1945: The Impact of Foreign, Military, and Religious Elites." Ph.D. dissertation, University of Connecticut, 1969.

Fried, Jonathan L. *Guatemala in Rebellion: Unfinished History*. New York: Grove Press, 1983.

Galich, Manuel. *¿Por qué lucha Guatemala? Dos hombres contra el imperio*. Buenos Aires: Editoriales Elmer, 1956.

Gall, Francis, ed. *Diccionario geográfico de Guatemala*. 4 vols. Guatemala City: Instituto Geográfico Nacional, 1976–1983.

Gálvez Borrell, Víctor. *Transición y régimen político en Guatemala, 1982–1988*. San José, Costa Rica: Facultad Latinoamericana de Ciencias Sociales, 1991.

Ganunza, José María. *Las sectas nos invaden*. Caracas: Ediciones Paulinas, 1978.

García Granados, J. *Evolución sociológica de Guatemala*. Guatemala City: Tipografía Sánchez y de Guise, 1927.

Garrard, Virginia Carroll. "A History of Protestantism in Guatemala." Ph.D. dissertation, Tulane University, 1986.

Garrard-Burnett, Virginia. "God and Revolution: Protestant Missions in Revolutionary Guatemala, 1944–1954." *The Americas: A Quarterly Review of Inter-American History* 46 (1989a): 205–223.

————. "Jerusalem under Siege: Protestantism in Rural Guatemala, 1960–1987." Texas Papers on Latin America 89-15, 1989b.

————. "Protestantism in Rural Guatemala, 1872–1954." *Latin American Research Review* 24(2) (1989c): 127–142.

————. "Positivismo, liberalismo e impulso misionero: misiones protestantes en Guatemala, 1880–1920." *Mesoamérica* 19 (1990): 13–31.

Garrard-Burnett, Virginia, and David Stoll, eds. *Rethinking Protestantism in Latin America*. Philadelphia: Temple University Press, 1993.

Garst, Rachel. *Ixcán: colonización, desarraigo y condiciones de retorno*. Guatemala City: COINDE, 1993.

Gill, Lesley. "Religious Mobility and the Many Words of God in La Paz, Bolivia." In Virginia Garrard-Burnett and David Stoll, eds., *Rethinking Protestantism in Latin America*, pp. 180–198. Philadelphia: Temple University Press, 1993.

Gillin, John. *The Culture of Security in San Carlos: A Study of a Guatemalan Community of Indians and Ladinos*. Publication 16. New Orleans, La.: Middle American Research Institute, 1951.

Gleijeses, Piero. *Shattered Hope: The Guatemalan Revolution and the United States, 1944–1954*. Princeton: Princeton University Press, 1991.

Goldston, James A. *Shattered Hope: Guatemalan Workers and the Promise of Democracy*. Boulder, Colo.: Westview Press, 1989.

Gossens, Gary H. *Symbol and Meaning beyond the Closed Community: Essays in Mesoamerican Ideas.* Studies on Culture and Society, vol. 1. Albany: Institute for Mesoamerican Studies, State University of New York, 1986.

Goubaud Carrera, Antonio, ed. *Indigenismo en Guatemala.* Guatemala City: Editorial del Ministerio de Educación Pública, 1964.

Graham, Richard, ed. *The Idea of Race in Latin America.* Austin: University of Texas Press, 1989.

Green, Linda. "Shifting Affiliations: Mayan Widow and Evangélicos in Guatemala." In Garrard-Burnett and Stoll, eds., *Rethinking Protestantism in Latin America,* pp. 159–179. Philadelphia: Temple University Press, 1993.

Greenleaf, Richard E. "The Mexican Inquisition and the Enlightenment." In Richard E. Greenleaf, ed., *The Roman Catholic Church in Colonial Latin America.* New York: Alfred A. Knopf, 1971.

Grenfell, James. "The Participation of Protestants in Politics in Guatemala." Master of Philosophy thesis, Oxford University, 1995.

Grieb, Kenneth. *Guatemalan Caudillo, the Regime of Jorge Ubico: Guatemala, 1931– 1944.* Athens: Ohio University Press, 1979.

Griffin, Charles S. *The Ferment of Reform, 1830–1860.* New York: Cromwell American History Series, 1967.

Griffith, William J. *Empires in the Wilderness: Foreign Colonization and Development 1834–1844.* Chapel Hill: University of North Carolina Press, 1965.

Grubb, Kenneth. *Religion in Central America.* London: World Dominion Press, 1937.

Guatemala. *Colección de los decretos y de las órdenes más interesantes que obtuvieron la sanción emitidas por la segunda legislatura del estado de Guatemala.* Vol. 1. Guatemala City: Imprenta de la Unión, 1830.

———. *Recopilación de las leyes emitidas por el Gobierno de la República de Guatemala.* Vol. 1. June 3, 1871–June 30, 1881. Guatemala City: Tipografía de "El Progreso," 1881.

———. Dirección General de Estadística. *Guatemala: Estimaciones y proyecciones de población, 1950–2025.* Guatemala City: Agencia Canadiense para el Desarrollo Internacional, 1985.

Guido, Yamileth. "Innovación en las iglesias o despertar neoconservador? *Revista Aportes* 18 (1984): 26–32.

Hall, Francis B., ed. *Los amigos en las Américas.* Philadelphia: Friends World Committee, 1976.

Hamilton, J. Taylor. "The Indians of Central America." *Missionary Review of the World* 5 (1918): 598–604.

Handy, Jim. *Gift of the Devil: A History of Guatemala.* Boston: South End Press, 1984.

———. "A Sea of Indians: Ethnic Conflict and the Guatemalan Revolution, 1944– 1952." *The Americas: A Quarterly Review of Inter-American History* 46 (1989): 189–204.

———. *Revolution in the Countryside: Rural Conflict and Agrarian Reform in Guatemala, 1944–1954.* Chapel Hill: University of North Carolina Press, 1994.

Harding, Joe R. "Cognitive Role Structure and Culture Contact: Culture Change in the Ixil Region of Guatemala." Ph.D. dissertation, University of California, 1973.

Haymaker, Edward H. "A Study in Latin American Futures." Mimeographed, 1917.

———. "Footnotes on the Beginning of the Evangelical Movement in Guatemala." Mimeographed, 1947.

Hays, Margaret N. *An Outline History of Fifty Years: 1922–1972.* Guatemala City: Primitive Methodist International Mission Board, 1972.

Heap, Gwladys. *Pioneering in the Petén.* Kansas City, Mo.: Nazarene Publishing House, 1972.

Herrick, Thomas R. *Desarrollo económico y político de Guatemala, 1871–1885.* San José, Costa Rica: 1974.

Hill, Robert M., II. *The Pirir Papers and Other Colonial Period Cakchiquel-Maya Testamentos.* Nashville, Tenn.: Vanderbilt University Publications in Anthropology, 1989.

Hill, Robert M., II, and John Monaghan. *Continuities in Highland Maya Social Organization: Ethnohistory in Sacapulas, Guatemala.* Philadelphia: University of Pennsylvania Press, 1987.

Hofstadter, Richard. *Social Darwinism in American Thought, 1850–1915.* Philadelphia: University of Pennsylvania Press, 1945.

Holland, Clifton L., ed. *World Christianity: Central America and the Caribbean.* Monrovia, Calif.: Missions Advanced Research and Communication Center, 1981.

Holleran, Mary P. *Church and State in Guatemala.* New York: Columbia University Press, 1949.

Howard, Oliver Otis. *Fighting for Humanity.* New York: F. Tennison Neely, 1898.

Hudson, James. *Guatemala: 60 Years.* Kansas City, Mo.: Nazarene Publishing House, 1976.

Huntington, Deborah. "God's Saving Plan." *NACLA* 18(1) (1984): 22–36.

Hvalkof, Søren, and Peter Åby, eds. *Is God an American? An Anthropological Perspective on the Summer Institute of Linguistics.* Copenhagen: Vinderup Bøgtrykker, 1981.

Iglesia Cristiana Verbo. Statement to the press. 10 August 1983.

Iglesia Evangélica Nacional Presbiteriana de Guatemala. *Apuntes para la historia.* Guatemala City: Iglesia Presbiteriana Nacional de Guatemala, 1980.

Iglesia Guatemalteca en Exilio. "Represión de los gobiernos militares de Guatemala al sector protestante 1982–1983." Communiqué, October 1983.

Immerman, Richard H. *The CIA in Guatemala: The Foreign Policy of Intervention.* Austin: University of Texas Press, 1982.

Ingersoll, Hazel. "The War of La Montaña: A Study in Reactionary Peasant Insurgency in Guatemala, 1837–1873." Ph.D. dissertation, George Washington University, 1972.

Izaguirre, Arnoldo. "Breve referencia histórica sobre la Iglesia del Nazareno en Guatemala." Guatemala City: National offices of the Iglesia del Nazareno, 1977.

James, Daniel. *Red Design for the Americas: Guatemalan Prelude.* New York: John Day Co., 1954.

————. "Church and State in Guatemala." *Commonweal* 62 (1955).

Janowiak, James. "Guatemalan President, Two Aides Return to Ministry after Coup." *International Love Lift Newletter* 8(8) (1983): 1–8.

Jonas, Suzanne, and David Tobis. *Guatemala.* San Francisco: North American Congress on Latin America, 1974.

Juárez Muñoz, J. Fernando. *El indio guatemalteco: ensayo de sociología nacionalista.* Guatemala City: Tipografía Latina, 1931.

Kepner, David, and Jay Soothill. *Social Aspects of the Banana Industry.* New York: Columbia University Press, 1936.

Knight, Alan. "Racism, Revolution, and Indigenismo." In Richard Graham, ed., *The Idea of Race in Latin America.* Austin: University of Texas Press, 1989.

Krout, J. A. *The Origins of Prohibition.* New York: Alfred Knopf, 1925.

Kuehn, Clarence T. "The History of the Lutheran Church–Missouri Synod in Guatemala until June 1949." Master's thesis, Concordia Seminary, 1950.

La Farge, Oliver. "Adaptations of Christianity among the Jacalteca Indians of Guatemala." *Thought* (2)(3) (1927): 476–495.

————. *Santa Eulalia: The Religion of a Cuchumatán Indian Town.* Chicago: University of Chicago Press, 1947.

Lalive d'Epinay, Christian. *Haven of the Masses.* London: Lutterworth Press, 1969.

————. "La iglesia evangélica y la revolución latinoamericana." Mimeographed, n.d.

Lange, Martin, and Reinhold Iblacker. *Witness of Hope: The Persecution of Christians in Latin America.* Maryknoll, N.Y.: Orbis, 1980.

Lannon, Frances. "'Modern' Spain: The Project of a National Catholicism." In Stewart Mews, ed., *Religion and National Identity.* Studies in Church History, vol. 18. Oxford: Basil Blackwell, 1982.

Latin American Mission. "An Urgent Communiqué to the LAM Family, San José, Costa Rica." Photocopy, n.d.

Lawrence, Robert. "Evangelicals Support Guatemalan Dictator." *Covert Action Information Bulletin* 18 (1983): 34–40.

Lawson, Guy M. "Flowers from the Ash: The Communities of Population in Resistance and the Process of Reintegration in the Ixcán Jungle of Guatemala." M.S. thesis, University of Texas at Austin, 1995.

Leonard, Thomas M. *The United States and Central America, 1944–1949: Perceptions of Political Dynamics.* Tuscaloosa: University of Alabama Press, 1984.

Lernoux, Penny. *Cry of the People.* London: Penguin, 1980.

Levine, Daniel. "Protestants and Catholics in Latin America: A Family Portrait." Paper prepared for the Fundamentalism Project, University of Chicago, 1991.

————. "Religion and Politics: Drawing Lines and Undertaking Change." *Latin American Research Review* 20(1) (1985): 188–189.

Lloret, Albert Julian. "The Maya Evangelical Church in Guatemala." D.D. dissertation, Dallas Theological Seminary, 1976.

————. "The Gospel in the Maya Culture of Guatemala." Mimeographed, n.d.

Lores, J. Ruben. "Manifest Destiny and the Missionary Enterprise." *Latin American Evangelist* 56(6) (1976): 4–6.

Lovell, W. George. "Surviving Conquest: The Maya of Guatemala in Historical Perspective." *Latin American Research Review* 23(2) (1988): 25–27.

Lovell, W. George, and Christopher Lutz. "Core and Periphery in Colonial Guatemala." In Carol A. Smith, *Guatemalan Indians and the State, 1540–1988*, pp. 35–51. Austin: University of Texas Press, 1990.

———. "Conquest and Population: Maya Demography in Historical Perspective." Paper presented at Latin American Studies Association Conference, Los Angeles, California, 1992.

———. "Conquest and Population: Maya Demography in Historical Perspective." *Latin American Research Review* 29(2) (1994): 133–140.

Luzbetak, Louis. "Christopaganism." *Practical Anthropology* 13 (1966): 115–121.

McArthur, Harry S. "La estructura politico-religiosa de Aguacatán." *Guatemala Indígena* 1(2) (1961): 41–56.

———. "El faccionalismo político-religioso en Aguacatán, Huehuetenango, 1966." *Cuadernos de Seminario de Integración Social Guatemalteca, Ministerio de Educación*, publication 21. 1966.

McCann, Thomas P. *An American Company: The Tragedy of United Fruit.* New York: Crown Publishers, 1976.

McCreery, David. "Coffee and Class: The Structure of Development in Liberal Guatemala." *Hispanic American Historical Review* 56 (1976): 342–460.

———. *Desarrollo económico y política nacional: el Ministerio de Fomento de Guatemala, 1871–1885.* Antigua, Guatemala: Centro de Investigaciones Regionales de Mesoamérica, 1981.

———. "Debt Servitude in Rural Guatemala, 1876–1939." *Hispanic American Historical Review* 63 (1983): 735–759.

———. "State Power, Indigenous Communities and Land in Nineteenth Century Guatemala, 1820–1920." In Carol A. Smith, ed., *Guatemalan Indians and the State, 1540–1988*, pp. 96–115. Austin: University of Texas Press, 1990.

———. "Caja, Cofradía, and Cabildo: The Transformation of 'Broker Institutions' in Nineteenth Century Guatemala." Paper presented at Conference on Ethnicity and Power in Mexico and Guatemala, Austin, Texas, March 1992.

McGavran, Donald Anderson, ed. *Church Growth and Christian Mission.* New York: Harper & Row, 1965.

McLeod, Marc Christian. "Railway Workers and Revolution in Guatemala, 1912–1954." Master's thesis, University of Texas at Austin, August 1993.

MacLeod, Murdo, and Robert Wasserstrom, eds. *Spaniards and Indians in Southeastern Mesoamerica.* Lincoln: University of Nebraska Press, 1983.

"La manipulación de la religión en Guatemala: testimonio del sector 'Libertad de Conciencia y Religión' de la Comisión de Derechos Humanos de Guatemala." Paper presented at Conferencia Latinoamericana de Personalidades Cristianas por la Dignidad y Soberanía, Mexico City, May 12–20, n.d.

Manz, Beatriz. *Refugees of a Hidden War: The Aftermath of Counterinsurgency in Guatemala.* Albany: State University of New York Press, 1988.

Marroquín Vélez, Carlos H., ed. *Así empezó . . . y creció. Crónicas de medio siglo de la obra Amigos en Centroamérica.* Guatemala City: Litografía CAISA, 1983.

Marsden, George. *Fundamentalism and American Culture.* New York: Oxford University Press, 1980.

Martin, David. *Tongues of Fire: The Explosion of Protestantism in Latin America.* Oxford: Basil Blackwell, 1990.

May, Stacy, and Galo Plaza. *The United Fruit Company in Latin America.* Washington, D.C.: National Planning Association, 1958.

Mayers, Marvin K. "The Two-Man Feud in the Guatemalan Church." *Practical Anthropology* 13 (1966): 115–125.

Mecham, J. Lloyd. *Church and State in Latin America: A History of Politico-Ecclesiastic Relations.* 2nd ed. Chapel Hill: University of North Carolina Press, 1966.

Melville, Thomas, and Marjorie Melville. *Guatemala: The Politics of Land Ownership.* New York: Free Press, 1971.

Menchú, Rigoberta. *I, Rigoberta Menchú: An Indian Woman in Guatemala.* Ed. Elisabeth Burgos-Debray; trans. Ann Wright. London: Verso, 1984.

Mews, Stewart, ed. *Religion and National Identity.* Studies in Church History, vol. 18. Oxford: Basil Blackwell, 1982.

Migdal, Joel S. *Strong Societies and Weak States: State-Society Relations and State Capabilities in the Third World.* Princeton: Princeton University Press, 1988.

Miller, Herbert J. *Iglesia y estado en el tiempo de Justo Rufino Barrios.* Guatemala City: Universidad de San Carlos, 1976.

———. "Catholic Leaders and the Guatemalan Revolution under Jacobo Arbenz Administration." Paper presented at SCOLAS Conference, San Antonio, Texas, April 1988.

———. "Conservative and Liberal Concordats in Nineteenth Century Guatemala: Who Won?" *Journal of Church and State* 33 (1991): 115–130.

———. "Church-State Relations in Guatemala, 1927–1944—Decline of Anticlericalism." Paper presented at Latin American Studies Association Conference, Guadalajara, Mexico, April 1997.

Millet, Artimius. "The Agricultural Colonization of the West Central Petén, Guatemala: A Case Study of Frontier Settlement by Cooperatives." Ph.D. dissertation, University of Oregon, 1971.

Minnery, Tom. "Why We Can't Always Trust the News Media." *Christianity Today* (14 January 1984).

Mondragón, Rafael. *De indios y cristianos en Guatemala.* Mexico City: Claves Latinoamericanos, 1983.

Montúfar, Lorenzo. *Reseña historia de Centro América.* Guatemala City, 1879.

Morrissey, James A. "A Missionary-directed Resettlement Program among the Highland Maya of Western Guatemala." Ph.D. dissertation, Stanford University, 1978.

Muñoz, Mardoqueo. "Las características para un líder en Guatemala." Paper presented at Universidad Mariano Gálvez, 12 January 1985.

Munro, Dana. *The Five Republics of Central America: The Political and Economic Development and Their Relationship with the United States.* New York: Oxford University Press, 1918.

Nájera Farfán, Mario Efraín. *Los estafadores de la democracia: hombres y hechos en Guatemala.* Buenos Aires: Editorial CLEM, 1956.

Nash, June. "Protestantism in an Indian Village in the Western Highlands of Guatemala." *Alpha Kappa Delta* (Winter 1960): 49–53.

Nash, Manning. *Machine Age Maya: The Industrialization of a Guatemalan Community.* Chicago: University of Chicago Press, 1958.

———. "The Relationship of Social Structure to the Problems of Evangelism in Latin America." *Practical Anthropology* 5(3).

Naylor, Robert A. "The British Role in Central America prior to the Clayton-Bulwer Treaty of 1850." *Hispanic American Historical Review* 40 (1960): 361–382.

Nelson, Wilton M. *El protestantismo en Centro América.* San José, Costa Rica: Editorial Caribe, 1982.

Nida, Eugene A. *Communication of the Gospel in Latin America.* Cuernavaca, Mexico: SONDEOS, 1969.

Noble, David W. *The Progressive Mind, 1890–1917.* Minneapolis, Minn.: Burgess, 1981.

"Obra misionera de la Iglesia Evangélica Presbiteriana 'Central' entre los hermanos Kek'chis de los años 1965 a 1978." Archives of the Iglesia Evangélica Presbiteriana Central, 1979.

Orellana, Óscar. "Evangelización-colonización." Pamphlet, Confederación, Sacerdotes, Diosesanos de Guatemala, n.d.

Orellana, Sandra. "La introducción del sistema de cofradía en la región del lago de los altos de Guatemala." *América Indígena* 35(4) (1975).

Organización del Pueblo en Armas (ORPA). "Los que matan en nombre de Dios." Communiqué, June 1983.

Painter, James. *Guatemala: False Hope, False Freedom.* London: Catholic Institute of International Relations, 1987.

Pérez, Louis A., Jr. "Protestant Missionaries in Cuba: Archival Records, Manuscript Collections, and Research Prospects." *Latin American Research Review* 27 (1992): 105–120.

Persky, Stan. *In America: The Last Domino.* Canada: New Star Books, 1984.

Piedra Solano, Arturo. "Evaluación crítica de la actual coyuntura evangélica centroamericana." *Vida y Pensamiento* 4(1 & 2): 3–20.

Pike, Frederick B., ed. *The Conflict between Church and State in Latin America.* New York: Alfred A. Knopf, 1964.

Pitti, Joseph. "Jorge Ubico and Guatemalan Politics in the 1920s." Ph.D. dissertation, University of New Mexico, 1975.

Proyecto Centroamericano de Estudios Socio-Religiosos (PROCADES). *Directorio de iglesias, organizaciones y ministerios del movimiento protestante: Guatemala.* San Francisco de Dos Ríos, Costa Rica: Instituto Internacional de Evangelización, 1981.

Quarraciono, Antonio, ed. *Sectas en América Latina.* Guatemala City: Consejo Episcopal Latinoamericano, 1981.

Ray, Harold. "Un breve resumen de la historia de la Iglesia del Nazareno." Mimeographed. Guatemala City: Iglesia del Nazareno, n.d.

Read, William R., et al. *Latin American Church Growth.* Grand Rapids, Mich.: William B. Eerdmans, 1969.

Reina, Rubén E. *Chinautla: A Guatemalan Indian Community.* New Orleans: Middle American Research Institute Publication 24, 1960.

———. *The Law of the Saints: A Pokomam Pueblo and Its Community Culture.* Indianapolis, Ind.: Bobbs-Merrill, 1966.

Reina, Rubén E., and Norman B. Schwartz. "The Structural Context of Religious Conversion in Petén, Guatemala: Status, Community and Multicommunity." *American Ethnologist* 9(1) (1974): 157–191.

Reinoso, Samuel. "Una síntesis histórica de la Iglesia Evangélica Presbiteriana en Guatemala." Archives of the Iglesia Evangélica Presbiteriana Central, n.d.

Ríos Montt, José Efraín. "Este gobierno tiene el compromiso de cambiar: no robo, no miento, no abuso." Press packet, July 1982.

Ríos Paredes, Mario. "Apuntes sobre la historia de la Iglesia Evangélica de Guatemala." Mimeographed, 1982.

Roberts, Bryan. "El protestantismo en dos barrios marginales de Guatemala." *Estudios centroamericanos,* publication no. 2, 1967.

———. "Protestant Groups and Coping with Urban Life in Guatemala City." *American Journal of Sociology* 73(6) (1968): 753–767.

Roberts, W. D. *Los auténticos revolucionarios: la emocionante historia de evangelismo a fondo.* San José, Costa Rica: Editorial Caribe, 1969.

Rodríguez, Mario. *A Palmerstonian Diplomat in Central America: Frederick Chatfield, Esq.* Tucson: University of Arizona Press, 1964.

Rojas Lima, Flavio. *La cofradía: reducto cultural indígena.* Guatemala City: Seminario de Integración Cultural, 1988.

Salazar, Ramón A. *Colección de tratados de Guatemala.* Guatemala City: Tipografía y Encuadernación Nacional, 1892.

Saler, Benson. "Religious Conversion and Self-Aggrandizement: A Guatemalan Case Study." *Practical Anthropology* 13 (1965): 107–114.

Samayoa Chinchilla, Carlos. *El dictador y yo.* Guatemala City: Imprenta Iberia, 1950.

Samayoa Dávila, Eugenio. *Memorias de la obra evangélica en Guatemala.* Mazatenango, Guatemala: N.p., 1980.

Sanborn, Helen J. *A Winter in Central America and Mexico.* Boston: Lee and Shepard Publications, 1886.

Schaefer, Heinrich W. "Una tipodología del protestantismo en Centroamérica." Unpublished, 1987.

Schlesinger, Stephen, and Stephen Kinzer. *Bitter Fruit: The Untold Story of the American Coup in Guatemala.* Garden City, N.Y.: Anchor Press, 1983.

Schneider, Ronald M. *Communism in Guatemala, 1944–1954.* New York: Frederick A. Praeger, 1958.

Schwemmer, Ora-Westley. "The Belgian Colonization Colony, 1840–1858." Ph.D. dissertation, Tulane University, 1966.

Scotchmer, David. "Convergence of the Gods: Comparing Traditional Maya and Christian Maya Cosmologies." In Gary H. Gossen, ed., *Symbol and Meaning beyond the Closed Community: Essays in Mesoamerican Ideas.* Studies on Culture and Society, vol. 1. Albany: Institute for Mesoamerican Studies, State University of New York, 1986.

———. "Symbols of Salvation: A Local Mayan Protestant Theology." *Missiology: An International Review* 17(3) (1989): 293–310.

———. "Symbols of Salvation: Interpreting Highland Maya Protestantism in Context." Ph.D. dissertation, State University of New York at Albany, 1991.

Scott, James C. *Weapons of the Weak: Everyday Forms of Peasant Resistance.* New Haven: Yale University Press, 1986.

Servicio Evangelizador para América Latina (SEPAL). "A History of SEPAL." Prepared for internal circulation, 1987.

———. "Retrato de SEPAL." Prepared for internal circulation, 1988.

Sexton, James D. "Protestantism and Modernization in Two Guatemalan Towns." *American Ethnologist* 5(2) (1978): 280–302.

Sexton, James D., and Clyde Woods. "Development and Modernization among Highland Maya: A Comparative Analysis of Ten Guatemalan Towns." *Human Organization* 36 (1977): 156–172.

Silvert, Kalman H. *A Study in Government: Guatemala.* New Orleans: Middle American Research Institute Publication 21, 1954.

Simalox S., Vitalino. "La evangelización y la cultura." Address to Conferencia de Iglesias Evangélicas de Guatemala, Programa de Asesoría Pastoral, June 1988.

Simon, Jean-Marie. *Guatemala: Eternal Spring, Eternal Tyranny.* New York: W. W. Norton, 1987.

Simons, Marlise. "Latin America's New Gospel." *New York Times Magazine* (7 November 1982).

Smith, Carol A. "Destruction of the Material Bases for Indian Culture: Economic Changes in Totonicapán." In Robert M. Carmack, ed., *Harvest of Violence: The Maya Indians and the Guatemalan Crisis.* Norman: University of Oklahoma Press, 1988.

———. "Origin of the National Question in Guatemala: A Hypothesis." In Carol A. Smith, ed., *Guatemalan Indians and the State, 1540–1988,* pp. 72–95. Austin: University of Texas Press, 1990.

———, ed. *Guatemalan Indians and the State, 1540–1988.* Austin: University of Texas Press, 1990.

Smith, Dennis A. "For Evangelicals in Central America, Religion Is as Polarized as Politics." *Religious News Service Special Report,* 16 January 1985.

———. "Whose Gospel? A Reflection on the Pastoral and Ideological Impact of Evangelical Broadcasting on Central American Christians." Paper presented at Conference on Evangelicals, the Mass Media and American Cultures, Wheaton College, 1988.

Spain, Mildred. *And in Samaria: A Story of Fifty Years Missionary Witness in Central America, 1890–1940.* Dallas: Central American Mission, 1940.

Spencer, Herbert. *Synthetic Philosophy: First Principles.* New York: D. Appleton, 1902.

Stahlke, Leonard. *Estadística religiosa cristiana de Guatemala.* Guatemala City: Iglesia Luterana, 1966.

Steigenga, Tim. "The Protestant Role in State-Society Relations in Guatemala: 1871–1989." Paper presented at the Latin American Studies Association Conference, 19 April 1989.

Stoll, David. *Fishers of Men or Founders of Empire? The Wycliffe Bible Translators in Latin America.* Cambridge, Mass.: Cultural Survival, 1982.

———. "La Iglesia del Verbo en el Triángulo Ixil de Guatemala, 1982." *Civilización* 3 (1985): 83–109.

———. *Is Latin America Turning Protestant? The Politics of Evangelical Growth.* Berkeley & Los Angeles: University of California Press, 1990.

———. *Between Two Armies in the Ixil Towns of Guatemala.* New York: Columbia University Press, 1993.

Strong, Josiah. *Our Country: Its Possible Future and Its Present Crisis.* New York: American Home Missionary Society, 1891.

Sullivan-González, Douglass. "Power, Piety, and Politics: A Cultural Analysis of Religious Discourse in Guatemala, 1839–1871." Unpublished, 1989.

———. "Power, Piety and Politics: The Role of Religion in the Formation of the Guatemalan Nation-State, 1839–1871." Ph.D. dissertation, University of Texas at Austin, 1994.

Summer Institute of Linguistics. "Informe anual del Instituto Lingüístico de Verano," 1984.

Sundberg, Juanita. "A History of Colonization Projects in Guatemala's Tropical Lowlands." Unpublished, 1993.

Suslow, Leo A. "Aspects of Social Reforms in Guatemala, 1944–1949." Latin American Seminar Reports 1. Hamilton, N.Y.: Colgate University, 1949.

Tax, Sol. *Penny Capitalism: A Guatemalan Indian Economy.* Washington, D.C.: Smithsonian Institution, 1953.

Taylor, James M. *On Muleback through Central America.* Knoxville, Tenn.: James M. Taylor Publications, 1913.

Teague, Dennis. "A History of the Church of God in Guatemala." Master's thesis, Trinity Evangelical Divinity School, 1975.

Toriello, Guillermo. *La batalla de Guatemala.* Mexico City: Cuadernos Americanos 39, 1955.

Torres, Carlos Alberto. *The Church, Society, and Hegemony: A Critical Sociology of Religion in Latin America.* Trans. Richard A. Young. Westport, Conn.: Praeger, 1992.

Treumann, Beverly. "A Righteous General, a Frightened People: Fulfilling God's Mandate in Guatemala." *Christianity and Crisis* (4 October 1982).
Troutman, Charles H. "Evangelicals and the Middle Classes in Latin America. Parts I and II." *Evangelical Missions Quarterly* 7 (2) (1971): 79–31; 7(3) (1972): 154–163.
Turner, Paul R. "Religious Conversion and Community Development." *Journal for the Scientific Study of Religion* 18(3) (1979): 252–260.
United States Information Service. "1984 Human Rights Report for Guatemala." Guatemala City: United States Embassy, 1984.
Varetto, Juan C. *Frederico Crowe en Guatemala.* Buenos Aires: Junta Bautista de Publicaciones, 1940.
Viadaurre, Adrián. *Los últimos treinta años de la vida política de Guatemala.* Havana: N.p., 1929.
Wadge, Gyl Catherine. "The Ríos Montt Regime: Change and Continuity in Guatemalan Politics." Master's thesis, Tulane University, 1987.
Wagner, C. Peter. *¡Cuidado! Aquí vienen los pentecostales!* Miami: Editorial Vida, 1973.
———. *Church Growth and the Whole Gospel.* San Francisco: Harper & Row, 1981.
Waldrop, Richard E. "Sinópsis histórica de la Iglesia de Dios Evangélico Completo: Cincuentenario 1932–1982." Guatemala City: República de Guatemala, n.d.
Wallace, Ruth A. "A Model of Change of Religious Affiliation." *Journal for the Scientific Study of Religion* 14(4) (1975): 345–355.
Wallstrom, Tord. *A Wayfarer in Central America.* Trans. M. A. Michael. New York: Roy Publishers, ca. 1955.
Walsh, Michael. *The Secret World of Opus Dei.* London: Grafton Books, 1989.
Warren, Kay B. *The Symbolism of Subordination: Indian Identity in a Guatemalan Town.* Austin: University of Texas Press, 1978.
Washington Office on Latin America (WOLA). "Guatemala: The Roots of Rebellion." Washington, D.C.: WOLA, Latin America Special Update, February 1983.
———. *Security and Development Conditions in the Guatemalan Highlands.* Washington, D.C.: WOLA, Report on a Mission of Inquiry, 1984.
Watanabe, John. *Maya Saints and Souls in a Changing World.* Austin: University of Texas Press, 1992.
Weber, Max. *Protestantism and the Spirit of Capitalism.* London: Allen & Unwin, 1930.
Weerstra, Hans. "Maya Peasant Evangelization: Communication, Receptivity and Acceptance Factors among Maya Campesinos." Doctor of Missiology dissertation, Fuller Theological Seminary, 1972.
Weigert, Andrew H., et al. "Protestantism and Assimilation among Mexican Americans: An Exploratory Study of Ministers' Reports." *Journal for the Scientific Study of Religion* 10(3) (1971): 219–232.
White, Alastair. *El Salvador: Nation of the Modern World.* London: Ernest Benn Limited, 1973.

Willems, Emilio. *Followers of the New Faith*. Nashville, Tenn.: Vanderbilt University Press, 1967.

Williams, Mary W. "The Ecclesiastical Policy of Francisco Morazán and the Other Central American Liberals." *Hispanic American Historical Review* 3 (1920): 119–143.

Williford, Mariam. "The Reform Program of Dr. Mariano Gálvez, Chief-of-State of Guatemala, 1831–1838." Ph.D. dissertation, Tulane University, 1963.

Wilson, Everett A. "Sanguine Saints: Pentecostalism in El Salvador." *Church History* 52 (1983): 186–198.

———. "The Central American Evangelicals: From Protest to Pragmatism." *International Review of Mission* 77 (1988): 94–106.

———. "Guatemalan Pentecostals: Something of Their Own." In Edward L. Cleary and Hanna W. Stewart-Gambino, eds., *Power, Politics, and Pentecostals in Latin America*, pp. 139–162. Boulder, Colo.: Westview Press, 1997.

Wingard, Roy A., Jr. "DAWN: After Three Years, Case Study: Guatemala." Paper prepared for John Knox Fellowship, London, 1987.

Winn, Wilkins Bowdre. "A History of the Central American Mission as Seen in the Work of Albert Edward Bishop, 1896–1922." Ph.D. dissertation, University of Alabama, 1963.

Winter, Ralph D. "¿Está perdida la Iglesia en el tiempo actual?" *El Noticiero Evangélico* (n.d.): 16–17.

———. "Two Reports on an Evangelical Indian Congress." *Practical Anthropology* 9(2).

Woodward, Ralph Lee, Jr. "Octubre: Communist Appeal to the Urban Labor Force of Guatemala 1950–1953." *Journal of Inter-American Studies* 4 (1962): 363–374.

———. "Economic and Social Origins of the Guatemalan Political Parties, 1773–1823." *Hispanic American Historical Review* 45 (1965): 544–565.

———. "Social Revolution in Guatemala: The Carrera Revolt." In Robert Wauchope, ed., *Applied Enlightenment: Nineteenth Century Liberalism*. New Orleans: Middle American Research Institute Publication 23, 1971.

———. *Central America: A Nation Divided*. 2nd ed. New York: Oxford University Press, 1985.

———. "Changes in the Nineteenth-Century Guatemalan State." In Carol A. Smith, ed., *Guatemalan Indians and the State, 1540–1988*. Austin: University of Texas Press, 1990.

———. *Rafael Carrera and the Emergence of the Republic of Guatemala, 1821–1871*. Athens: University of Georgia Press, 1993.

Ydígoras Fuentes, Miguel. *My War with Communism*. Englewood Cliffs, N.J.: Prentice-Hall, 1963.

Zapata Arceyuz, Virgilio. *Historia de la obra evangélica en Guatemala*. Guatemala City: Génesis Publicidad, 1982.

Index

Abzug, Robert, 63
Acción Católica. *See* Catholic Action movement
Acción Social Cristiana, 87–88, 93
Acul, 151
Adams, Richard N., 73, 123, 174n.15, 193–194n.11
Africa, 29, 41, 43
Agnosticism, 17, 20
Agrarian Reform Law (Decree 900), 91–94
Agriculture, 6, 48–49, 84, 85, 112, 113. *See also* Coffee cultivation
Aguilar, Calletano, 39
Ajucum, Juan Augustín, 39
Alcohol: and cholera epidemic, 5; and conversion, 162; and folk religion, 105; and Indians, 5, 47, 53, 62–63; and ladinos, 53; and Ríos Montt, 141; as social problem, 62–63; and temperance, 63–65, 124, 182n.51; and urban migration, 123
Alcoholics Anonymous, 122

Alta Verapaz Department: colonization in, 112; and Comity Agreement, 32, 177n.29; and earthquake relief, 121; education in, 83; German immigrants in, 186n.25; guerrilla movement in, 131; Maryknoll and Sacred Heart Orders in, 129; and Pentecostal-Nazarene church, 28; and Presbiterio Kek'chi, 107; public violence in, 103; and Roman Catholic Church, 57; and unionism, 84
Altiplano: armed popular movements in, 111, 128; and Catholic Action movement, 106; and Church of God, 38; earthquake relief in, 192n.6; and land shortages, 112; and literacy programs, 82; and Presbyterian Church, 31; Protestant growth in, 132. *See also* Los Altos; Western highlands
American Bible Society, 24
American Hospital, 33, 114

Día de la Raza, 152
Dialect ministry, 51–54, 65, 69. *See
also* Indian-language ministry
El Diario de Centro América, 62
Díaz, Porfirio, 12, 13, 16
Dillon, H. C., 25
Dispensationalism, 24–25
Dulles, John Foster, 188n.40
Dunn, Henry, 7, 174n.23
Durkheim, Emile, xi, 18

Earthquakes: church response to, 120,
134; and guerrilla movement, 127–
128; and missionary personnel
problems, 43; and Protestant
growth, 121–125, 127; and Quetzaltenango mission, 27
Eastern Europeans, 24, 182n.51
Economics: and anticlerical legislation, 3; and Arévalo, 79; Barrios'
policies on, 10; and conversion, 60;
and crop diversification, 112; and
democracy, 163; and depression of
1893, 24; economic reforms, 19; and
Escuintla, 31; and Estrada Cabrera,
65; export economy, 10; and Good
Neighbor policy, 74–75; and
Indians, 19, 49, 156; international
economic development, xii; and
Pentecostalism, 165; and Protestantism, xi, 123–124; and Ríos
Montt, 159–160; and Roman
Catholic Church's power, 6; and
rural communities, 119; and textile
industry, 60; and Ubico, 74; and
wage economy, 48
Edinburgh Conference, 186n.26
Education: and Arbenz, 91, 101; and
Arévalo, 80–81; bilingual instruction, 81; and CAM, 34; and Crowe's
school, 8, 14; and cultural values,
35, 46; and Haymaker, 17, 33; and
Hill, 14–15; and Indian assimilation, 68; of Indians, 48; and Ki'ché

language, 70; and Liberal Party, 13,
13–14; and Mayan languages, 70;
and missionaries, ix, 68, 82; and
mission finances, 42; and North
American curriculum, 35; and Presbyterian Church, 33; and Protestantism, 13–14; role of, 34–35; and
Roman Catholic Church, 11, 13,
101; schools as secular projects, 33;
vocational training, 35. *See also*
Literacy programs
EGP (Guerrilla Army of the Poor,
Ejército Guerrillero de los Pobres),
127, 132, 134, 135, 144, 152, 195n.37
El Salvador: Catholic activists in, 130;
and Indian communal land, 48;
and ladinos, 174n.15; and Liberation Theology, 129; rebellion in,
72–73, 76, 78; and United Provinces of Central America, 2
Elim Church, 168, 199–200n.62,
200n.3, 201n.11
Elim Mission, 117, 134
Elites: and alcohol consumption, 62;
and Carrera, 6; and cholera epi-
demic, 5; factionalism of, 9; and
Freemasonry, 17; landholdings of,
6; missionaries' salaries compared
to, 14–15; and Pentecostalism, 165–
166; and politics, 2–3, 4; and Presbyterian Church, 40; and public
land sales, 49–50
English language, 15, 35
Enlightenment, 3, 9
Enríquez, Antonio, 39
Enríquez, José María, 39
Epidemics, 3, 4–6, 28
Episcopal Church, 121
Episcopal Presiding Bishop's Fund
for World Relief, 192n.6
Escrivá de Balaguer, Josemaría,
187n.33
Escuela Politecna, 75, 138–139, 140
Escuintla Department, 31, 86, 177n.29

Robertson, Pat, 140, 157
Robinson Bible Institute, 70
Robles, Mariano, 39
Rockefeller, David, 165
Rodó, José Enrique, 79–80
Rojas Lima, Flavio, 59
Roman Catholic Church: and anti-
 clerical legislation, 3–4, 56–57;
 anti-Protestant rhetoric of, 68; and
 Arbenz, 93; and Arévalo, 87, 88;
 Carrera's policy on, 6–7, 8, 11; and
 Castillo Armas, 100–101; and
 church-state relations, 2; in colonial Spanish America, 1–2; and
 Conservative Party, 2; and conversion, 162; and elites, 165; and Good
 Neighbor policy, 75; and Guatemalan identity, vii, 7, 19–20, 41; Haymaker on, 50; and Indians, 55, 105;
 and individual, 50; and international conservatives, 86–87; and
 Liberal Party, ix, 3, 7, 11, 19, 56–57;
 missionaries' anti-Catholic rhetoric, 55–56; missionaries of, 87; and
 neo-Pentecostalism, 117; and
 political violence, 128–131; and
 politics, 2, 87, 102, 105, 168–169,
 187n.34; and positivism, 11; Presbyterian Church compared to, 27;
 priest shortage of, 123, 151; and
 Protestant hostility, 86, 88; Protestants united against, 29; reformation of, x; and Renovación, 155; and
 Ríos Montt, 150, 158; secular power
 of, 6–7, 11; social activism of, 113,
 123; and Social Gospel, 16, 17;
 spiritual hegemony of, 7, 11, 12, 19,
 119, 161; and temperance, 182n.51;
 and Ubico, 75; ultraconservative
 Catholic lay factions, 102; and U.S.
 conservative Christians, 108; and
 Vatican II, 112, 118, 128–129, 131
Roosevelt, Franklin D., 74–75

Rossell y Arellano, Mariano, 86, 101–
 102, 104
Rural communities: and alcohol use,
 62; and CAM, 83; and earthquake,
 122; and economic reforms, 19;
 and economics, 119; education in,
 91; and land reform, 93; and literacy programs, 82, 91; and Lucas
 García, 129; and Pentecostalism,
 118; policies towards, 67; political
 violence in, 144–145; and Protestantism, xii, 153, 164; and Roman
 Catholic Church, 57; Roman Catholic priests in, 123, 193–194n.11
Russell, Charles, 29
Russellites, 29, 35, 36
Russia, 76

Sacatepéquez Department, 177n.29
Sacred Heart Order, 87, 105, 113, 123,
 129
Salesian Order, 105, 123
Salvadoran Party, 188n.40
San Andrés, 106, 190n.17
San Andrés Xecul, 39
San Antonio Aguascalientes, 34, 53,
 70, 156
San Antonio Illotenango, 106
San Carlos University, 68, 128
San Cristóbal, 39
San Francisco El Alto, 39
San Francisco Nentón, 197n.19
San Juan Cotzal, 153
San Juan Ostuncalco, 70, 94, 125
San Marcos Department, 31, 51, 57,
 83, 177n.29
San Pedro Charcá, 103
Santa Cruz del Quiché, 134
Santa Eulalia, 62
Santa Mária Chiquimula, 39
Santa Rosa Department, 177n.29
Santiago, 106
Santiago Atitlán, 103

CPSIA information can be obtained at www.ICGtesting.com
Printed in the USA
LVOW06s0738190514

386266LV00001B/68/P